IN ABOR JUNGLES

HOURS OF EASE AT PUAK CAMP.

In background (left).—Captain Poole, D.S.O., Official Correspondent; (facing camera) Major-General Hamilton Bower, C.B., Commanding Expedition. In foreground (lying down).—Major Hutchinson, Chief Staff Officer; Captain Smithers, Orderly Officer; (sitting on rock) Major Wilson, 1st Batt. 8th Gurkha Rifles. Note the war dog!

IN ABOR JUNGLES

BEING AN ACCOUNT OF THE ABOR EXPEDITION
THE MISHMI MISSION AND THE MIRI MISSION

BY

ANGUS HAMILTON

FELLOW OF THE ROYAL GEOGRAPHICAL SOCIETY
AUTHOR OF "KOREA," "AFGHANISTAN," "PROBLEMS OF THE MIDDLE EAST," "SOMALILAND," ETC.

WITH ILLUSTRATIONS AND A MAP

LONDON
G. BELL & SONS, LTD.
1912

CONTENTS

CHAPTER VII

CHAPTER VIII

CHAPTER IX

CHAPTER X

CHAPTER XI

CHAPTER XII

CHAPTER XIII

LIST OF ILLUSTRATIONS

To face page

TO

THE OFFICERS, NON-COMMISSIONED OFFICERS AND MEN

OF THE

ABOR EXPEDITIONARY FIELD FORCE

AND OF THE MISHMI AND MIRI POLITICAL MISSIONS

THIS NARRATIVE OF THE WORK ACCOMPLISHED

BY ALL CONCERNED

RESPECTFULLY IS DEDICATED

IN ABOR JUNGLES

CHAPTER I

The Lands of the Abors—Tribal Life—Manners—Customs—Dress—Methods of Fighting.

THE lands of the Abors, which served as the theatre of war for the operations which Major-General Bower recently conducted on the north-east frontier of India, have been hitherto almost unknown to white men. Geographically, they may be said to fall between the eastern watershed of the Dibong River and the western drainage of the Subansiri River, and to extend from the course of the Brahmaputra River in the south to the water-parting in the north which divides Assam from the plateaux of Tibet. Aborland is only a few hundred miles square, but it comprises between the slopes of the snow-clad northern uplands and the jungle-covered banks of the mighty river some of the most difficult country in the world for purposes of war. Varying very much in character, it reveals between north and south extremes of heat and cold, vast stretches of dense jungle, deep barren valleys, patches of alluvial plain and many ranges, the lower rising seven thousand feet, while the higher ones, snow-clad and wooded from base to summit, exceed ten thousand feet.

The lands on the west of the Dihang are low-lying. The belt between the Dihang and the Dibong is traversed by the mountains, and contains only an occasional indication of cultivation, and few villages. Beyond Kebang, the valley of the Dihang is more open. Between Dijmur and the mouth of the Dibong to the foot of the hills, the country is flat, and overgrown with an almost impenetrable jungle forest in which giant ferns, bamboos, and plantains grow side by side with entangling thorns and poisonous creepers.

In addition to the dense vegetation, the region is distinguished by its rivers—at least four being quite large—and by what has been hitherto an entire absence of roads. Such pathways as did exist were mere animal tracks, while the best "roads" were the chasms through which the rivers flowed. When the traveller was not wading waist-deep through these, he was crawling along narrow ledges cut out of the face of high precipices. Now and again he came to places where there was no ledge, while the path, such as it was, was continued by a rude gallery contrived out of the face of the cliff, or he found himself compelled to climb perpendicular cliffs with the aid of cane ropes.

The Abors are divided into a number of clans, of which the principal are the Minyongs and the Padams; in addition there are the Komkar, Karko, Panggi, Pasi, Doba or Galong, Simong, and Aieng.

The Padam, or, as they are more often called, the Bor—which means "great"—Abors, occupy a zone which is bounded on the south by a line from Bomjur on the Dibong River to the mouth of the Yamne River; on the east by the Sesseri River; on the west by the Yamne River. There is no definite line to the north where the Milangs, who are closely allied with the Padams, are found. The chief village of the Padams is Damro. The clan is reported to have a fighting strength between five and six thousand strong.

The Aiengs occupy a few villages situated along the foothills east of the Dihang River opposite Pasighat. In a measure, they have encroached on the territory of the Padams.

The Komkars control a strongly stockaded group of villages lying between the Yamne and Dihang rivers. Occupying a central position they do not concern themselves with the affairs of any of their neighbours. Their country, accordingly, is regarded as a haven of refuge from the more turbulent areas surrounding it.

The Karkos inhabit three villages to the west of the Komkars. They are more or less independent.

The Panggis, who at first "sat on the fence," and only came in when they saw how the "cat was jumping," hold a thickly populated belt of country between the Dihang and Yamne rivers, having Sibhum for their principal stockade.

The Minyongs, lying to the south and west of the Panggis, possess villages on both banks of the Dihang River; from Rengging near Pasighat to Pankang. The Ledum villages are also under Minyong authority. Their chief village, Riga, fearing the fate of Kebang, which was burnt, ultimately climbed down, though at one time it was much inclined to fight. Other villages were Puging and Rikol in the far north.

The Simongs occupy a few villages on the left bank of the Dihang, and though friendly with the Minyongs, are separated and quite distinct from them.

The Pasis live in a group of villages near Pasighat. They are dominated by the military police post at Balek, and from that fact profess a friendship for the British which it is known they are far from feeling.

The Galongs, the remaining section, occupy the basin of the Dijmur River where they have been ever since they were driven off the left bank of the Dihang by the Padams. They are divided into four groups: the Rimens, Taipudias,

AN OLD ABOR.

PASIS FROM PASIGHAT.

Dobangs, and the Taduns. The Taduns are allied with the Minyongs. The Dobangs, on the other hand, are distinct from the Taduns. They are friendly with the British.

Many sections of the Abor tribesmen name themselves after the tracts of country in which their particular clan has settled. This is the case with the Pasis, Panggis, Karkos and Komkars. Other clans have inter-married so freely that it is difficult to tell where the possessions of one group end and those of another begin. It is, perhaps, because of this excessive inter-relationship that tribal feuds are specially bitter among the Abors. Jealousy prevents any possibility of tribal combination, and together with lack of opportunity restrained the clans from uniting against General Bower. If they had done so, from ten to fifteen thousand fighting men would have been available. To this total the Pasi Minyongs would have contributed some 6500 men, and the Padams a rather less amount, when a much more formidable resistance would have been possible. As it was, the Abor defence was by no means insignificant, though gaining nothing from the few muzzle-loading guns which Tibetan traders had introduced to the tribesmen during the last two or three years. In point of fact the expedition was brought to a successful conclusion only by the patient and laborious co-operation of all ranks in the plans which General Bower laid in the face of very great difficulties.

For a long time past the Abors have been cocks of the Assam border. Very independent and quarrelsome, they had come to regard themselves as the rulers of this far-distant corner of India from the fact that so many of the Miri and the Mishmi tribes had submitted to their exactions. It is to be feared, too, that the success of the expedition has been a sad blow to their self-esteem, for it has brought peace where before peace was an unknown quantity.

The Abors are of Mongoloid descent, though their characteristics differ considerably. The men of the north stand over six feet, while those of the southern clans are short and squatly built. All are lithe and active, with symmetrically shaped, well-developed limbs. They have lank black hair, which they wear closely cropped, and cut by laying across the blade of a sword, and beating it with a stick ; saffron or brown complexions, high cheek-bones, and oblique brown eyes. They employ in speaking a mixture of Tibetan with dialects of their own that differ so radically among the various groups into which they are divided that the men of one clan do not as a rule understand those of another. They are slow talkers, intoning words and giving them a certain sonorous cadence that makes what is said very clear and distinct.

While the Abors speak with the deliberation of a

typical savage people, their manners and customs no less reveal their primitive state. If not quite so degraded as the Sunthals of Bengal—who, on occasion, have been known to devour human flesh, though as a rule they feed off dogs, bats and animal refuse—they run them a close second. They live off the smaller wild life of the jungle, and favour frogs, lizards, snakes, rats, dogs, monkeys, cats and mice. An animal that has died a natural death is as acceptable to them as the best butcher's meat, while the flesh of the tiger is reckoned particularly good—for men, though it is denied to women on account of its supposed passion-rousing qualities.

Abors prefer their food to be smoke-cured, and use but little water in its preparation. Both sexes are inveterate smokers. They begin when they are four or five years old and never leave off the practice until they die. They inhale the smoke ; but their greatest treat is to add a little water to the nicotine that is precipitated in the bowl of the pipe, and then to drink it ! They have no other use for water, for they consider dirt an antidote to cold, and avoid removing the one lest they should take the other. Both sexes tattoo, the men wearing a cross on the forehead between the eyebrows ; the women a smaller cross in the hollow of the upper lip immediately under the nose.

During the greater part of the year the only dress

of the Abors—and this applies both to men and women—is a loin-cloth of bark. In some of the villages the men wear a sleeveless cloth jacket, while the women favour a skirt of cloth, the two garments being woven out of jungle products. They also make great play with bamboo. At all times scantily clad, when they do have resource to bamboo it is put to an infinite variety of uses. On state occasions, for example, the Abor belle dons a small petticoat, or skirt, made of filaments of cane closely woven together. It is only about a foot in breadth, and is fastened so tightly round the lower part of the thighs as to impede the free action of the legs. In a measure, therefore, Abor women may be cited as the inventors of the hobble skirt.

Another direction in which bamboo is seen is as an ankle-band of finely plaited cane, the object of which is to set off to the best advantage the curve of the bare leg. Abor girls particularly favour such ornaments while both the married and the unmarried encircle their waists with bamboo girdles, from which depend a number of small, bell-metal discs—*boyops*—which are imported from Tibet. These clank and jangle at every movement, the sound resembling nothing so much as the harsh tinkling of the bells that farmers hang round the necks of their wethers.

The principal thing which the men make out of bamboo is a head-piece in the shape of a jockey-cap,

1

HAIR-DRESSING EXTRAORDINARY.

1. Looking for trouble.
2. Hair-cutting. The method employed is to put a dhao under the lock of hair and then to strike it with a bit of wood.

TUBULAR BAMBOO BRIDGE OVER THE DIHANG RIVER.

ANOTHER KIND OF ABOR BRIDGE.

which is worn on the back of the head with the peak slanting down the neck. The cap is generally adorned with a " bheem-raj " of king crow's feather, or of cock's feathers, boar's tushes, *mithun* skin or yak's tail. It is made so well that it is capable of turning a direct or even a glancing cut from sword and spear. Like their women-folk, the men coil strips of bamboo round their arms and legs. Each sex is very partial to necklaces of turquoise stones, and to all kinds of beads.

Bamboo, however, figures not only in the dress of the men and women. It is the essential factor in everything appertaining to the daily life of Aborland. Bridges over turbulent torrents, if crude and uninviting, owe their existence to this pliable though very endurable cane, as do the houses in the village, the weapons of defence and the implements of husbandry. In regard to bridges, the Abors favour two methods of construction. The commonest kinds are swing-bridges, made of cane, which they walk across. Another form is made by stretching a bamboo across a river at a considerable height. A bamboo basket is then slung on to this cane, and the Abor pulls himself across hand-over-hand like a monkey. Rivers of fifty or sixty yards are crossed in this way. A bridge of the other kind over the Dihang, near Komsing, was three hundred yards long.

For purposes of protection, the Abors largely use

panjees, or pieces of bamboo, hardened to the toughness of steel by being placed in hot ashes. When thoroughly fired the stakes are sharpened at one end and stuck into the ground at an angle that just catches the foot of any unobservant walker. In this state they easily penetrate a soft boot or gaiter, and are disastrous to a barefooted coolie. They are laid in thousands all round a village, or are concealed under leaves about the paths leading to it. Somewhat similar pieces of bamboo, but placed horizontally some two or three feet from the ground, are also employed ; while the rock chute or "booby trap" is a very favourite device. An Abor village is never without its cordon of chutes formed of huge boulders, which are so hidden that they are released by the enemy himself as he advances along a jungle-path, or through some defile leading to the village. He is, of course, crushed to death. Abors select very inaccessible places for their villages. Surrounded with bamboo palisades, or protected by a stockade of tree trunks, with all approaches carefully "panjeed" and flanked by chutes, the villages present very formidable positions to an attacking party.

An Abor village is an entirely independent entity over which the Gam or headman exercises absolute authority. The houses are laid on piles and raised some few feet from the ground. The roofs, like the walls, are made of plantain leaves placed one upon the other like tiles in our own houses. The floors are bamboo. The space beneath is used as a latrine or as a lumber store, and also provides accommodation for poultry, pigs and the *mithun*: a much-prized species of cattle, strong, handsome, white legged, and resembling both the ox and the bison in shape and size.

In the heart of the village is the "moshup," a spacious building, where the inhabitants attend to discuss the business of the community. It is also used as the place where the unmarried men of the village sleep, and as a guard-house, where they take duty by turns at night in order to protect the village from sudden attack. Among the Abors only married men have the privilege of possessing a hut for their own use, the arrangements serving as a strong incentive to the young "bloods" of the town to throw off the parental yoke for that of the connubial hearth. To judge from the careworn expression of the women, who are pretty enough to deserve a better fate, the system is not altogether to their liking.

Abor implements of peace, like Abor weapons of war, are made from bamboo. For purposes of agriculture they use a bamboo spike to scrape the earth, or to make the holes in which they drop the seeds. When a clearance has been made in the forest and the ground between the fallen logs has been scratched over, it is planted with Indian corn, tobacco, opium, pumpkins, melons and, of course, rice.

For arms they possess bamboo shields, cross-bows, ordinary bows and arrows with iron tips poisoned with aconite, very long spears, daggers, and the strong, straight-cutting swords (or dhaos), which are reported to come from Tibet. It was with these weapons moreover that the tribesmen endeavoured to check the progress of the punitive columns. Though their arms were not modern arms of precision, in the hands of the Abor expert they could be, and were, extraordinarily serviceable.

From the moment that the clansmen knew that a military force was to be dispatched against them a state of wild excitement prevailed in Aborland. All the principal gams or headmen assembled in council at Kebang; and, after prolonged discussion, agreed upon certain measures, which, if of a somewhat elementary character, undoubtedly resulted in General Bower's advance being met by substantial resistance. In the first place, fords across the rivers were removed; strong stockades, constructed out of trunks of trees felled for the purpose, were thrown across the valleys; and palisades of green bamboo erected round the villages. Foot-traps, in the form of shallow pits, lined with poisoned *panjees* and carefully covered over, were sunk in the jungle tracks, and formidable chutes were built up on every con-

Photo] *Colonel Lumsden.*

ABOR WARRIORS.

ABORS ROASTING "BIG" MEAT.

AN ABOR WOMAN.

AN ABOR WOMAN.

ceivable position. Indeed, a thorough spirit of defiance was aroused by the prospect of war, and the gams of Yemsing, Pongging, Riga, Rengging, Yekshi, Sissin, Panggi, Komsing, Riu, and Mopit at once declared that they would support Kebang.

As the weeks passed, and General Bower's forces made no appearance, the impatience of the clansmen steadily increased, and imperious orders were sent by Kebang to the men in the lower villages to leave the fighting men to it, while the others attended to the coolies. "We shall be tired of eating pig, and chicken is not food for fighting men," was the purport of one message. "We want the big meat, so leave us the white sepoys," was the sense of another message. Pig, chicken, and big meat or *mithun* represent the principal dishes in the feast that is given by an Abor warrior on his return from a war where he has killed in combat a sepoy of the Native Army, a coolie, or a soldier of the British Service. Dancing and merriment attend such celebrations, which are kept going one, two, or three days, in accordance with the standard of the repast.

A variation on the foot-pit was an ingenious adaptation of the spring trap, fitted with arrows in place of the customary blunderbuss, and much used by Abor hunters. In this unwieldy, though pretty reliable contrivance, hollow lengths of bamboo, each fitted with a poisoned arrow, were fixed in bows which were fastened to bamboos growing conveniently near a jungle path. From the bows lines of bamboo fibre were carried across the path at various elevations from the ground: from a few inches to two or three feet. The lines were strung tightly, and so placed that the lightest touch discharged a flight of arrows. For any ordinary purpose a hunter seldom sets more than a pair of arrows. In warfare, or as a defensive measure along a path leading to a village, both sides of a section of the track, perhaps two or even three hundred yards in length, would be closely planted with the traps, the bow-strings so adjusted that they released an irregular fire of poisoned arrows from many angles and at varying distances. Another popular, though less reliable, trap was formed by cutting nearly through some tree that overhung the track, and connecting its top with the path by a length of bamboo fibre in such a way that the trunk crashed to the ground if the least strain were put upon the line.

In addition to ambushes, the Abors rely largely on their prowess as bowmen and spearmen, while they are adept also in wielding heavy dhaos, which vary in length between one and four feet. It is as bowmen, however, that they are most distinguished, and Abor archers can pick off an object with unerring precision at a couple of hundred yards. The arrow used is the long, heavy bolt common to most parts of Asia. In many cases the arrow-heads are flanged and grooved, and detach themselves on impact. For purposes of extraction the bolt must be pushed through for, as a rule, it cannot be pulled out without the head remaining behind, the wound being badly torn.

The Abors obtain the poison with which they anoint their arms from aconite, deadly nightshade, or the flesh of decomposing carcasses of animals—or enemies, whichever might be most handy. The mixture is smeared on the weapons, which are then varnished and slow-dried. Once treated in this way, the arms retain their deadly character for a considerable period, and can be used again and again. The action of the poison, too, is very rapid—sometimes less than one hour, and rarely more than six hours. Violent convulsions are set up, and tetanus supervenes. With a view to the treatment of any arrow wounds which might be received during the course of the expedition, all hospital details were furnished with phials of crystals of permanganate of potash together with metal syringes, while precise instructions for the application of the remedy appeared in Force Orders. From these it appeared that when the arrow had been pushed out of the body, its track had to be swabbed out with pure carbolic acid and then syringed with permanganate of potash.

In order to secure the destruction of the enemy's "defences," it was intended to equip the Field Force with some light artillery and a supply of hand-bombs of the "Martin-Hale" pattern, which combine the advantages of a grenade which may be slung or thrown, as the user may prefer, or discharged from a rifle. While it was very doubtful whether artillery or bombs would make any direct impression on the enemy's protective works, it was thought that the moral effect on the tribesmen themselves, produced by a shell or bomb which, skimming prettily over their defences, burst in their very midst, would be very telling. The happiest results therefore were anticipated from the dainty little Martin-Hale grenade, and it was distinctly unfortunate that this well-made, handy little bomb did not arrive in time to prove its value.

In appearance these bombs seem little more than a few inches of brass tubing charged with a high explosive and fitted with a percussion-cap. At the same time they make a "surprise packet" of peculiar deadliness, for the tube is packed with small shrapnel bullets. It weighs when fully charged nearly two pounds, and is an inch in diameter. Thrown by hand, it can be hurled about sixty yards or more; when shot from a rifle, to which it is fastened by a steel rod which passes into the barrel at the muzzle and is ejected by the explosion of the cartridge, its duration of effectiveness is regulated by the "set" of the fuse and is usually up to four hundred yards. The value of bombs, however, in modern warfare is always rather doubtful. In the South African and Russo-Japanese campaigns where they were used by both belligerents, as also in the Balkans where the Macedonians affected them, their use was ever more picturesque than practical.

CHAPTER II

Our Relations with the Tribes — Earliest Visit to Aborland — Major-General Babbage — Treaty of 1862 — "Inner" and "Outer" Lines — Mr. Needham's Activities — Advent of Mr. Williamson.

THE story of our relations with the tribes of the north-east frontier of India admirably illustrates the difficulties under which the task of safeguarding the marches of Hindustan proceeds. It is a vivid and deeply interesting chapter of Indian history, to which another page has now been added by the Abor operations.

It was in the early years of the last century that the country of the Abors was first reported upon by British explorers. Though the visit of Captain Bedford in 1826 was but a brief one, the year in which it was made deserves more than the passing reference which it receives from the pens of historians. Little appears to be known about its circumstances; but it would seem, even at the date when Captain Bedford's journey took place, that the Abors had made their reputation felt and their position secure among their neighbours.

By claiming an inalienable right to all the fish and gold found in the streams which flowed from the Miri lands, the Abors exercised almost feudal powers over many sections of the Miris. The oppressive effect of this power by 1826 had caused an exodus of the Miris from their tribal lands to Sadiya, where they placed themselves under the protection of the old Assam Government, who refused to assist the Abors to get them to return. This state of affairs engendered friction between the Assam Government and the Abors; and when efforts were made in 1847 after we had taken possession of Assam, to establish trading posts on the Dihang, the Abors objected, and emphasised their objection by kidnapping a number of Miri gold-washers.

After considerable difficulty and some fighting, in which the Abors made a determined night attack, Captain, now Major-General, Babbage, and Major Vetch, Political Officer at Sadiya, effected a rescue. In the following year, with a view to peace, the Abors were granted a fixed annual *posa*, or allowance, and passed under the care of a Government whose protection ever since they have been content to defy or to accept, as circumstances warranted.

The Major-General Babbage mentioned here, is happily still alive, and contributed to a recent issue of *The Times* the following letter, which deals in detail with the work of his column :—

"More than sixty years have passed since I was sent in command of a detachment of over a hundred men of the 1st Assam Light Infantry to support the Governor-General's agent in Upper Assam against the hill-tribe of Abors, who are now giving trouble. These tribes look on the flat country at the foot of their hills as their territory, and hunt, fish, and cut wood there freely. In the 'forties some of the natives in the plains earned a precarious living by washing the sands of the rivers coming from the Himalayas for gold; the Abors claimed a share of what they considered their gold, and in 1848, not being satisfied, carried off ten of the gold-washers. Negotiations failing, active measures were adopted, and the detachment under my command was sent against the Abors.

"We started in February with six regimental elephants, about 150 coolies, and no camp equipage; the agent and myself had one tarpaulin to sleep under. In Assam the beds of the minor streams, which in the winter season are at their lowest, are the roads of the country. The elephants therefore could only travel three or four marches; sometimes they were up to their knees in running water, sometimes there was a stretch of sand with small boulders, but the banks were always either perpendicular rocks or steep slopes covered with jungle. One day one of the elephants, carrying rice for the men's rations, slipped over a boulder and fell; the bags got wet and were handled by low-caste men, so the Hindus would not touch the rice, but they cheerfully agreed to eat the coarse rice provided for the elephants, and the latter got the fine rice. When the elephants could go no further we formed a depôt at the best place available and pushed on, leaving a weak guard to be reinforced from regimental headquarters. Our way was now up one of the hill spurs, and we passed one night on the ridge without water, except what we could carry ; a long march next day brought us down into another valley, somewhat more open than the previous one. Very soon the Abors brought in the ten gold-washers and begged the agent to go back, but he did not see it that way. Next day we crossed another hill and got into the broad sandy bed of another stream, whose banks as usual were covered with thick jungle. Here the village headmen came with presents and submission. What was in the mind of the agent I do not know, but he kept the headmen (some seven or eight) in camp for the night, instead of letting them go to the village, which was close above us, and he did not take their 'dhaos' from them.

"When evening came I had to make arrangements for the night, so that half the detachment should be always awake and alert, and after dark I had the 'dhaos' taken from the Abors without consulting the agent. The night was very dark, there was no moon and not a star was visible. In the middle of the night one of the headmen gave a whistle ; he and his fellows bolted to their village, and from the opposite side some forty men rushed on us with heavy 'dhaos.' It was the affair of a moment ; we were prepared, and beat them off. One sepoy was badly, but not fatally wounded, and two coolies were killed.

"When daylight came we formed order of march —half the sepoys first, with the agent to direct ; the coolies (with loads decreased day by day) in the middle, and the remainder of the force with me. On clearing the narrow belt of jungle which skirted the river bed, we saw the village above on the hill-side. The women had been removed, and the men who had stayed speedily took to flight to the height above, from which they watched and abused us. The houses (about thirty to forty in number) were, under the instructions of the agent, set alight, and the rear-guard halted for an hour or more to keep the Abors from returning. About half-a-mile further up the hill was another village, which as a measure of policy we did not burn. But the Abors were forbidden to enter our territory, and their trade was stopped.

"We then resumed our march down a narrow valley, from whose steep sides the Abors above us sent down flights of poisoned arrows, which had, however, no metal heads, so that I was obliged to send out a few skirmishers to keep them at a distance. In due course we reached the place where the captives had been released. Continuing our homeward march, we found our depôt all safe, and reached Dibrooghur after about three weeks' absence."

For the first ten years of their relations with the Political Officer at Sadiya, the Abors treated his wishes with respect, and kept the peace of the border with self-denying regularity. But in 1858 they relapsed into their raiding habits; and, in an attack on the Beeah village of Sengajan, a party of Kebang and Romking Abors killed a baker's dozen. Sengajan lay within a few miles of Dibrugarh, and so daring a breach of the peace necessitated instant punishment. Within a few weeks a light column, composed of 16 Naval Brigade, 16 local artillery and 104 Assam Light Infantry, took the field. The force arrived at Pasighat on March 20th ; it failed to reach Kebang, and the operations were regarded officially as a complete fiasco. Accordingly, in the following year, a second column set out, consisting of 75 British and 300 native soldiers, two mortars, two twelve-pounder howitzers, 25 gunners, 18 elephants, a coolie corps, and a boat's convoy.

The enemy's stronghold, perched on a hill and protected by eleven stockades—many of which were held until their garrisons were expelled at the point of the bayonet—was breached on February 27th, with a loss to the attacking column of one killed and forty-four wounded. After this fight the column made a general reconnaissance of the Abor country and withdrew, when a few other villages had been destroyed.

The effect of these operations on the Abor tribesmen was merely temporary. In 1862, Romking braves again came within a few miles of Dibrugarh in a raid which they made upon an Assamese village. Eleven villagers were killed. As the attacking party had crossed the Brahmaputra to secure their victims, the challenge to the troops at Dibrugarh, presented by such effrontery, was taken up. On this occasion a force of 300 sepoys, 50 gunners and two twelve-pounder howitzers was dispatched. Proceeding as far as Lalluchapri, a halt was made, as overtures for peace had been submitted by the Abor chiefs. After considerable discussion a treaty of peace was arranged under which, in return for an annual *posa* of iron, salt, opium and other articles, equivalent in value to three thousand rupees per annum, an "Inner" and "Outer" line of frontier was set up. For the future this new line was to be taken as describing, in regard to the former, the area of British administration, and, in connection with the latter, the limits of a semi-independent tribal zone. At the same time, the tribes between the "Inner" and the "Outer" line were within the political jurisdiction of the frontier.

By this treaty the great bulk of the Abor tribes came under the British flag, and the frontier on the north-eastern border of India became coterminous with that of Tibet and China, save where it was broken by the occasional inter-section of the lands of one or other of the outlying hill-clans, who wished still to preserve complete independence. Four years later, in 1866, fourteen of these outlying tribes —the mountain clans—signified their adherence to the terms of the treaty of 1862 by sending their chiefs to Sadiya for the purpose of signing it. If the terms of the treaty of 1862 had only been observed by the chiefs of the Abor tribes, the years which since

Photo] [*Colonel Lumsden.*

THE GAM OF RIU ADDRESSING A GATHERING OF THE VILLAGERS.

Photo] [*Colonel Lumsden.*
THE GAM OF KOMSING WHO RECEIVED THE LATE MR. NOEL WILLIAMSON AND COLONEL LUMSDEN WITH GREAT FRIENDLINESS IN 1909.

A GAM OF DAMRO WHO CAME INTO SADIYA TO SEE MR. DUNDAS ON BEHALF OF THE PADAMS.

have passed would have seen a considerable difference in the aspect of the country that lies between the banks of the Brahmaputra and the Chino-Tibetan hills. Trade would have flourished and the tribes at peace beneath the Imperial ægis waxed rich. As it happens, the treaty has been repeatedly violated by the lowland Abors, with the result that the land has been as a closed book.

For several years peace was absolute, and the *hookum* of the British *raj* up and down the frontier was instantly obeyed. In 1876, as if tired of their good behaviour, the Abors began again to cast covetous eyes on the possessions of their neighbours. Five years later the terms of the treaty of 1862 had been so strained that it was found advisable to establish posts of 300 men at Bomjur and Nizamghat to prevent the Abors from crossing the Dibong into the lands of the Chulikatta Mishmis. In 1884 Mr. Needham, Assistant Political Officer at Sadiya, visited Balek and other villages, though his reception only tended to show that the Abor tribesmen were becoming rather "above themselves" again. A few more years were to pass before any actual breach of the peace occurred, and it was not until 1888 that anything very serious took place. In that year a band of Pasi Minyong Abors from Yemsing and Ledum decoyed four Miris over the "Inner" line and killed all of them. Heavy fines were levied on the recalcitrant tribesmen ; but four years later, in April 1892, the offence was repeated by Bomjur Abors when three Miris were captured and enslaved. In the following year, Abors from Dambuk and Silluk attacked in rapid succession the patrols of military police that were watching the border.

In face of these acts of insubordination a punitive column, consisting of 100 sepoys of the 44th Gurkhas, 300 Lakhimpur Military Police, 100 Naga Hills Military Police and a coolie corps of 1500 carriers, was organised at Sadiya in January 1894 under the command of Captain Maxwell and the political direction of Mr. Needham. The primary objectives of the column were the villages of Bomjur, Dambuk and Silluk, whence the raiding parties had issued. A stout resistance was offered but the three centres were eventually punished, a feature of the enemy's defences being an immense stockade of tree-trunks, extending over a mile in length, against which the mountain guns with the expedition made little or no impression. This and other similar stockades were carried by storm, and the expedition turned north towards Damro, the most populous and influential village of the Bor Abors.

Damro was in sight after an arduous march, when news reached the column of a treacherous attack on a party of camp-followers and sick who had been left with a small guard at the village of Bodak.

Retirement, prompt and absolute, was necessary, so the little force retraced its steps, leaving the Abor citadel untouched. After a perilous march to Bodak it was discovered on arrival that neighbouring tribesmen, professedly friendly, had undertaken to carry up supplies to the column advancing on Damro. The garrison of Bodak, suspecting nothing, had readily granted admission to the camp, where, after waiting their opportunity, the Abors had caught the sepoys off their guard and massacred them and the camp-followers, killing in all forty-five. One man alone escaped to tell the tale. Reprisals were at once effected, but the force returned to British territory leaving the heart of the Abor country untouched. In view of the behaviour of this group of the Abor tribes, the payment of the annual *posa* to the chiefs was suspended upon conclusion of the operations, and has remained ever since *en l'air*.

Once again an interval of ten years was to pass before the peace of the north-eastern border of India was disturbed to any serious extent, the next occasion occurring in the spring of 1903, when a party of Doba Abors crossed the line and carried off a quantity of stock. After considerable discussion with Mr. Needham, the warring tribesmen returned their booty and the headmen paid over a certain sum in fines. In spite of the penalties inflicted by Mr. Needham the Abors continued to give us trouble.

In 1904 the headmen of the Pasi Minyongs began to levy blackmail on the contractors who were cutting timber for the Meckla Nadi Saw Mills. When complaint of these proceedings reached Mr. Needham, that officer ordered a police post to be established at Laimakuri, a precaution, however, which brought but little improvement, for, in 1906, the Pasi Minyongs interfered with the Sissi Saw Mills; while, in 1907, they turned their attention once more to the Meckla Nadi Saw Mills.

Mr. Needham had now retired, and in 1908 his successor, the late Mr. Noel Williamson, tried other ways to cultivate the good graces of the Abor chiefs, and accordingly made a brief tour of the "Inner" line. Starting from Pasighat, Mr. Williamson passed through Ledum and Dijmur to Laimakuri, personally visiting a number of the chiefs. In 1909 he repeated the experiment when, in company with Colonel D. M. Lumsden, C.B., and Mr. W. L. B. Jackman, a member of the American Mission at Sadiya, he passed up the Dihang River to Kebang, where the further progress of the party was checked by an inter-tribal war.

Turned back in 1909, Mr. Noel Williamson made his third tour in the spring of 1911, when, accompanied by the late Dr. Gregorson and 47 coolies, he set out in March with the intention of visiting the Minyong Abors, for whom he carried

Photo] [*Elliott & Fry.*

COLONEL D. M. LUMSDEN, C.B.

THE LATE DOCTOR GREGORSON (CENTRE). TAMBA, TIBETAN SERVANT (ON RIGHT).

a number of gifts and medicines. Crossing the Dihang on March 22nd, Mr. Williamson halted at Sissin until March 29th, when he broke camp and pushed on to Komsing, which he reached early on March 30th, while Dr. Gregorson, with some sick coolies, remained at Sissin. Unhappily no further advance was to be made for Mr. Williamson at Komsing and Dr. Gregorson at Sissin were treacherously murdered by Minyong Abors on March 30th, together with the majority of their party.

CHAPTER III

Frontier Regulations — Previous Tours — Correspondence with Government—Tribal Treachery—Massacre of Mr. Noel Williamson, Dr. Gregorson and Party—A Gam's Story.

THE orders relating to projected tours beyond the area of political control on the north-east border of India are summed up briefly in the rule that the sanction of the Local Government must first be obtained in all cases. Where such tours are likely to involve complications of a nature that may render a punitive expedition necessary, the tour is not to be permitted without the previous approval of the Government of India. These rules were laid down in May 1900; they were reiterated in January 1904, in connection with a tour of the Naga Hills that was just then under consideration. On the 29th June, 1909, suggestions were made by the Government of Eastern Bengal and Assam to the Government of India for a visit by Mr. Williamson to certain villages in the Abor country, the farthest of which from the "Outer" line was Kebang. Sanction was given on the 7th September, 1909. For various reasons the tour could not be undertaken, and was finally abandoned in favour of the tour between the "Inner" and "Outer" lines, to which reference is made in the previous chapters. This was reported to the Government of India in a letter dated the 6th March, 1911, from which the following is an extract :—

"On the 19th January, 1909, you approved the draft instructions to be issued to the Assistant Political Officer, Sadiya, for his guidance when touring between the Inner and Outer lines of the Lakhimpur district. Owing to pressure of work in other quarters of the north-east frontier the Assistant Political Officer has not yet undertaken the tour contemplated in these instructions, and since these instructions were issued, the attempts to levy black-mail on timber-cutters have ceased. Mr. Williamson reports that there is no reason why he should not inform the villages who are cultivating within the Outer line that if they continue to cultivate they must pay poll-tax to the Government. Two at least of these villages will, he thinks, pay without demur. Under these circumstances His Honour would recommend that Mr. Williamson should visit this area during the course of one of his ordinary tours and arrange with the hillmen for the payment of poll-tax for land cultivated within our territory."

To this letter the Government of India telegraphed to the Government of Eastern Bengal and Assam, under date 22nd March, 1911, as follows :—

"Your letter of 6th instant. Do Lieutenant-Governor's proposals contemplate Mr. Williamson proceeding beyond the Outer line on present occasion?"

As they were uncertain of his intentions, the Government of Eastern Bengal and Assam telegraphed to Mr. Williamson under date 23rd March, 1911, as follows:—

"Presume that when touring between Inner and Outer lines it will not be necessary for you to cross Outer line?"

As no reply came, the message was repeated on 30th March by the Government of Eastern Bengal and Assam as follows:—

"My telegram, dated 23rd March, regarding Inner and Outer lines tour. Please wire urgent whether you propose to cross Outer line or not?"

No reply was received from Mr. Williamson. It appears now that he had left Sadiya on the 14th March, though the first information that he had crossed the "Outer" line and had penetrated into Abor country was contained in the telegram from the Political Clerk, Sadiya, reporting his death. The tour originally contemplated, to which reference has been made above, included the employment of a large military police guard. Mr. Williamson, however, had visited Kebang without a guard on a previous occasion when he had been received in a most friendly manner by the hillmen, and had been given a cordial invitation from Madu and other Gams to visit Komsing and Riu. In view of these circumstances Mr. Williamson concluded that he ran little risk by his visit, and dispensed with an escort. In the fullest confidence, too, that he would be received in the amicable spirit that had been shown before, he provided himself with a gramophone, a magic-lantern and a medicine chest.

The party accompanying Mr. Williamson consisted of one military police orderly; one coolie sirdar named Lal Bahadur; thirty-five Nepalese coolies; two servants; one Miri interpreter and three other Miris. He was also accompanied by Dr. Gregorson, a successful doctor in medical charge of the European and native staff of an important block of tea gardens at Tinsukia, in the Lakhimpur district, who took a deep interest in frontier tribes; and by the latter's Tibetan servants. The party left Jonakmukh at the mouth of the Sirki on the 19th March, and, according to the statement in the White Paper, the itinerary of the journey was as follows:—

March 19th	To camp below Rengging.
,, 20th	To camp near Rotung.
,, 21st	To Siring-Rengak-Yippor.
,, 22nd	Crossed the Dihang to Sissin.

March 23rd to 29th	Halted at Sissin.
„ 29th	To camp near Komsing.
„ 30th	To Komsing.

Mr. Williamson avoided Rengging, Rotung, Kebang and the neighbouring villages because of a bad outbreak of smallpox. During the halt at Sissin the coolies were sent back to Jonakmukh for rations. On the 30th March, Dr. Gregorson, with some sick coolies, including the sirdar, Lal Bahadur, were left at Sissin, and Mr. Williamson resumed his march. He had been received in such a friendly manner that his suspicions were entirely lulled, and during the march his rifle and revolver were with his bedding. Madu, the Gam of Komsing, who had been foremost in inviting Mr. Williamson to visit his village in 1909, met him on his arrival. The baggage was put down and the coolies taken to a large house, where a quantity of drink was produced. Mr. Williamson warned the coolies not to drink too much, and was then conducted by Madu Gam to the place where he was to camp. His Naga servant, Vichey, followed him at some little distance.

As they turned the corner out of sight of the coolies the latter were invited to enter the house. Suddenly Vichey came running back shouting "the Sahib is killed." As if this had been a signal a pandemonium ensued in the village, where it is said that 1000 Abors had assembled. The panic-stricken coolies burst out of the house but were cut down with long swords, one survivor escaping by jumping out of the back of the house and running to the other end of the village. Vichey and the cook succeeded in finding two guns and a little ammunition, and with the few surviving coolies retired from the village. With the aid of their guns they held off the Abors until ammunition ran short. The White Paper states that the cook shot himself with the last cartridge, while the fates of Vichey and of the orderly were unknown. Of the whole party, only five got away, and they fled through the jungle chased by Abors with dogs; eventually they reached the river at Sissin where they saw no sign of the doctor. His tent had disappeared, and an ominous gathering of vultures hung over the encampment.

The last news was contained in a letter written by the Miri interpreter to his wife in Sisserimukh. He informed her that he had arrived at Pangighat and had heard that the Kebang Abors objected to the party proceeding farther. He added that the Burra sahib insisted on going on, and that his impression was that they would never return. The interpreter's "impression," however, was right only in one direction, for his master did not intend and made no effort to visit Kebang. Apart from the fact that the village was stricken with smallpox, Mr. Williamson had visited the place on an earlier trip.

Further light on the massacre is thrown by the statements of two of the survivors of the party with Mr. Williamson. An extract from the statement of Randhojo Thapa (Thakur) is as follows :—

"On the morning of the 17th (Friday) we reached an Abor village—Komsing—at about ten a.m. There were some Abors with us carrying the baggage. In the middle of the village there was a big basha house, in which we were told to keep the baggage. The Burra sahib's tent was pitched a little distance from the godown. After pitching the tent, etc., we went into the godown to rest. At about twelve o'clock about 1500 Abors came armed with spears, dhaos, bows and arrows. They began to shout, and entering the godown began massacring us with dhaos, spears and arrows. In the *mêlée* I took out my kukri, and flourishing it in my hand escaped into the jungle. The Abors chased me a little distance with dogs, and then went back. I do not know what happened to the Burra sahib. I heard five shots fired from his tent. I saw several of our men being killed. While escaping I wounded one or two of the Abors with my kukri, but not seriously. I ran through the jungle, and in the evening I was joined by three other Nepalese coolies on the river-bank. We made a bamboo raft and tried to cross the river, but the raft sank. At about ten o'clock in the night we came across a raft made by the Abors. This raft was found by us on the night of the 18th day. While crossing in this raft one of our men got drowned. We passed the

Doctor sahib's camp in the night. I heard a lot of shouting and saw a number of Abors going about with torches. We lay down flat on the raft for fear of being detected. I did not hear any shots being fired from this camp. We did not know how to row, so we let the raft float, and the next day touched the other bank at a bend. We were afraid of being seen, so followed the course of the river through the jungle. We camped that night at the foot of the hill. It was raining all night. Next morning we again followed the same course. On the 21st day we saw some Abors coming in a boat towards us, so fearing lest they should murder us we ran in all directions and separated. I ran up a hill and passed the night in a tree, in the rain. On the morning of the 22nd I came down and again followed the course of the river. Some Abors meantime had come across one of our party and brought him along with them. They now encountered me and took me also along with them. My companion, being afraid, got off on the pretence of attending to the call of nature. I do not know what became of him subsequently. Me the Abors took to their village, and after giving me something to eat told me they were going to cross me to the other side. They crossed me in a boat and took me to a Miri village. We passed the night there, and next morning the Abors, accompanied by some Miris, took me in a boat to the steamer."

The statement of Narsing Thapa, another survivor, runs :—

"On the 7th day we halted in a village—Komsing—where the Abors gave us a house to put the *mal* (kit), and the Burra sahib told us not to leave the *mal* on any account. The sahib camped in a tent quite close to our house. We reached this village about ten a.m. About one or one-and-a-half hours after reaching the village the Abors assembled with dhaos and spears. There was shouting of Abors. They entered our house and began to use dhaos and spears on us. I did not see the sahib then and don't know where he was. God knows whether he is killed or not. We left the Doctor sahib two days' march behind this village. The Abors surrounded us. I myself saw five men killed inside. I don't know how many men were killed outside. I jumped off the back machan, which was the height of two elephants. I went through the jungle, and at ten o'clock that night I came to the spot where we had left the Doctor sahib. I did not see the Doctor sahib or any of his *mal*, only Abors. I heard two shots from this camp. I can't say whether the Abors in the Doctor sahib's camp had guns in their hands. About four miles from the village I met two other men who had gone with us and the Burra sahib to the village. I did not see any of the men who had been left with the Doctor sahib. The Burra sahib's orderly bolted with me for about 200 yards, but we lost one another in the jungle. I went along the river-bank in the jungle for five days. For two days I followed the left bank of river and crossed below a big village on a bamboo raft. Three of us crossed.

It is not one of the villages we passed through on the upward journey. After two days and one night wandering in the jungle after crossing the river we came out on to a river to drink water, where we met some Pasi Abors, who took us to their village and gave us food, and then took us three or four hours in a boat, where they put us on a steamer.

"The Burra sahib had a pistol, the doctor's servant had a magazine rifle, the Burra sahib's orderly and cook had each a magazine rifle, and Vichey (Mr. Williamson's Naga servant) had a Martini-Henry rifle. The Doctor sahib had a pistol. The Doctor sahib stayed behind to look after three sick coolies.

"In the village where we were attacked there were thirty-three of us in the godown and the Burra sahib, Malina (a Miri interpreter or servant of Williamson) and two Miri chokras—boys—outside. I did not hear any cry from the Burra sahib owing to the cry of the Abors. When I had run for about 300 yards I heard only one shot. We were sitting talking in the godown when the Abors attacked us. We drew our kukris and defended ourselves as well as we could. Not less than 1000 Abors attacked us.

"The village is about as big as Kohima in the Naga Hills. I cut three men with my kukri.

"After leaving the doctor we marched from early morning till late in the evening, when we camped by a small nulla with a little water in it. There the Abors brought fowls to the Burra sahib, and forty to fifty of them remained in camp with us.

"The Abors of this side (right bank) of the river helped us to cross the river.

"The Burra sahib employed some Pasi Abor coolies in addition to us in carrying loads, and they stole things on the march. They went with us as far as the river and then went back.

"I was struck by a dhao on the right thigh.

"The path was very steep and in many cases it was necessary to climb up steps.

"The river where we crossed was about 200 yards wide, easy current, very deep.

"The village where we were attacked was about three hours' march from the place where the Abors brought in presents to the Burra sahib and camped with us.

"The attack was on a Friday.

"When we bolted the Abors put dogs on us to pursue us. I heard and saw some dogs. The Abors chased us for three days."

In tracing the story of the massacre with the help of the details that appear in the Parliamentary papers on this subject, as has been done up to this point, the action of the Abors must seem to have been carried out in a spirit of most wanton aggression. Investigation on the spot, however, showed too that the murders were almost entirely unpremeditated. Many reasons were put forward at the time to explain the crime, though few were of any value, and it is necessary to accept the story of the gam, which appears on another page, for the true explanation of the deed. Colonel Sir Thomas Holdich, the eminent authority on the frontier problems of India, put forward the view that the tribesmen were incited to the deed by their belief that we had been "kicked out" of Tibet, a country immediately contiguous to their own, after an ineffectual attempt to establish ourselves in the valley of the Upper Brahmaputra.

Another theory was that the more savage Abors were jealous of the intrusion of the white man, and took the drastic step of slaughtering Mr. Williamson and his party merely to indicate their displeasure at his persistent advance into their country. In support of this it was explained that all hillmen on the Indian frontier desired to act as middlemen for the tribes more distant than themselves from the plains, and resented any action that might lead to the establishment of direct communication between their northern neighbours and the marts from which rice, salt, iron, and cloths were obtained.

A third opinion suggested that the Pasi Minyongs may have felt indignant over the way in which they were treated after the Bor Abor expedition of 1894, and saw in the presence of Mr. Williamson's party an opportunity to give vent to a long-smouldering bitterness. In explanation of this reasoning it should be stated that in 1894 a blockade of the Padams was instituted, which, on Mr. Needham's recommendation, included the Pasi Minyongs on the ground that, if they were allowed free access to the plains, they would supply their neighbours with necessaries, and render the blockade ineffectual. This is in accordance with the policy laid down in Sir Alexander Mackenzie's standard work on the *North-Eastern Frontier of Bengal.* At the same time the "posas," or allowances of both tribes, were stopped, in spite of the fact that it was not proved that the Pasi Minyongs had joined the Padams in resisting the march of the punitive column. Mr. Needham subsequently withdrew his recommendations, and the blockade was gradually allowed to fall into abeyance. At the same time the "posa" of the Pasi Minyongs was not restored to the tribe, who have always regarded its stoppage as an act of injustice.

Interesting as these suggested motives for the massacre may be, it is to be feared that they throw less light upon the causes of the crime than that cast by the explanation of an Abor gam which is published for the first time in the pages of this volume. The sequence of events as recorded by this gam, who was well known to the members of the party, will be found to differ in so many important particulars from that set forth by the extracts from the White Paper with which this chapter opens, that it is easy to believe it bears the impress of the truth, and is, in fact, a correct record of the events which culminated in the massacre. In a measure the statement by the gam is a vindication of Mr. Williamson out of the mouth of an Abor.

It is offered here because, in the absence of adequate and accurate information, public opinion has been inclined to attribute the loss of his own life, as well as those of his companions, to Mr. Williamson's admitted contravention of the spirit of the regulations in respect of the Inner and Outer lines of India's north-eastern frontier. If the gam's version of the murders makes one point clearer than another, however, it is the fact that the motive for the outrage had its sole origin in the loquacity of the Miri letter-carrier, over which, as will be seen, Mr. Williamson could exercise absolutely no control. If it had not been for the Miri runner's unfortunate interpretation of the colours of the three envelopes, it seems humanly probable that Mr. Williamson and his party would have been alive to-day, justified by the results of the visit in the opinion that the Abors of Komsing intended to be, wished to be, and would have been both peaceful and amicable in their reception of their visitors.

To understand the course of events, to which the gam's narrative alludes, it is necessary to go back to the morning of March 22nd, when Mr. Williamson and his party were preparing to cross from their camp at Komlinghat on the right bank of the Dihang to Sissin on the left bank. Orders had been issued for the camp to be struck and the coolies were piling the kit into their baskets when four youths appeared on the scene with messages from Takat Gam of Kebang. These messengers stated that they had been ordered by Takat Gam on no account to allow Mr. Williamson's party to cross the river as, if it was to do so, unfriendly Abors would certainly attack the travellers. When it was learnt that four men from Kebang, where a very virulent type of small pox was raging at the time, had come into the lines, Mr. Williamson was alarmed, and, explaining that he had already seen Kebang and did not wish to see it again he bade the messengers keep away from his camp. In the meantime Mr. Williamson continued his preparations for crossing the river. Acting on their conception of the instructions given to them by Takat Gam, the four youths now proceeded to line up before him as though to bar the way to the river, whereupon Mr. Williamson stated that his movements were no concern of theirs and ordered the youths to stand aside. The leader of the four youths, by name Lalo, at first demurred though finally he acquiesced and, with his companions, returned to Kebang, while Mr. Williamson and his party crossed over to Sissin.

With the river successfully negotiated, the further advance of the travellers was delayed for a few days by the sickness of some coolies, Mr. Williamson and Dr. Gregorson assisting to build a temporary hospital for the accommodation of the sufferers. After the halt of a week at Sissin, it was decided to send back the worst cases to Pasighat; accordingly, on March 29th, three Nepalese, accompanied by one Miri who, it seems, was carrying three letters began the return journey. When the three Nepalese and the Miri had been safely started, Mr. Williamson left Dr. Gregorson behind in charge of the sick coolies and began his journey to Komsing. After an uneventful progress he camped at nightfall, on March 29th, in the jungle a few miles from his objective. When the news of Mr. Williamson's presence reached Komsing presents of fowls were sent to him by the Gam of Komsing, and some two score of Abors belonging to the place joined him.

Unlike Mr. Williamson who, hampered by the difficulties of the way, was travelling slowly, the three Nepalese coolies and the Miri moved rapidly. After their departure from Sissin camp with the first signs of light on the morning of March 29th, and the river safely crossed, the party pushed ahead and reached Rotung village by nightfall. The welcome extended to them at Rotung was friendly, and both food and quarters were provided for the strangers. Stimulated by the interest taken in their presence in the village, the Miri who was carrying the letters began to descant upon the importance of his charge and flourished the envelopes before the eyes of his host, whose curiosity was at once aroused by a variation in the colours of the envelopes. The Abors are accustomed to convey news by symbols ; as one letter was contained in the red envelope of the Telegraph service ; another in a black-bordered envelope, and a third in a grey envelope, the Rotung villagers readily believed that the three letters bore special significance. Gratified by the sensation the missives had created, in reply to the inquiries of the villagers the Miri letter-carrier explained that death lurked in the red envelope as it was an order for troops to be sent to punish the men of Kebang for attempting to prevent Mr. Williamson from crossing the river ; that the black-bordered envelope called for guns which would crumble mountains and pass through stockades as a stone through water ; finally that the grey envelope was an instruction to Mekir, the Gam of Pasighat, to arrange coolies to carry the rations of the sepoys referred to by the red envelope.

Alarmed by what they had heard, the villagers communicated the news to their headman, who decided that at all costs letters of such dire consequence must be intercepted, and with that purpose in view he laid his plans. Ignorant of the far-reaching effects of his foolish story, the Miri letter-carrier with his companions left at daybreak on the morning of March 30th for Pasighat. Everything proceeded quietly with the party and the returning travellers were approaching Royi Hill, in the vicinity of Old Rengging, when they were overtaken by a body of Rotung braves and killed before resistance could be offered.

With so much accomplished, the tidings were sent off hot-foot to Babuk and Kebang, whither a report concerning the meaning of the letters carried by the Miri runner already had been dispatched by the Gam of Rotung. The result of the action of the Rotung men was awaited not without impatience in Kebang, where, when the news of the success of the ambush was received, a council of state was summoned. At this meeting the warlike spirit of those attending was evidenced, but Takat Gam, who had sent the friendly warning to Mr. Williamson in the first instance, endeavoured to prevent his men from having anything to do with the business. The fighting blood of Kebang was aroused, however, and Takat Gam was over-ruled, while at the instigation of Lomgah Gam, a brother of Lombeng Gam of Komsing, it was decided to attack the travellers at once.

With this object in view, a large party of armed men, estimated at five or six score, crossed the

Dihang at Rebhing Ghat and came up with Dr. Gregorson at Panggi, to which place he had moved from the camp at Sissin. Dr. Gregorson was accompanied by his Tibetan servant, Tamba; by the coolie sirdar Lal Bahadur, and by an interpreter, Moria. Tamba was cooking; Lal Bahadur was suffering from headache and was lying down; Dr. Gregorson was sitting on his bed in his tent engaged with Moria when, without any warning, the Kebang men rushed in. No defence was offered by Dr. Gregorson or his interpreter, and the pair were cut down before either of them had time to realise their position. Tamba was killed at once, but Lal Bahadur was only wounded and escaped to become the chief guide to Major-General Bower.

From Dr. Gregorson's camp, the Kebang men hurried on to Komsing, where they found a dense throng of men, women and children regarding Mr. Williamson's tent with curiosity. The Kebang men arrived as Mr. Williamson was moving off with Lombeng Gam and among them, highly indignant at the fruitless character of his previous journey, was Lalo, the leader of the four messengers that Takat Gam had sent to Komlinghat. Up to this point Mr. Williamson's reception had been friendly and he was invited to the gam's house, while the rest of the party and the kit were taken to the moshup. Meanwhile Mr. Williamson had ordered a hot bath, which the cook was preparing, and he was dressed in a vest, a pair of shorts and chaplies in readiness for it. He had no watch upon him and his firearms were in the tent. When Mr. Williamson entered Lombeng Gam's house he noticed that Lalo and three or four other Kebang men had followed after him and that one and all were armed. As neither he nor the gam were carrying arms, and the attitude of the village was friendly, the presence of armed men from Kebang in his host's house surprised him, and he asked the gam—

"What are these men from Kebang doing in Komsing?"

Lombeng Gam was unaware of the presence of any large party of Kebang men in Komsing and said so to his guest. As the gam replied one of the Kebang men flourished his dhao, and Mr. Williamson then asked—

"Why do they come armed into my presence? They are wearing swords: do they intend to attack me?"

Lombeng Gam knew nothing of the dastardly intentions of the Kebang party, and replied casually—

"No, sahib; it's Kebang custom for them to carry swords."

While the gam was speaking, one of the Kebang men then drew his dhao and began to point a piece of bamboo. As though this were the signal agreed upon between themselves, Lalo, who was standing a little to the rear of Mr. Williamson, slashed suddenly at his right arm, wounding him just above the wrist. Lombeng Gam was overwhelmed with surprise at the attack, but Mr. Williamson tried to catch the dhao with his left hand when he was killed by a stroke on the head, which brought him to the ground. The Kebang party then raised an alarm of fire; and, while the Komsing people came pouring out of their houses with chatties of water, the Kebang men dashed into the moshup and began cutting down the Nepalese. General uproar followed for a little time, though nobody tried to prevent the Kebang men from killing the coolies.

At the moment of Lalo's attack on Mr. Williamson, the servant Vichey was cleaning his master's guns in the tent. Suddenly some one shouted, "The Sahib is cut!" whereupon Malinar, an interpreter, and Bhudhiman, the cook, joined Vichey in the tent and, grabbing as many cartridges as they could get, the three men began to fire on the crowd. Two old men were killed inside their houses by bullets passing through the walls, and Yassan, a woman, and Sagon, a young man, were wounded in the open. When he saw what was happening, Lombeng Gam shouted to the three men not to shoot in the village and ordered them to go outside.

THE MAN WHO ACTUALLY KILLED MR. NOEL WILLIAMSON, IN CHARGE OF AN ESCORT OF MILITARY POLICE.

THREE OF THE MURDERERS UNDER GUARD OF MILITARY POLICE.

Reading from left to right.—1. Morsang, who cut down Doctor Gregorson. 2. The Gam of Rotung, who gave the order for the massacre of the letter-carriers. 3. One of the men who cut down the letter-carriers.

The three men thereupon retired, and, covering their retreat with their rifles, made good their escape to the river, where they were joined by four Nepalese coolies who had escaped from the moshup. For three days the seven fugitives sheltered under the bank of the Dihang near Panggi, and kept the Abors at a distance while the cartridges lasted. On the third day Malinar, having exhausted his ammunition, threw away his rifle and swam the river. Reaching Babuk in safety, he at first was given food and drink by the headman of the village, but when it was found out who he was he was seized and pounded with stones till nearly dead, when a small boy was ordered to cut his throat. His body was thrown down one of the hills.

When Bhudhiman had finished his cartridges he, too, threw away his rifle, but he was shot with an arrow while swimming the river. Vichey and one of the Nepalese coolies made their way along the bank of the river as far as Sissin, where they took shelter among the branches of a large tree. They were discovered by two Sissin men who were returning from hunting. One of these made overtures to Vichey, and offered him some rice in a leaf with his left hand, while he held his dhao ready in the right. Vichey saw this and shot the man dead. The coolie then made a dash from the tree to get the dhao from the Sissin man's body, and on returning found that Vichey had been killed by the second Abor, who had climbed up and cut him down whilst the gun was being reloaded. The coolie then ran away to the river and, carrying the dhao in his teeth, swam across and escaped, as the Sissin man had no arrows and the rifle had been rendered useless by the sword cut. Out of the seven who escaped only three survived.

Two Miris, Tanyong and Dhaniram, who had been cutting boats for Mr. Williamson at Komlinghat, and were not in Komsing, were attacked by men from Babuk, and killed. When all the party had been wiped out the Kebang men claimed the credit for the deed, and had Mr. Williamson's property handed over to them. They took it with them to Kebang when they returned and, on their arrival there, celebrated their success by deposing Takat Gam from his position as chief of Kebang and by installing Lomgah Gam in his place.

In what he did Mr. Williamson no doubt was in error. Yet, if nothing had happened to his party, his technical "breach" of the spirit of the official regulations would have been regarded as of such small consequence that any information gained by the journey would have been accounted to his credit. While his tour may have been a little untimely, nothing in it can justify the characteristically petty strictures passed upon it by Mr. Frederic

Mackarness in a letter that he contributed to the *Westminster Gazette.* Even Sir Lancelot Hare, the Lieutenant-Governor of the Province, and head of the department of the Government of India most concerned in the developments which sprang from the massacre, refrained from criticism, while every other fair-minded person followed suit. At the very least Mr. Mackarness might have held his peace until the facts were before him. As it was he preferred to jump to conclusions, and to ventilate his ignorance in a letter to the press that was cruel, cowardly and contemptible.

In a measure Mr. Williamson, in paying his visit to the Minyong Abors, was acting in the best interests of his work. It is one of the duties of the Assistant Political Officer at Sadiya, which position Mr. Williamson filled, to maintain relations with the tribesmen that inhabit the foothills of the Himalayas and their offshoots surrounding the crescent-shaped valley in which the plains of Upper Assam terminate. Beginning at the southern end of the crescent these tribes are as follows: Rangpang and Sarkari Nagas, Singphos, Khamptis, Digaru and Meju Mishmis, Chulikatta and Bebejiya Mishmis; then directly north of Sadiya, the Bor Abors; and west and south of them, mostly on the right bank of the Dihang River, the Pasi Minyong Abors. West of these again come other tribes of Abors of a less turbulent character, such as the Doba or Galong Abors of the Dijmur and Sissi Rivers. Beyond the Sissi River reside various tribes of hill Miris as far as the Ranganadi River. Across the river are found the Daflas, who stretch far down the frontier of the Darrang district, and somewhat behind these, in the hills above the North Lakhimpur station, are the Apa Tanangs, into which country an expedition was led by Mr. Macabe in 1896.

Mr. Williamson himself was a man of proved tact and of more than twenty years' experience in dealing with the tribes that have just been enumerated, so that it becomes fairly certain that the catastrophe resulted from unforeseen circumstances. He was specially selected in 1905 to succeed Mr. F. J. Needham, who had held the same difficult post with great distinction since its creation in 1882. He was a member of the Indian Police Service. Before his promotion to Sadiya he had had a long and distinguished career in similar semi-political posts in savage hill tracts in Lushailand and in the Naga Hills district; while, since 1905, he had made many successful journeys by which the influence of the solitary European representative of the British power at Sadiya had been greatly extended. In particular he had established most friendly relations with the Digaru and Meju Mishmis, lying between Sadiya and Rima. He had conducted two punitive promenades against the Rangpang Nagas in 1909 and November 1910, outside the immediate sphere of his activity, in the Dafla Hills on the Darrang border. He had journeyed thrice to the borders of Tibet, in 1907, 1909, and 1911; on the latter occasion actually reaching Rima, through the assistance he received from a Tibetan servant of Doctor Gregorson, who, by the way, was among those killed at Komsing.

In addition to performing these and other journeys, Mr. Williamson, who was a scientific cartographer, trained in the use of the theodolite at the establishments of the Government of India's Survey Department at Dehra Dun, had prepared reliable maps of his routes, supplementing and extending the frontier work of the Survey Department. In this manner he had mapped the course of the Lohit branch of the Brahmaputra as far as the borders of the Meju Mishmi country, discovering a very distinct change in the course of the river as hitherto shown. He had also laid down the unexplored course of the Dihang River from the plains of Assam as far as the village of Kebang, and he had fixed from a distance the position of Riu.

His friend and companion on this ill-fated journey, Doctor Gregorson, was no less experienced in intercourse with hillmen. He had travelled very extensively in Sikhim, besides up and down among the hill-folk of the north-eastern border for many years past. He was a student of Tibetan, and had three or four Tibetans in his employ for the purpose of studying their language. One of these Tibetan servants had been lent to Mr. Williamson on the occasion of that explorer's trip in 1909 towards the frontier of Tibet *via* the Meju Mishmi country; and again in 1911.

Widely known and universally liked, Doctor Gregorson was mourned by every one in the Province. He has been succeeded at Dibrugarh by Doctor Roberts, a medical man from Australia, who has made himself popular. Natives take very kindly to European medical men, and trust them under conditions where no amount of official representation would carry any weight. In time, too, Doctor Roberts will more than fill the position held by his predecessor as he has the quick intelligence and broad sympathy necessary to a frontier doctor. Doctor Gregorson, however, had to spend the best years of his life among the people on the north-eastern frontier of India before he received their confidence, and Dr. Roberts will no less have to 'bide a 'wee.''

On receipt of tidings of the outrage, Mr. Harrison, the manager of the Meckla Nadi Saw Mills, at once started up the Dihang in the hopes of affording assistance to any possible survivors. He succeeded in rescuing the three Nepalese, two of whose statements appear on a previous page. The news of the massacre reached Dibrugarh on April 5th, whereupon Mr. Bentinck, the Deputy-Commissioner of Lakhimpur, and Captain Sir George Duff-Sutherland-Dunbar, Bart., Commandant of the Lakhimpur Military Police, at once pushed off with a movable column of 150 men. They travelled *via* Saikhwaghat, and thence up the Dihang to Pasighat in boats, while an officer of the 114th Native Infantry, with an escort and a party of signallers, was sent to Saikhwa to keep open communication with Pasighat.

On receipt of the news at Shillong, the Lieutenant-Governor, Sir Lancelot Hare, consulted Major-General H. Bower, C.B., the officer commanding the Assam Brigade and a soldier who had had great experience of frontier expeditions. Major-General Bower advised, as there was no hope for any of the party except those who had already reached the plains, that the small force that had already taken the field should stand fast at Pasighat until the rains were over; and that any advance into the Abor country to punish the villages concerned in the massacre and to arrest the murderers should be deferred until the beginning of the cold weather. A little later Mr. W. C. M. Dundas, who was ultimately placed in charge of the political mission that was sent to the Mishmi tribes, succeeded the late Mr. Noel

Williamson as Political Officer at Sadiya ; and, on April 18th, Major-General Bower started on a tour of inspection of the disaffected region as a preliminary to taking up the task of organising the punitive columns that were to form the expedition.

CHAPTER IV

The Plan of Campaign—The Troops Employed—The Career of Major-General Hamilton Bower, C.B., General Officer Commanding the Operations.

THE plan advocated by Major-General Bower in the forthcoming operations favoured the employment of an expedition that could be separated into three or more mobile columns, made up of one R.M.L. seven-pounder gun with crew, a corps of bomb throwers, a body of pioneers, and four companies of infantry with maxim detachments. It was suggested that the advance of the troops as far as the advanced base at Pasighat should be by two divisions: a main force which should march in two columns; and a supporting force, constituting a column similar in strength with the two halves of the main body and serving as a safeguard against any attack on the western flank of the advance, that should move by way of the Poba River and the Ledum villages.

When the two parts of the main column and the Ledum force had united at some point on the river, a direct advance upon Kebang was favoured after which it was intended that the force should break again into small columns. Broadly speaking, while one column was expected to cross the Dihang and proceed against Komsing and Riu, other columns were to operate on the right bank and to be ready for any special mission that the situation might demand. In addition to these field columns, Major-General Bower required a force at Pasighat that would be strong enough to act as escort to the supply trains, to guard the base depôt, or to be used as a containing line against the Bor Abors should they move in support of the Pasi Minyongs. Finally, as the expedition would have to remain some time in the hills, he pointed out that the services of a Pioneer regiment for improving the lines of communication would be necessary.

As the views of Major-General Bower were endorsed by the Government of Eastern Bengal and Assam, which was supported in turn by the Government of India, the Secretary of State approved the proposals, and, on July 24th, 1911, sanctioned the preparations for the expedition. Public opinion was at first slow to concentrate itself upon the Abor operations; but, so soon as the precise nature of the theatre of war was realised, the greatest possible attention was aroused by the character of the campaign. Jungle warfare was not unknown to India. All the same, it was necessary to go back many years to find a parallel with the contemplated expedition for, though there had been "little wars" innumerable on the north-west frontier of India, the hills, rivers, and the wide areas of primeval forest, which make up so much of the north-east frontier, were quite unlike the regions in which the wily Pathan has his home.

Under these circumstances popular interest in the preparations which Major-General Bower had in hand grew rapidly, and satisfaction was universally expressed at the fact that the bulk of the troops was to be drawn from the Gurkha Battalions of the Indian Army. There was no special reason for this distinction beyond the fact that the Assam Brigade, which forms a part of the Eighth Division, is largely a Gurkha Force. The Gurkha is the "handy-man" of India, and Gurkha sepoys are deservedly most popular figures with the "man in the street." Short and sturdy, they are as active as cats on the hills, and take to bush warfare instinctively; in fact, as naturally as do the Yaos, who figure so prominently in the operations of every African field force.

The details of the force finally chosen were as follows:—

Two 7-pounder R.M.L. guns worked with infantry crews.

No. 1 Company, King George's Own Sappers and Miners.

Detachment 31st Signal Company, Sappers and Miners.

32nd Sikh Pioneers.

1st Battalion 8th Gurkha Rifles with maxims.

1st Battalion 2nd King Edward's Own Gurkha Rifles with maxims.

Four hundred Lakhimpur Military Police with maxims.

Detachment of Assam Valley and Surma Valley Light Horse with maxim.

Native Carrier Transport; Boat Transport Detachment.

One section of Indian Field Ambulance.

Two Mule Transport Corps.

From time to time other details were added to the strength, though, from first to last, the expedition never lost the appearance of a compact punitive body. In all, some 3000 troops and 3500 to 4000 Naga coolies were employed.

The principal staff officers comprised :—

Major C. A. R. Hutchinson, 41st Dogras; General Staff Officer (2nd Grade).

Lieutenant J. H. Knight, Royal Artillery; Brigade Signalling Officer.

Major J. Davidson, I.M.S.; Assistant Director of Medical Service.

Deputy-Commissioner Mr. A. Bentinck, I.C.S.; Assistant Political Officer.

CAPTAIN POOLE, D.S.O.
Official Correspondent.

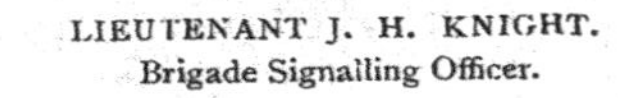

LIEUTENANT J. H. KNIGHT.
Brigade Signalling Officer.

SURVIVORS OF THE MASSACRE.

Reading from Left to Right.—1. Degum, an ex-Abor slave, used as an interpreter and guide. 2. Narsing Thapa, one of Mr. Williamson's coolies who escaped. 3. Lal Bahadur, who was cut down but escaped to become chief guide to Major-General Bower.

Captain W. B. Hore, 120th Rajputana Infantry; Intelligence Officer.

Colonel D. C. MacIntyre; Administ.-Commandant base and Inspector line of communications.

Major E. G. Vaughan, Supply and Transport Corps; Assistant Director of Supplies.

(Major Vaughan had had war service in the Chin-Lushai expedition of 1889–90; Burma; British East Africa; North-West Frontier.)

Captain L. H. S. Smithers, 17th Infantry (the Loyal Regiment); Orderly Officer to Major-General Bower.

Captain C. W. F. Melville; Staff Surgeon to Major-General Bower.

Captain Becher, 2nd Gurkha Rifles; Provost Marshal.

Captain O. H. B. Trenchard, R.E.; Director of Surveys.

Other officers included:—

Supply and Transport Officers:—

Major H. M. M. Brooke; Base Supply and Transport Officer.

(Major Brooke belongs to the Supply and Transport Corps, and is a Deputy Assistant Director of Transport, Quartermaster-General's Branch.)

Captain M. Synge.

(Captain Synge had seen service in Tibet.)

Captain W. B. Dunlop.

(Captain Dunlop had seen service in Tibet.)

Officers of Coolie Corps :—

Captain C. W. Hext. Captain Geoghegan.
Captain Price. Captain Timbrell.
Captain G. W. Bond.

Survey Officers :—

Lieutenant G. F. T. Oakes, R.E.

Attached for scientific purposes :—

Mr. I. H. Burkhill, Botanist.
Mr. S. W. Kemp, Zoologist.
Mr. R. Hodgart, Anthropologist and Geologist.

Over all as the officer commanding was Major-General Hamilton Bower, C.B., who had commanded the Assam Brigade at Shillong since December 1st, 1908, and was quite rightly a soldier in whom public, military and official circles had complete faith. Every one knew, too, that General Bower possessed the confidence of his men in a most complete degree; and, further, that he had a very thorough knowledge of the tribal and physical peculiarities of the Assam border, so that there was nowhere heard two opinions upon the wisdom of the appointment.

No one was less liable than Major-General Bower

to make mistakes in the very difficult task which awaited him, and his tact and *savoir faire* in delicate circumstances cannot be better illustrated than by recalling the story of his career. By a strange coincidence it may be said to have begun with a mission from the Government of India to avenge the murder of a British officer in the wilds of Asia. On that occasion Major-General Bower was asked to hunt down a man who had all Asia before him in which to cover his tracks.

It was many years ago, and in the days when the question of a remunerative commerce between India and the wealthy districts of Chinese Turkestan was busily discussed. Amongst the earliest pioneers and the most strenuous advocates of this trade were men of the stamp of Dalgleish, with whom were associated a few others who risked their lives in an earnest quest for geographical knowledge, and a determined effort to turn that knowledge to practical account. On the 8th of April, 1888, Dalgleish with his caravan had reached the northern side of the Karakorum Pass on his way to Yarkand. The camp was pitched in snow, and all seemed peaceful. Suddenly Dalgleish was attacked by a Pathan named Dad Muhammad, who had joined the party *en route*, and there and then hacked to pieces without a hand being lifted in rescue. Dalgleish's faithful dog seized the murderer by the leg, and was killed for his pains,

Dad Muhammad wandering forth from the camp unmolested, nor was any effort made by any Central Asian authority to arrest him.

Eighteen months afterwards, Lieutenant Bower —he was then a subaltern in the 17th Bengal Cavalry—was at Yarkand on a shooting expedition, when he received instructions from the Government of India to bring Dad Muhammad to justice. It seemed to be quite a futile suggestion, but, as the event proved, the quest was not so hopeless as at first it had appeared. Setting to work, Bower gathered information from all quarters, and dispatched agents westward to Afghan Turkestan to head off the murderer in that direction, whilst he himself scoured Chinese Turkestan to the east. Rumours of Dad Muhammad seemed to flow in from all sides.

From Yarkand to Kashgar and Aksu the trail seemed clear, but at Aksu the murderer had apparently doubled back through the Kirghiz country between the Russian and Chinese posts. Then came news of a man in hiding in the wild jungles of Karashahr, and Bower prosecuted his hunt eastwards. He hunted through the Kuchar and Bagur districts, making important discoveries by the way which opened up the first glimpses of that strange tragedy of sand-buried cities (the lost and forgotten centre of Buddhism) which has since been so remarkably verified by the researches of Sven Hedin and of

Stein. Finding himself on a false scent, Bower returned to Kuchar, wandering through a strange land within sight of the snowy ridges of the Thian Shan, and exploring as he went the subterranean ruins of Mingoi. Working by night for fear of interference, he secured none the less the packet of those ancient manuscripts, now known as the Bower manuscripts, which ever since have aroused the envy and curiosity of all the leading Orientalists in India and England.

At Kuchar he awaited news from his scattered agents. It was clear that Dad Muhammad had not gone eastwards, so Bower lost no time in returning by Awat and Maralbashi to Kashgar, which city he reached on the 1st of April, 1890. Whilst at Kashgar he received news of the success of his quest westward through Balkh and Afghan Turkestan. His agents had picked up the trail of the murderer at Balkh, and had hunted him through Chinese Turkestan into Russian territory, when by a lucky chance Dad Muhammad was recognised in the bazaar at Samarkand. Having been provided with letters to the Russian Governor of Samarkand, Bower's agents demanded official help, which being forthcoming secured the arrest of the fugitive who was promptly lodged in a Russian gaol to await extradition for the murder he had committed two years before. He did not await it: he hanged himself with his belt, and thus closed one of the strangest episodes in the history of Indian frontier crime.

Shortly after the successful termination of his pursuit of Dad Muhammad, Bower, in 1891, embarked on an expedition across Tibet from west to east, which was very rich in important discoveries. At a later date he returned to the scenes of his hunt, adding some remarkable travels in the Pamirs to the record of his earlier explorations in the deserts of Chinese Turkestan.

In 1899 he became the recipient of the Founders' Gold Medal of the Royal Geographical Society. His interest in the Abor operations therefore was manifestly twofold; for, a keen soldier, he was also an intrepid explorer.

Known in the service as Buddha Bower because of the unusual solemnity of his expression, General Bower cuts a very dignified figure. His hair is grey. His skin is tanned and roughened by exposure, while his face is prematurely wrinkled, though distinguished by large thoughtful-looking eyes and an attractive ruggedness about his nose and chin. Slow in speech, placid in manner, cautious in action, his study of languages—for he is the master of several—has given him a taste for detail, which naturally caused him to see that every part of his expedition was in smooth-running order before he embarked on the troublesome task of crushing the Abors.

A giant in height, but of delicate physique, he is good-tempered, and possesses the knack of winning the confidence of people wherever he goes, and of putting every one at ease. His success in the army has been well earned, and is due to merit rather than to any friendly influence. Although his earlier years in the Service were occupied with exploring work in the uplands of Asia, he has taken his career very seriously, and can look back to having been one of Kitchener's men at Suakim during the Egyptian operations of 1896. Four years later he went through the Boxer crisis of 1900, being present at the relief of Tientsin and Pekin, though his chief opportunity came with his work in the Chinese Wei-Hai-Wei Regiment, of which he was the colonel, and for which he received his C.B.

Though Chinese themselves, the men of the Wei-Hai-Wei Regiment did not object to smell fire under the Union Jack against their fellow country-men. Moreover, they showed their spirit and willingness in many a sharp fight. Keen as mustard, they wept "buckets" on parade when Colonel Bower, as he then was, read out the notice which terminated their service and put an end to an interesting experiment.

Major-General Bower's selection for the post of Commanding Officer of the Chinese regiment was in recognition of the spirit which had prompted him to make himself proficient in Chinese and, in point of fact, has sustained him all through his career. Other officers of the Indian establishment have since taken up the study of the Chinese language, promptly pocketing upon passing the Government grant of 1500 rupees, which is the prize for success. Colonel Bower entered into it upon his own initiative, and he is now-a-days one of the most important of the group of officers serving with the Indian Army who speak, read and write the tongue of the Son of Heaven.

The Abor Expedition may have been from the point of view of some people only a minor matter; but it should be remembered that there were influences at work along the Chino-Tibetan border of India which might have caused the limits of the operations to have been extended. Under such circumstances there is little doubt that the presence in the supreme command of India's north-eastern frontier of a pastmaster in the difficult speech of India's northern, and—at this time of writing—strangely aggressive, neighbour, would have been of the greatest value.

In North China, Colonel Bower was a member of the International Provisional Government of Tientsin. From 1901 to 1906 he commanded the Legation Guard at the British Legation in Pekin. Since then he has steadily advanced in the Service. He was made a Brigadier-General and given command of the Assam Brigade at Shillong on December 1st, 1908; while, on February 15th, 1909, he was promoted Major-General. A few months later Major-General Bower was appointed to the Bareilli Command, which is by way of being a step up the ladder of preferment from Shillong. With the possibilities of a "show" in the Abor country looming in the future, the gallant officer elected to remain in the Assam command, and thus lead in war the corps he had so patiently trained in peace.

CHAPTER V

The Lands—Manners—Customs—Marriage-Laws—Popular Beliefs of the Miris and the Mishmis.

In addition to the punitive measures to be taken against the Abors, it was decided to dispatch political and surveying missions to the tribes who occupied the country between the Dihang River and Bhutan on the western flank of General Bower's operations, and to the Mishmis, who held the territory to the east and had been subjected to interference by parties of Chinese soldiery from Rima.

Divided into those who occupy the hills and those who have settled in the plains, the so-called Miris of to-day are grouped in four chief clans: the Ghasis, who live east of the Subansiri; the Saraks, who live on the right bank of that river; the Panibotias and Tarbotias, who inhabit the country further to the west. Each section is broken into many minor branches, but, though the term "Miri" is employed officially to describe them, it is undoubtedly a misnomer. It is necessary to emphasise the fact that a wide ethnic divergence distinguishes the tribes of

MAJOR-GENERAL HAMILTON BOWER, C.B. (FACING THE CAMERA), COMMANDING THE ABOR FIELD FORCE, TALKING WITH COLONEL WIDDICOMBE, 114TH MAHRATTA INFANTRY.

LEFT TO RIGHT.—MAJOR HUTCHINSON, CHIEF STAFF OFFICER; CAPTAIN MOLESWORTH; CAPTAIN GIFFARD.

POST OF THE MIRI MISSION AT GOCHUM IN COURSE OF CONSTRUCTION.

the Kamla-Subansiri region and the Miris of the plains, who are really only Abor emigrants from the Dihang Valley.

Little is known about the country of the hill tribes and even less about themselves or their customs. Their origin, like that of most of the tribes on the north-eastern frontier, is veiled in considerable mystery. As an ethnic unit, they are believed to be members of the Tibeto-Burman family, and are said to have settled originally in the hills to the north of Lakhimpur, between the Dafla and the Abor territory. According to their own account, they descended with the Chutiyas, when first they conquered Lakhimpur, and retired again with the Chutiyas into their mountain fastnesses, when they were finally defeated in the sixteenth century by the Ahoms.

In appearance the Miris of the Assam border are Mongoloid, but their faces are by no means unpleasing. In general, too, they are strongly built, with finely developed limbs, and complexions that often have a distinctly ruddy hue. They are cleaner in their persons than many of the Tibeto-Burman tribes, and the more progressive among them appreciate the advantages of an occasional bath. Ever since the advent of the British in Assam, the Miris have shown themselves amenable to civilising influences, though this quality is not shown by the hill tribes who still preserve no little independence.

In the plains the Miris seem to prefer to live near running water, although in doing so they usually frequent the most malarial spots. As a rule they settle upon the newly-formed alluvial islets in the rivers, in which they fish, or upon the banks of the marshes, where they graze their goats, pigs, and cattle, and support themselves by raising crops of summer rice, mustard, millet, pulse, and sweet potatoes. In spite of their surroundings, or perhaps on account of their active lives, their diet of fish and flesh, and the character of their houses, they enjoy an enviable immunity from disease. Miri villages are built in two long rows, the houses being as much as forty yards in length, with accommodation for twenty or thirty inmates. They are raised on piles. Unlike an Assamese village there are neither fruit trees nor gardens near them.

The Miris who have colonised the Assam border describe themselves as Hindus. At the same time they have liberal notions with regard to diet, eating pork and drinking rice beer without hesitation. Where they are not Hindus, they are Animists sacrificing to the sun, moon, and earth. Doctor Tiele, in some interesting observations on the aboriginal beliefs of the hill tribes, describes Animism as :

"A belief in the existence of souls or spirits, of which only the powerful, those on which man feels himself dependent, and before which he stands in awe, acquire the rank of divine beings and become the objects of worship. These spirits are conceived as moving freely through earth and air, and either of their own accord, or because conjured by some spell and thus under compulsion, appearing to men. But they may also take up their abode either permanently or temporarily in some object, whether lifeless or living it matters not, and this object, as endowed with higher power, is then worshipped or employed to protect individuals or communities."

In this direction the Rev. P. H. Moore has collected an instructive account of their version of the Creation. According to this :

" A long time ago, two gods, Hemphu and Mookrang, held a consultation to decide about creating the universe. They determined the limits and set four great posts to show the boundaries of the world, which remain to this day, as they were fastened immovably with six hairs which the two gods got from their mother. Having set the limits, they proceeded to plan the creation, but they had no seed that could produce an earth, so they called in one hundred other gods and their wives to advise them, and after long consultation decided to send one of the wives to get a little earth from the god Hajong.

" Hajong refused to give any seed to help a rival earth to be formed, and sent the goddess away empty, but as she returned she noticed the little bits of earth at the holes of the earthworms, and stole a small piece and hid it in her bosom. Even with this half-pound of mud the gods were not able to make an earth, so they sent for the king of the earthworms, who worked so well at the bit of mud, that in one day it became about ten feet in diameter, and eventually grew into our globe. Even then, however, another difficulty confronted them. It was only worm mud, so soft that no one could travel on it, so Kaprang was called, and he with a blacksmith's bellows caused a wind to blow that eventually dried the mud to solid earth. The gods then brought seeds from the far west, and from them grew reeds and trees and all kinds of vegetables; then came the creation of animals. The elephant, being the greatest, was told to be the servant of man, and to the tiger was entrusted the duty of eating the wicked.

"Last of all came man, who was provided with two wives, one a Mikir, the other an Assamese. The descendants of this Adam increased and multiplied exceedingly, and, tired of the mastery of the earth only, they determined to conquer the stars. With this object they began to build a tower to reach unto heaven, but the gods, in fear lest they might attain their purpose, confounded their speech and scattered them to the four corners of the earth, and it was from this time that man began to speak different languages."

Some of the tribes regard the creation of the world as the work of a goddess named Nastoo, who sprang from a self-begotten egg. Streams of water issued from her womb and became rivers; all kinds of reeds and grasses sprang up; then came fish, reptiles, birds, animals, and, lastly, man. Amongst nearly all the tribes there is a belief in beneficent gods, who, as they entertain friendly feelings towards men, do not require much in the way of sacrifice. The thing which impresses itself most forcibly and painfully upon the mind of the uneducated hillman is the existence of apparently unmerited pain and trouble. He is confronted with the problem, to which no satisfactory solution has yet been found, of innocent persons suffering misfortune, sickness, and death. He attempts to solve the difficulty by assuming the existence of malignant spirits, who take delight in tormenting man and have to be propitiated by any means that are likely to prove acceptable.

Not unnaturally it is believed that for each of the class of evils to which men are commonly subject a special demon is responsible. Among the Padam Abors, Mr. Needham states, it is believed that these malignant spirits are appeased by offerings of *mithun*, pig, and poultry. The chief spirits are Apom or Epom, and his younger brother Pomsa. Their habitat is the rubber tree, and they are chiefly propitiated when sickness occurs. Urom is another malignant spirit, who is said to reside in unclean places. He has the power of attacking people after dark; of causing various aches and pains. By way of a peace-offering, he is given bones and liquor.

Other spirits are the Kilu Dele (male and female),

who are supposed to reside underground and turn their attention to destroying crops and other field produce. Sacrifices to these spirits are usually made under a granary, and require two cooked fowls, pounded rice, tamul, pān, etc. Nipong is a demon who is essentially bent on harming females, so almost all ailments from which women suffer, especially at the time of parturition or menstruation, are attributed to him. Although Nipong pays particular attention to females, he is not thought to spare males. All cases of haemorrhage, intestinal troubles and physical ills afflicting man are credited to him. He is said to live in plantain groves and to exist on the seeds of stinging-nettles.

Although special demons are appointed to preside over special classes of misfortune, it is generally thought advisable to call in a person learned in these matters to decide who is responsible for the trouble, or to ascertain what particular form of sacrifice is required. There are various methods in force for obtaining the desired information. Of them all the one most popular is that which calls upon the divining powers of a hen's egg. An expert is set down before a board, in the centre of which he places an egg on a few grains of rice. After invoking the egg to speak the truth, he sweeps the rice off the board with the exception of one grain which is left on any spot that his fancy dictates. Naming a particular spirit he asks, if that spirit is the cause of the evil, that a part of the shell of the egg may be deposited near the grain of rice ; he then strikes the egg sharply on the board. This process is repeated, if necessary, till the desired information is obtained. The next thing is to discover what sort of offering will be acceptable to the spirits. This is ascertained in a precisely similar way, but the desired result is often not arrived at till much time and many scores of eggs have been wasted. Among the Miris a different system is in force.

Two spear-headed leaves, which should point to eastward or northward when about to be picked (those dropping to the westward and southward are alleged to be untrustworthy), are plucked and drawn through the right hand in order to wither them. When withered, the two leaves are slit into six strings with the right thumbnail and left attached to their stalks. Each leaf in turn is now taken up in the left hand, held aloft and adjured to prognosticate truly, after which, gathering the six strings in his right hand, and drawing them through it a few times to make them more pliable, the diviner proceeds to twist them several times round and round, and then to tie four of the string ends into two pairs.

When both leaves have been treated in this fashion, he untwists the strings and examines the lay of the two loops and the spare strings, the right-hand loop representing the house of the patient and the right-hand string the patient himself, while the left-hand loop represents the abode of the spirits supposed to be causing the sickness and the left-hand string the spirit itself. Should the two loose strings fall inside the patient's loop or house it is a very bad omen, as the spirit afflicting him is actually closeted with him. If the string representing the spirit is outside, and on the right hand of the patient, it is likewise a bad omen.

If satisfaction is not obtained from eggs and spear-shaped leaves, reference is not infrequently made to the liver and entrails of a fowl, which are supposed by many tribes to hoard the secret of the future. Other signs of approaching misfortune are indicated by the way in which a fowl that has been throttled crosses its legs at the moment of death ; while dire calamity is believed to visit the person unlucky enough to see a dog drag its hind-legs along the ground.

At one time the Miri tribesmen were torn between the principles of endogamy and exogamy ; but tribal restrictions are fast disappearing, and now-a-days the most rigid disciples of the old order are the first to be influenced by Hindu observances in matters matrimonial. Marriage is an expensive affair, and entails upon the families of the contracting parties a considerable expenditure in food and entertainment.

In the first case the rites are regulated by a number of curious observances which differ considerably among the various tribes.

The Miris, for example, never countenance a betrothal, unless at the same time a female belonging to the bridegroom's family is promised for some male member of the bride's. For instance, if A. desires B.'s daughter as a wife for his son, he must agree to give B. some female member of his family in marriage to some male member of B.'s. It does not necessarily follow that the two marriages take place simultaneously. Indeed it will often happen that one of the contracting parties has no female of age at the time. When this is the case complications are frequent.

Let us suppose that A. after promising a female from his own family, has secured B.'s daughter for his son, and that the marriage has been completed according to custom; that two years or so later B. finding that A.'s daughter (or some other female promised) has reached the age of puberty, asks for her as a wife for his son, or other male relative, and the reply from A. is, "she has gone off with some one else," what happens?

Acting strictly according to the custom of his tribe, B. takes back his daughter from A.'s son, although she may have had children by him, and makes her over to C., who promises his sister, or some other female relative, in exchange for her. If C. in the fulness of time likewise fails to fulfil his part of the contract, B. takes her away from C. and makes her over to D., and so on until cases have been known where a girl has been married to four or five different men, and has had children by each one.

In many cases marriage is by purchase; in others by service, the conditions showing as many variations along the different sections of the frontier as the scale of prices asked for a wife. Among Kacharis a girl costs from Rs. 60 to Rs. 100. The Mikirs and Lalungs of Nowgong think that a feast to the villagers is sufficient, while the Padam Abors only mulct the groom in a few dried squirrels. The Garos prefer their brides to be of tender years; the Lhotas look for virgins, while the Hojais impose a fine, though a light one, for unchastity. Among the Kukis, where marriage by service is common, cohabitation is freely permitted during the time that the lover is serving in the house of his prospective father-in-law. Pregnancy in these circumstances entails no disgrace, though the girl may not bring forth a living child. The matter is arranged with the help of an old woman who locates the position of the baby's head in the womb and strikes it a sharp blow with a flat stone, with the result that the child is born dead.

Among the Miris complete freedom of action is allowed to the unmarried girls of the village, little or no disgrace attaching to the birth of illegitimate children if the parentage is acknowledged. Where the bride is unable to swear to her virginity, she has to be content with a comparatively quiet wedding. Similarly, and preserving a link with polyandrous days, adultery is only considered of importance if the offence has been committed with some one outside the circle of the husband's family.

The penalty for adultery among the tribes living in the plains is that the co-respondent should pay twice the cost of the wedding ceremony, after which he is allowed to take his mistress openly to his own house. The same practice is reported from the hills, with the significant reservation that, if the gay Lothario is unable to make the necessary reparation, the guilty couple are tied face to face, pierced with a bamboo stake, and thrown into the river. The bodies of these unfortunate lovers are not infrequently brought down by the Subansiri, when the river rises during the monsoon.

Although adultery among the Mishmis may be settled by the imposition of a fine of a pig or by the payment of a few rupees, among the Miris it is regarded as an extremely serious offence, and it is usual to hold an inquiry into the conduct of the woman. If the village elders, who confer about the matter, are of opinion that she has courted rather than avoided the attentions of her lover, she is stripped, tied up in the moshup and publicly subjected to a form of physical punishment, which, to the savage mind, seems peculiarly appropriate to her offence.

In some of the Miri villages, the husbands of expectant mothers affect couvade, that remarkable custom, now almost extinct, by which men lie abed, pretending to experience the agonies of childbirth, while the mother shuffles off to work in the fields. Similarly, as a throw-back to the days of exogamy, it sometimes happens, where the price demanded for the bride is in excess of what the youthful swain can afford to pay, that the girl arranges that she shall be abducted. By special request, her lover and a few of his friends are in waiting at some appointed place, when, as the artful maiden passes with her companions, she is captured and carried off amidst tears and lamentations. Marriage quickly takes place, whereupon, as the groom has overcome all obstacles and is in possession of the prize, the bride's parents usually find it politic to come to terms.

In the present unsurveyed state of the Mishmi country it is difficult, if not impossible, to define its precise extent. Accepting the four great tribal divisions—viz., Midus or Chulikattas, Bebejiyas or Mithuns, Taius or Digarus, and Mejus—as an indication of the Mishmi boundaries, the Chulikattas occupy both banks of the Dibong River, many of the larger and more affluent villages lying close to the Tibetan border. They are found also in the ranges north of Sadiya from the Sesseri River on the west to the Digaru River on the east. The Bebejiyas frequent the valleys of the Ithun and Ithi Rivers, holding the country to the north of the Sihi Range and Saruba Peak, and to the east of the Chulikattas. They are bordered on the north by the ranges of the Southern Tibet, and on the east by the possessions of the Digarus. The Digarus lie to the east beyond the Digaru River. The Mejus are further east again, towards the Zayul Valley, a sub-prefecture of Lhassa.

The four tribal divisions are split into numerous clans.

The Chulikattas, who claim to be descended from the Abors, and do not intermarry with the Bebejiyas, are divided as follows :—

In the Dibong valley :—

Mepu, Menda, Migi, Lingi, Mili, Maikaron, Epoyia, Lingaru, Meton, Pulu, Mimi, Meenee, Elapran, Mendon, Mison, Miku, Mema.

On the Tibetan border :—

Mihun, Mitaiya, Melonga, Miku, Emohon.

The clans of the Bebejiyas, who are descended from the Digarus, are :—

Miaga, Mison, Miaton, Mpe, Mderen, Minli, Mimi, Mikatson, Mongon, Michen.

The clans of the Mejus, who intermarry with the Digarus, are :—

Lapa, Prun, Manlo, Nai, Samle, Hago, Towa, Ro, Tumblu, Lamat.

In general the Mishmi country is mountainous, greatly cut up by watercourses, and difficult of access. The mountain valleys are covered with dense jungle and the crests of the ranges are hidden in snow. Trade is poor and cultivation scanty. The tribesmen are of uncertain temperament; though friendly with us, they are frequently at war among themselves. Mongoloid in feature, light complexioned, stunted in stature, and of picturesque appearance, their manners are as simple as their clothing, while their primitive manners are preserved in a variety of ways. Less naked than the Nagas, their dress resembles that favoured by the Abors.

It comprises a short, sleeveless Tibetan jacket and an attenuated skirt made from the *Rhea nivea*, which with other jungle nettles is made into a rough, tough, and very fibrous cloth. The Chulikattas and the Bebejiyas follow identical fashions; but there are certain tribal differences of dress in the styles of the Digarus and Mejus, and peculiar to them. In their

A MIRI TRIBESMAN.

DIGARU BELLES FROM SAMPÜN VILLAGE, LOHIT VALLEY.
(Note the head-dress of the two women in the foreground.)

MISHMI WARRIORS ON TREK, CARRYING BOW, QUIVER OF POISONED ARROWS, DHAO AND SPEAR.

head-dress the Mishmis follow the mode of the frontier, for Abor, Miri and Mishmi alike wear cane helmets, ornamented on grand occasions with bear-skin, feathers, or beads, and sufficiently strong to resist direct or glancing cuts by sword, dhao, or spear.

In addition to their dhaos, the Mishmis carry the usual bow and quiver of poisoned arrows ; in war time they sport a shield and spear. Unlike the Nagas the spear is carried only in full war-dress. Each of the four tribal divisions affects a distinctive coiffure, which varies between a straight fringe across the forehead just above the ears to a sweep some inches broad from the nape of the neck to the eyes and from ear to ear, by which a very bizarre and altogether novel effect in hair-dressing is achieved.

In their domestic life the Mishmis follow lines of their own, both in regard to the construction and character of their houses and in their relations with women. Polygamy is popular, and widely practised among all sections of the tribe. Sexual morality is not imposed on men or women until after marriage. The inevitable result is that the great majority of women have large and happy families, though only the minority possess husbands. Where the lady boasts a lover, and honours her intercourse with him after the eternal fashion, some sort of permanent alliance is set up. Such an arrangement is optional none the less; more often than not it is disregarded.

Where marriage does take place, the women are supposed to act with decent restraint, though the custom is not viewed with favour by the ladies of polygamous households. In rare cases the formal consent of the parents is asked to a contemplated union. Where it is given the happy man is compelled to make many gifts to the family of his choice. The expense is on the other side so soon as the wedding has been solemnised, for the parents have to make over to their son-in-law in other gifts the value of those he has already presented to them. The nuptial ceremony is only partially completed by the exchange of presents. The final touch comes with the return of Benedict to his village, when all the inhabitants turn out and build the future house of the happy, or unfortunate, couple, as the Fates may disclose.

Since marriage is almost ideally simple among the Mishmis, it is in the natural order of things that divorce should not be difficult. Where reasons for divorce are supposed to exist—one would think that they would be hard to define—the husband—not the wife, who has no right of petition—summons the village sorcerer, an object of dignity, decorated about the neck, arms, and legs with bells and ornaments, to purify the woman. The evil spirit, in the guise of a bird who lives in the armpits of erring wives, is caught, plucked alive and eaten raw, the woman being cleansed immediately of her guilt. When the sorcerer has gone, the husband usually emphasises the character of the visitor by beating his wife before admitting her to the marital mat. Generally, too, he takes an early opportunity to mulct the co-respondent in cooking-pots and dhaos ; in buffaloes or swine, if he should own any. It seldom happens that the price of the family honour is rated in cattle. More often it is appraised no higher than a pregnant sow.

The houses of the Mishmis vary in size as much as do their villages. A small house is forty feet long : a large one two hundred feet ; but they are all about twelve feet in width. As a rule they are raised on piles four feet from the ground, the space beneath being used for pigs and poultry, or for refuse. The house in its interior economy is divided into narrow compartments according to the number of wives and the size of the family, a narrow passage running the whole length and affording a means of exit and admission. Each compartment possesses one smoke-hole, while hanging from the roof is a tray upon which any food that requires to be dried is stacked. Other impedimenta are stored on shelves suspended from the walls. The houses are thatched, constructed from bamboo, and so low pitched that it is impossible to stand upright in any of them. As a precaution against attack, each house is isolated from its neighbour and screened by a patch of bamboos and trees.

Villages, as a rule, number from three to forty houses. They are smaller than the Miri villages, just as the houses in them are inferior to those of the Abors. Unlike the Abors, the Mishmis adopt no communal defence. Some of the Chulikattas and Bebejiyas encircle their villages with palisades and, on occasion, stockade their houses. It is never done among the Mejus and Digarus.

Curiously enough, for a community where the primary conditions of life are so exceedingly simple, the last phase of a Mishmi is attended with considerable state. When a birth is expected the happy mother is removed from the village proper to a hut specially built in some isolated spot in the jungle, where mother and child are kept ten days. Superstition has it that if twins of one sex are born one is sure to die. In death the whole village mourns; no one works or goes out until the burial has been completed. The bodies of elders are kept for three days, during which time the circle of relatives takes turn and turn about in fanning the remains. Graves are placed down-stream below a village, the dead being interred in the ground in rude coffins hewn out of trees and lined with leaves. Dhaos, a sword, a bow and arrows are put in the coffin, but no food. If the deceased should have been killed in battle he is buried where he falls, though as far from a path as possible. The bodies of wealthy Mishmis are burnt. Those of slaves are thrown into the river, the latter ending a life of misery in a miserable way.

CHAPTER VI

Preparations at Calcutta, Shillong and Dibrugarh—Gathering of the Troops—Across India to Aborland—Indian Military Police—The Spirit of the Planter—The Cup that Cheers—Lumsden's Lambs.

ALTHOUGH sanction to the dispatch of a punitive expedition against the Abors was given in July by the Secretary of State for India, it was not until the early days of the September following that the task of preparing the force was actively pushed forward. Long before September, however, Major-General Bower had intimated his requirements to Army Headquarters, but the impossibility of moving through the jungles of Aborland in the rains had necessitated delay. Many difficulties lay ahead of the expedition, not the least of which was contained in the twin evils of supply and transport, and in the fact that the early conditions were not unlike those which accompany a river war. As the scene of operations lay across the Brahmaputra, and supplies were non-existent in the Abor country, everything had to be carried by water to the theatre of hostilities.

Pending the laying out of a base there was no site on the north bank—the Abor bank—of the river, where anything could be stored. Supplies, therefore, were dispatched by steamer from Calcutta, or by road from Shillong, and accumulated on river "flats," a variety of barge with large holds, at the steamer piers at Dibrugarh. From Dibrugarh, when the base camp had been prepared, the stores were transported direct to Kobo or unloaded into country bottoms and ferried across.

The supply of country boats at the best of times is very inadequate. At the outset of the expedition it was unusually disorganised, as the boatmen, impressed for service when the first advance to Pasighat was made, had been badly frightened. In the interval, the Hindustani boatmen had decamped to their *dais*, while the Assamese and Miris had concealed their boats up the creeks of the stream and buried themselves in the depths of the jungle. None the less, the supply and transport officers were not to be beaten. Major Vaughan, who, together with Captain Dunlop, was in charge of the work of collecting the supplies, took over from the Sissi Saw Mills a forty-foot Thornycroft motor-launch, and passed many a tiresome hour among the malodorous and malarial marshes of the river rounding up recalcitrant or reluctant boatmen. Lieutenant Hay Webb carried out somewhat similar duties at Gauhati.

Dibrugarh itself is not troubled by the question

of communications. Through possession of a local railway which joins at Tinsukia junction with the Assam-Bengal Railway system, it is in direct connection with Lower Assam, Calcutta, and the sea at Chittagong. Troops destined for Dibrugarh thus had a choice of routes, and in the main travelled by steamer from Calcutta, the vessels of the River Steam and India General Inland Steamers Company being chartered for the purpose. Among the boats used were the s.s. *Mirani*, which carried Surgeon-Captain Melville, 9th Hodson's Horse, and one hundred and forty men of "A" Section of the 168th Field Ambulance Corps; Captain Tylden Pattenson, R.E., and one hundred and twenty men of No. 1 Company of the Bengal Sappers and Miners, with fifty mules from Roorkee; the s.s. *Battani*, which conveyed thirteen officers and eight hundred men of the 32nd Sikh Pioneers, under the command of Major E. H. Cullen, with sixty-three mules from Lahore; the s.s. *Sherani*, which brought the 1st Battalion of the 2nd Gurkhas, and details of the 31st Sappers and Miners Signal Company; the s.s. *Scinde*, which loaded Naga coolies at Kokilamukh, and the s.s. *Pagan*, which came up with general stores.

For a time Calcutta was very busy with the task of provisioning the expedition; at Fort William, at Prinsep's Ghat, Baloo Ghat and other piers, there were daily scenes of the greatest animation. But everything was not quite plain sailing. Reports of the simple, though complete, savagery of Master Abor had reached Calcutta, and had had the effect of so terrifying the local sweepers, water carriers, cooks, etc., that one and all declined to have anything to do with the "show." In the end the military authorities had to make up the necessary complement of followers by recruiting them elsewhere.

As the preparations at Fort William neared completion many officers, who were on leave, and were to take part in the expedition, found it necessary to return in hot haste. From distant quarters of the world they hastened to rejoin their regiments. Major-General Bower himself, who, since returning from his preliminary tour of the border had made a flying trip to London, went back to Shillong. Major Hutchinson, the Chief Staff Officer of the expedition, hurried from New Zealand; Captain Hutchison, the Adjutant of the Assam Valley Light Horse, who had just reached England, hastily retraced his steps; Captain Molesworth, of the 1st Battalion of the 8th Gurkhas, by losing three months of his leave, caught his battalion as it marched out of Shillong *en route* for the front; while Lieutenant-Colonel F. H. Peterson, D.S.O., Lieutenant I. Burn-Murdock, and Lieutenant A. T. G. Beckham, all belonging to the 32nd Sikh Pioneers, joined at the base of operations. Others, too, sped east: Captain

Poole, D.S.O., as correspondent for Reuter's Telegram Company, and myself, as correspondent to the Central News Agency, anticipating with enjoyment the experiences of a campaign in India.

Although the voyage to India was conventional, the journey of eighteen hundred miles by train and river, from the sea at Bombay to the banks of the Brahmaputra at Dibrugarh, was a memorable experience, revealing as it did India verdant beneath the monsoon. To my mind, under no other condition is India quite so picturesque as when the land has been refreshed by its periodic rains. Sun-baked and exhausted at other times, it is an inspiring panorama that unfolds itself beneath the encouragement of the monsoon : a vision splendid of cities, villages, temples, and peoples seen through a riot of vegetation.

Unfortunately, whatever the circumstances, the trip across India by railway, on account of the antiquated condition of many of the lines, has several drawbacks. Food is bad and the rolling-stock most inadequate ; many of the first class carriages being filthy, badly ventilated, insufficiently illuminated, and quite unsuited to a tropical country. The passing hours, therefore, are impressed with much unnecessary discomfort, for which even the spectacle of monkeys, barking deer, black buck, and the somnolent "mugger" on its mud-bank, does not altogether compensate. Numerous changes have to be made, for the trans-Indian traveller is carried over the metals of many companies. From Bombay to Jubbulpore the system used is that of the Great Indian Peninsula Railway Company; from Jubbulpore to Calcutta that of the East India Railway Company; from Calcutta to Amingaon, where a ferry to Gauhatti is taken, that of the Eastern Bengal State Railway Company; from Gauhatti to Tinsukia that of the Assam-Bengal Railway Company, and from Tinsukia to Dibrugarh the final link belongs to the Dibrugarh-Sadiya Railway Company.

It is possible, of course, to proceed by water from Calcutta. If the river service is not particularly expeditious, it is at least much cleaner and more comfortable. From Calcutta to Dibrugarh the journey by steamer occupies from ten days to two weeks, according to the rate of progress permitted by the state of the river. For the first two days the time is spent in negotiating the myriad creeks, swamps, and tiny islands which form the Sunderbunds, and make up one of the most fever-stricken spots in Asia. Covering some 5500 square miles of the Ganges delta, they lie between the mouth of the Hugli and the mouth of the Meghna.

The passage is at first very dreary, and an occasional patch of cultivation on the banks of the Meghna strikes a welcome note after the impassive flats of the delta. As the steamer proceeds by many devious twists and turns, some suggestion of Burma creeps into the colouring of the low-lying banks and the vivid green of the vegetation. Though the tortuous course gives way to the broad bosom of the sacred Ganges, recollections of the Irawaddy crowd the mind until the captain, steering deftly between mud-flats and negotiating with pretty skill some dangerous sand-banks, drops anchor before Goalundo. Here mosquito-infested creeks and jungle-covered swamps make room for miles of paddy fields, picked out with patches picturesquely populated ; and river craft dance to the swirl of the Brahmaputra.

Above Goalundo the breadth between the banks varies from one to four miles. The current flows ordinarily at about three knots per hour, though, when in flood, the stream has the speed of a modified mill-race. From every point of view magnificent, the Brahmaputra is also dignified and independent ; it sweeps everything out of its way and overflows its banks with a graceful inconsequence that gives it a somewhat treacherous character. It is, too, a river that reflects in many ways the energy of those who go down to the sea in ships. Flotillas of fishing boats dot its broad reaches : fishing in the waters of the river, and growing rice in the fields inundated by its overflow apparently being the two chief industries of the region. The fish is good. The fish are large, though slightly muddy in flavour.

DOCTOR ROBERTS AND HIS "STAR" CAR.

At the wheel.—Doctor Roberts ; Captain Becher, Provost Marshal. At the back (left).—Captain Molesworth ; (right) Captain Giffard.

THE PLANTERS' STORES, DIBRUGARH.

BAZAAR AT SAIKHWAGHAT.

The crops are wonderful, the rice-fields extending uninterruptedly mile after mile.

From Goalundo the river bends towards the north to Dubrighat, a riverside town of some importance, where it turns east and enters Assam. Beyond Dubrighat the Brahmaputra is barely a mile across, and there is a further change in the appearance of the course. The hills of Assam loom up on the right: green, jungle-covered and inviting; but to the north the country is entirely different. Unoccupied by reason of the propinquity of the independent tribes, it is uncultivated and abandoned. Tall grass, rank and rough, growing in places seven or eight feet in height, springs up from the water's edge and stretches in an undulating line to the northern horizon; on the Assam bank it only reaches to the foothills. Fishing boats are fewer; for roving crocodiles have spoilt the fishing industry and only an occasional market boat spins by, floating on the current, or passing up-stream poling laboriously.

The heat is the same; and the insects, which make night a torment and day a disillusion, seem to become more concentrated in their attentions. Nothing else disturbs the harmony of the river, the passage proceeding peacefully to where the life and bustle of the bank show that the steamer is reaching the starting-place of the ferry service between Amingaon, the terminus of the Eastern Bengal State

Railway, and Gauhatti. In the dim distance across the river the smoke of railway workshops and the whistle of engines indicate the position of Gauhatti, where the metals of the Assam Bengal Railway Company begin. The broad river divides the two systems. Passengers must perforce dismount from their carriages and embark upon the ferry steamer. Fanned by river breezes, the change from the heat of the trains seems delightful.

From Gauhatti the passage to Dibrugarh by water occupies four days, as progress is impeded by low-lying mud-flats, upon which the boats more often than not run aground. In view of the advantage which water transport possesses over rail carriage it seems a pity that the rivers of Eastern Bengal have been neglected so much in the past. They are Bengal's natural channel of communication. For a long time now they have been out of favour, and railways have been extended until a network of lines radiates eastwards from Calcutta. Intended primarily for strategic reasons, the lines have been built at a cost of millions sterling, a tithe of which would have removed the difficulties which impede river navigation. The steamer service is cheap and convenient. The boats are capable of holding large cargoes ; yet ten millions sterling were spent on laying down the Assam-Bengal Railway in the face of difficulties which must make the upkeep of the permanent way a perpetual source of anxiety, if not an altogether hopeless prospect.

As the government authorities have projected railways on the north-eastern frontier of India as a military precaution, they might just as well provide the region with a commercial and, at the same time, a more reliable channel of communication and give attention to the condition of the waterways. Nothing could be worse than the existing system of railways on the Assam border. Unreliable and incomplete, it is without a parallel in the world, and it is by no means surprising that, under the pressure imposed by the preparations for the Abor columns, the military authorities should have fallen back upon the river vessels. The circumstance becomes a feather in the caps of the river steamer companies.

If the Government of India wishes to interest itself in the question of the riverine communications of the north-east frontier there is no need for it to go far in quest of information. Close at hand is an expert authority in the shape of Mr. Bramley, a police official of the United Provinces, whose work has brought the opportunity of studying the river system of Bengal. Only last summer Mr. Bramley read a paper before a large London audience on this very subject. The points raised then can be commended to the notice of the Indian Government.

Life on the river steamers that were carrying the

troops to the seat of war was not by any means a time of ease and peace. Every day the troops were put through their exercises, and the decks of the "flats," towed by the vessels, resembled for the nonce miniature parade grounds. Bayonet exercises and rifle-drill were performed by the sepoys; the signalling section practised "flag-wagging" and telephoning; hospital orderlies busied themselves in dressing imaginary wounds, bandaging casualties, and in carrying the disabled. The scene always afforded amusement to any passing vessel, not unusually provoking loud shouts of derisive encouragement. Nevertheless it was in a good cause, and from sunrise to sunset the hours were filled with solid work, which undoubtedly reflected the keenness and ability of the men.

Aboard the steamers every one lived in shirt-sleeves and "shorts," at once a comfortable, as well as a serviceable, kit. Later on, the "shorts" of some details were changed for breeches as, owing to the fierceness of the leeches in Aborland, uncovered knees invited too much attention from these and other pests of the jungle. At the same time, the appearance of the troops in field kit made it impossible to avoid the reflection that the uniform of the British soldier was the best in the world. Suited to all the purposes of war, and adapted to any climate, it is immeasurably in advance of anything possessed by other armies.

As is usual with the British and Native service, the Abor Field Force was khaki clad : officers appearing in khaki shirts, collars and ties, khaki coats, khaki "shorts" and khaki putties. The Sikhs wore khaki shirts and breeches, and the Gurkhas khaki shirts and "shorts."

As the days passed afloat, the activities of the troops brought very definite impressions of the various men. Next to the Gurkhas, whose fitness for the work in Aborland already has been described, the most interesting units were those representing the Indian Military Police, of which a composite battalion drawn from the Lakhimpur Battalion and the Naga Hills Battalion, under the command of Captain Sir G. D. S. Dunbar, of the 31st Punjabis, was included in the strength of the expedition. Although most of the Police details moved by train to Dibrugarh, a few came up by water, one and all regarding with extreme pleasure the prospect of a scrap.

It was not the first time that the men of the Military Police had campaigned in the Abor jungles. As a matter of fact, scarcely a year passes in which one or other of the Police battalions on duty on the north-east frontier does not see active service. In the forthcoming operations, while they were to bear a share in General Bower's immediate activities, they were to furnish, under Captain Graham and Major

Charles Bliss respectively, the sole escorts to the two political missions which were to move through the Miri and Mishmi marches.

So many references to the efficiency of the Military Police details participating in the expedition, and to the very capable officers who commanded them, will be found in the succeeding pages of this volume that no excuse is made for giving a brief outline of the history of the corps. The origin of the force may be traced to the anxious times of 1857–58, when the old native civil police broke away from their allegiance to the *raj*, and threw in their lot with the mutinous sepoys. In 1861, three years after the old East India Company was transferred to the Crown, this new semi-military police force, which had performed very valuable service in the restoration of law and order, was converted into a civilian organisation. From that it has gradually grown and developed into the present highly disciplined and efficient body.

Although under one head, it practically comprises nine different divisions, each varying in its training and organisation, according to the requirements of the particular district or province in which it is located. The divisions are : the Madras Presidency, Bombay Presidency, Bengal, the United Provinces of Agra and Oudh, Eastern Bengal and Assam, the Central Provinces and Behar, the Punjab, and the North-West Frontier, in addition to small bodies at the headquarters of certain political agencies.

Recruited from a variety of creeds and castes, the force numbers some 5000 European and native officers, and about 170,000 sepoys. Some are purely civilian, others are armed. Some are mounted, others again, are boatmen ; while in certain parts, chiefly on the frontiers in Burma and in the unsettled tracts, there are Military Police battalions, commanded and trained by officers of the Indian Army and differing distinctly from the armed Civil Police. The armed police of the United Provinces form a corps d'élite of over 50,000 men and officers, who for physique, efficiency, and discipline can more than hold their own with the finest regiments of Indian Infantry. The mounted police are recruited from none but the best Rajputs, Sikhs, and Mohammedans. They are constantly on active service against armed bands of dacoits and cattle lifters.

The life of the European Police Officer in India is one that should appeal to most young Englishmen. It is passed in the open air, and is not unaccompanied by excitement and adventure, while blessed with opportunities for sport of all kinds. The pay is good ; promotion is secure ; and reliance can be placed on a reasonable retiring allowance. No influence is required. Its ranks are open to any decently born well-educated young man between the ages of nineteen and twenty-one, of sound physique. He must be of European descent, unmarried, and able to pass a competitive examination much on the lines of that for the Royal Military College, Sandhurst. The following are the subjects of examination, of which not more than five, including English, may be taken up: English; Mathematics; Latin; Greek; French; German; History; Science. Freehand drawing is optional.

In addition to having to pass a test of medical fitness, each candidate, before being accepted as a probationer, must produce a certificate of his ability to ride. He must be able to saddle and bridle a horse; to mount and dismount; to trot and canter. He must be able to ride at a trot without stirrups; at a trot with stirrups but without reins; to go easy over jumps. If all goes well, he is appointed a probationer for two years at a salary of 300 rupees a month; if finally approved, he becomes an assistant superintendent. His further promotion to the ranks of superintendent, district superintendent, deputy inspector general, and inspector general—the latter drawing salaries of 3000 rupees a month—depends entirely upon his seniority and professional ability.

The regulations in regard to short and long leave, and retiring pensions are of a reasonable character. The latter can be earned at the age of fifty-five; after thirty years' service; in case of illness not attributable to irregular or intemperate habits. These retiring allowances are supplemented by means of a provident fund, to which all officers are compelled to subscribe. Compound interest at 4 per cent. is allowed, the accumulated amounts becoming the absolute property of the officer on retirement from the Service. In the event of his death, they go to his legal representative.

Until some place on the north bank of the Brahmaputra had been prepared as a base camp, Dibrugarh served as the point of concentration for the men and stores that were required for the expedition. Situated on the south bank, and some forty miles down-stream from Kobo, the little station soon became a centre of military activity. In itself, Dibrugarh is a straggling settlement in which the civil and military elements are subordinate to the interests of the tea-planting community. Pretty and prosperous, it boasts an excellent hospital, race-course, golf club, railway station, a well-equipped branch of the Assam and Planters' stores, and a District Club which serves as the headquarters of the tea-planters and is a centre from where is dispensed a generous hospitality, somewhat stronger in character than the cup that cheers.

The country round Dibrugarh is entirely devoted to tea-growing, the planters' gardens extending in one unbroken stretch mile after mile in every direction. One and all of the tea-gardens is worthy of inspection, the visit being spent in instructive explanation of the processes of tea-growing, enlivened with excellent fishing, some capital shooting and motoring. If nowhere else, a call at least must be paid upon Mr. Lamb, uncrowned King of Assam and the presiding genius of a famous garden, whose cleverness in speeding the hours while staying the feet of his guests is accomplished with the aid of a wonderful cook, and a cellar that is the envy of the province.

In the spirit of the planter and throughout Assam there is more of the atmosphere of the Australasian colonies than of India proper. In a measure this is due to the absence of the service element—Civil, Military, and Political—which becomes sometimes just a little oppressive in the life of the ordinary hill or plains station of India. For the rest it may be attributed to the fact that tea brews in the planter much the same spirit of jovial independence and hospitality that the breeding of sheep and cattle does in the colonial run-holder. The parallel between the two professions is a close one. Assam is a country of infinite distances, and tea-gardens are as isolated as sheep-runs. Before the advent of the motor-car communication was often difficult and invariably slow, so by force of circumstances the planter became a law unto himself, while his bungalow was

MR. LAMB, A POPULAR AND FAMOUS TEA-PLANTER IN ASSAM, WITH HIS FAVOURITE ELEPHANT.

A VIEW OF TEA BUSHES IN MR. LAMB'S GARDEN.

TEA-GARDEN WOMEN.

TEA-GARDEN CHILDREN.

regarded as the fount of all justice. Since the time of Lord Curzon, the Indian Government has endeavoured to make the native believe that the "ipse-dixit" days of the planter have passed. The coolie knows otherwise; he still sees in the "garden sahib" not only his mother and father, but his salt.

Without exception, too, planters hold either independent or else highly remunerative positions, and are upright, honourable men. As they supply tea-garden coolies with board and lodging, with medical assistance in time of ill-health, with educational facilities, and invariably treat them with kindness and consideration, it is not surprising that, as a body, planters have no patience with officialism or that they should be intolerant of red tape. Correspondingly, no little vigour and directness in the expression of their views is to be expected. In general, it might be said that the distinguishing note of the planting community is a certain fearless independence, which unites in its expression the qualities of justice, honesty and common-sense.

The care that the various stages of tea receive is shown by the prices obtained in the auction rooms of Mincing Lane. Garden management demands exacting and unremitting attention, success in tea-planting, as in everything that is worth while, being possible only after years of protracted toil. Capital and courage, too, are wanted in almost equal shares, for the life of a tea-bush is as delicate as any flower, and the stages of progression from the garden to the cup are menaced by lurking dangers all the way.

A dozen stages are passed through before the leaf becomes the beverage that we know. In the first instance there is the "plucking" or gathering, when the leaf is taken from the bushes by coolies, many hundreds of whom are employed for the purpose. Each coolie carries a basket which, when filled, is deposited at the weighing house, which is the second stage. As the leaf cannot be "rolled" until it has been "withered," for the third process the "pluck" is spread out on large canvas trays in the withering houses, which are large sheds containing from eight to twelve tiers of trays open to the air on all sides.

From the withering stage the leaf passes to the rolling machine where, if it has not been properly withered, it breaks and just so much of the crop as has been treated is spoilt. The fifth stage is "fermenting" or oxidisation, which is followed by "firing" and then "sorting," upon which depends the market price of the season's harvest. When the sorting is finished, a "final firing" is given, after which the different grades are sampled by the tasters. From the tea-tasters the crop passes to the packers; from them to the dispatchers, after which, as the final phase of its evolutions from the garden to the table, it is shipped to Mincing Lane for consumption by the public.

The planters around Dibrugarh were at first only indirectly interested in the preparations of General Bower's force. Matters changed, however, when it became known that a detachment from the local corps of Volunteers was to be permitted to join the expedition. This regiment is known as the Assam Valley and Surma Valley Light Horse and its needs are entirely provided for by planters in the two districts. When the strength of the Abor Field Force was first decided upon, no hint was given that any details from the Assam Valley and Surma Valley Light Horse would be invited to participate in the operations, though it was an open secret that the Indian Government had been much impressed by the representations of General Sir James Willcocks, commanding the northern army, and of Major-General Bower, C.B., as well as by those of Colonel Jessop, the present Commanding Officer of the A. V. S. V. L. H., and of Major Grimston, V.D., the second in command.

The receipt of the invitation came with the force of a surprise, and filled the corps with an excitement which vastly increased when it became known that the party was to take with it the maxim gun which Colonel D. M. Lumsden, C.B., had presented to the Assam Valley Light Horse in 1910. After much discussion it was decided that the strength of the contingent would have to be limited to twelve men and an officer; and, as every man in the full muster of the regiment, some six hundred and fifty-five, had a particular reason why he himself should be included, recourse was made to lottery. Even then two officers resigned their commission and reverted to the ranks in order to cut in; while four men, whose applications for permission to go on active service were refused by the head offices of their companies, took French leave and forthwith threw up their positions, acting with a spirit that equally animated the entire corps.

The twelve "good men and true" to be selected were: Squadron-Sergeant-Major and Sergeant-Instructor Webster, Sergeant Davies, Corporal Ashe, Troopers Whitten, Henning, Lemon, Southon, Falconer, Kilgour, Floyer, Hardwicke, Middleton. The officer in charge of the twelve men was Captain Cecil Lennox Lovell, of the Nokhroy Tea Estate at Tinsukia, while Sergeant Davies and Trooper Middleton were the two officers who had resigned their commission as subalterns in the regiment, in order to go on active service with their colleagues. Corporal Ashe and Trooper Lemon served with Colonel Lumsden in Lumsden's Horse, and wear the South African medal.

Great pleasure was derived from the permission

to include Colonel Lumsden's machine gun which, by the way, was of the latest Vickers pattern, and made so that it could be broken into four sections and man-carried—as it had to be in the jungles of Aborland. Maxim practice on the Dibrugarh range filled the hours of the happy twelve during the last few days of their stay, and excellent shooting results were obtained. In point of fact, their record shows that from first to last they were always in the thick of the hard work and earned conspicuous reference to their keenness and bravery in Force Orders, as well as in Dispatches.

While Major-General Bower's compliments were highly appreciated by all concerned, they were not unexpected, for the Assam Valley and Surma Valley Light Horse is noted for the hard riding, straight shooting, and the good fellowship of its men. Similarly the regiment looks for these fine qualities in its adjutant : the officer of the regular service who trains them in times of peace in the way they should go in times of war. Fortunately, Captain Hutchison, 38th Central India Horse, the present adjutant of the corps, is admirably suited to the duties of the post. Responsible for the appearance of the regiment on parade and for its efficiency in the field, he sent to the front a group of men who, in stamina, resolution, and training required a lot of beating, and were never sick nor sorry.

In many ways the position of the A. V. S. V. L. H. party was unique. It was the only "white" unit among the details composing the Abor Field Force. As Aborland is by no means a white man's country, the detachment to which the soubriquet of "Lumsden's Lambs" was given, was "up against it" all the time—but the "Lambs" never bleated! In explanation of their name "Lumsden's Lambs," it should be said that General Bower found something shorter as the official style of the corps, the Assam Valley and Surma Valley Light Horse was so much of a mouthful. Employed with every accent of good feeling, the new title stuck; and, since it served as an affectionate reminder of the fact that Colonel Dugald McTavish Lumsden, C.B., a gallant planter of the old school, had been associated with the Assam Valley Light Horse from its earliest days, it was very popular.

As all the world knows now, Colonel D. M. Lumsden, C.B., raised a contingent of excellent shots and capable riders, under the title of Lumsden's Horse, for service in the South African War. Lumsden's Horse was chosen from all India; it proved itself a well-disciplined and reliable body: a veritable chip of its veteran sire. "Lumsden's Lambs" came only from the Assam Valley and the Surma Valley. In actual result, however, the "Lambs" were a close second to the men of

Lumsden's Horse. They displayed the same soldierly qualities that had endeared the larger force to the Army Chiefs in the Transvaal and brought to one and all a well-deserved place in the history of that war.

CHAPTER VII

Selection of Kobo—The Base Camp—Its Appearance and Possibilities—The Transport Coolie.

WHILE it was easy for the authorities to give assent to an expedition against the Abors, it was no light task to select the point from which the punitive columns should be launched. Where the jungle did not present an unsurmountable obstacle to a landing-party, the banks of the river shelved into the stream in a way that made them unapproachable by boat, so that in either case the work of making a choice offered many difficulties. After careful examination, however, a spot was found near the junction of the Dihang and Lohit-Brahmaputra, where, though the jungle was exceedingly dense, the low-lying mud of the foreshore gave way to strata of sand that at least would be absorbent in the event of rain.

Once chosen no time was lost; and, when a space some six hundred yards square had been blazed, the task of clearing began. Work started in August, and, under the combined exertions of the 32nd Pioneers, the Sappers and Miners, and the Lakhimpur Military Police, assisted by elephants, coolies,

THE MAXIM OF THE ASSAM VALLEY AND SURMA VALLEY LIGHT HORSE.

MEN OF THE ASSAM VALLEY AND SURMA VALLEY LIGHT HORSE
WHO SERVED WITH THE EXPEDITION.

SCENES IN KOBO CAMP. (I.)

Top (left).—Gurkha sepoy felling timber; (right) Drawing tree-stumps with the aid of elephants.
Bottom (left).—Gurkha sepoy at work on the stockade; (right) Gurkha sepoy of the Lakhimpur Military Police acting as sentry over working parties.

and the inventive genius of Captain Beeman, order was soon evolved from the chaos of the virgin jungle. While the coolies cleared the undergrowth or chopped their way through the opposing walls of giant bamboo, the Military Police erected an encircling stockade with look-out towers at the corners, and a Crow's Nest, one hundred and fifty feet high, in the centre; the Pioneers bunded the river bank; the Sappers and Miners built a landing-stage, and elephants coaxed the tree-stumps from dank, tenacious depths. In a very short time a space large enough to receive a brigade, a big base supply depôt, "lines" for four thousand coolies, and a hospital was ready.

As Kobo had no previous existence, and there was no village or encampment of any kind near the site, the skill, enterprise and originality exhibited were really wonderful. Of course every one worked with a will, for time was pressing and the first week in October had been arranged as the date of the advance. Yet, long before the hour appointed for the advent of headquarters, everything was in readiness, a perfect camp having risen in but forty working days. From so phœnix-like a metamorphosis of the banks of the Brahmaputra nothing was wanting; neither fresh water, which was provided from a twenty-foot tube well; nor the telephone, over which Lieutenant J. H. Knight, R.A., presided as signalling officer, while the first telegram, over a specially laid line from Kobo to Dibrugarh, was handed to Major-General Bower as he stepped, on October 5th, from his railway carriage to the platform of Dibrugarh station, *en route* for the front.

Welcomed by Lieutenant-Colonel Widdicombe, senior officer commanding at Dibrugarh, and other officers of the 114th Mahratta Infantry, and entertained to luncheon in the mess of this distinguished regiment, Major-General Bower spent the afternoon in inspecting troops, examining stores, and in putting the finishing touches to his plans for the immediate concentration of men and supplies at the base camp. As all stores had to be portered by the Naga coolies through the jungle, careful packing was an important feature of the transport arrangements. Everything was put up, therefore, in loads of fifty or sixty pounds' weight, particular interest attaching to the tea consignments.

The tea was Lipton's, of very good quality and the subject of a somewhat daring experiment, as the well-known firm had been permitted by the Government of India to provide supplies of compressed tea for the use of the expedition instead of the loose leaf that hitherto had been favoured. A special machine was sent to India for the purpose of compressing the tea; and, as it was the first time that troops on service in India had been given compressed tea, the military authorities were taking a keen interest in the experiment. Happily the departure from the customary methods of carrying tea was a great success and it is pretty certain that compressed tea will be employed in future wars. The advantage in transport was very obvious, a chest of forty-five pounds only measuring 20 inches by 15 inches by 8½ inches.

When his inspection was completed Major-General Bower, accompanied by Major Hutchinson, chief staff officer, Captain Smithers, orderly officer, Captain Becher, provost marshal, Mr. A. Bentinck, political adviser, embarked on the s.s. *Battani*, on which the 1st Battalion of the 8th Gurkhas had already taken up its quarters for passage to Kobo. This fine regiment was particularly fortunate in seeing service so soon again, as it had only recently been employed in Tibet, where, by the way, it had been brigaded with the 32nd Pioneers, who were also participating in Major-General Bower's operations.

The battalion was commanded by Lieutenant-Colonel F. Murray, D.S.O., who had with him the following officers :—

Major J. A. Wilson.
Captain D. H. R. Giffard.
Captain A. L. M. Molesworth.
Captain D. S. Orchard.

Captain A. T. Pridham, I.M.S.
Captain J. F. S. D. Coleridge.
Lieutenant H. R. Harington.
Lieutenant H. Kennedy.
Lieutenant M. A. C. Kennedy.
Lieutenant H. R. C. Meade.
Lieutenant E. J. Ross.
Lieutenant G. C. B. Buckland.

The decision of headquarters to travel by the s.s. *Battani* was not communicated to Colonel Murray until the last moment lest a change of plans should have to be made. Coming with all the force of a surprise to the battalion, the news soon spread through the ship, officers and men collecting wherever they could find room to extend a rousing welcome to their distinguished fellow passenger. Moreover, word was passed to the masters of the river steamers, to the drivers of the engines on the adjacent railway, and to the police band, who doubled with celerity to the ghat, so that when Major-General Bower and his staff appeared, driven by Doctor Roberts himself in his "Star" car, which the genial physician had placed at the staff's disposal, there was so much din that the heroic efforts of the band to play independent versions of "There'll be a hot time in the old town to-night" went unnoticed. When every Abor for miles round had been scared by the pandemonium of cheers, whistles, and false notes, the gallant old veteran went aboard, deeply touched by the sheer spontaneity of his reception; his obvious pleasure pleasing every one concerned in the demonstration.

Owing to the many snags in the river and the difficulty of picking up in the dark the channel through the sand-banks, the s.s. *Battani* did not break berth until the following morning. By nightfall she arrived within four miles of Kobo camp, further progress being impossible until daylight again appeared. With dawn came a storm of rain; a dense fog that enveloped everything in an impenetrable screen and a flood with a current running at ten knots per hour. It was impossible to move. Though the boat stood fast, every now and then some giant tree from the upper reaches of the river collided with the steamer and threatened to carry away the moorings. In time, however, the rain stopped, the fog lifted, and the anchor was weighed. But the stream was so strong that four hours were spent in getting within two hundred yards of the landing-stage, from where, after the *Battani* had struggled with the current for two more hours without making headway, another steamer put off and gave assistance.

In spite of what had been reported at Dibrugarh, no one, not excepting so experienced an officer as Major-General Bower himself, was prepared for the magnificent accomplishment which, despite torrential rains and unparalleled floods, the working parties had achieved at Kobo in something less than six weeks. Nothing had been omitted from the planning of the camp that would be conducive to its safety and to the well-being of the force; and, though the rain and floods had converted the site into a veritable quagmire, the spirits of the troops rose superior to unavoidable discomforts.

The Staff was met by Colonel MacIntyre who, as officer commanding the lines of communication and base commandant, displayed the miracle that had been performed. Major-General Bower gasped with astonishment when it was explained that Force headquarters had been placed in the centre of "The Mall —to the left of Piccadilly, Sir." "Piccadilly!" said the General; "Well, I'm——." The Staff coughed; discretion happily is still an essential element in Staff college training. With corresponding appositeness the Military Police had been given Scotland Yard, and the hospital section Harley Street; while the gallant and good-looking "bloods" of the various battalions of the Gurkha regiments looked out upon a somewhat desolate Piccadilly. There was, too, an Oxford Street where the contingent, which the Assam Valley and Surma Valley Light Horse contributed to the expedition, was stationed.

Reference to the most delightful fancy of all has

been left to the last. It concerns the name of the camp and shows again how great is the affection and interest of the Native Army in the Throne. It had been easy to bridge the distance between the heart of the Empire and its most recent and far-distant outpost by giving to its newly cut roads the distinction of metropolitan nomenclature. The task of finding a name for the clearing itself was another matter. Many were suggested until Kobo, the name of a Miri hunter who lived in the neighbouring village of Poba and was known on the Brahmaputra as a capital sportsman, was selected. Just at this moment the native officers submitted "Coronation Camp." Their happy inspiration was welcome, but the impossibility of reducing the suggestion to any corresponding native term, which would have been intelligible to local natives, made its adoption impossible.

While the outward sign of the good fettle of the force was manifested in the cheerful humour which distinguishes the soldier the world o'er so soon as a chance of the real thing comes within rifle-shot, it must not be imagined for one moment that there was no undercurrent of seriousness. Without a lightness of heart and brightness of disposition among the Sappers and Miners, and the Pioneers, the tasks set these gallant fellows would have quite broken their spirits. Time and again the work, which their fatigue-parties put in during the day on the landing-stage and along the bank of the river, was swept away by some "fresh" that came down from the upper reaches during the night. In such circumstances there was every need of good spirits; for, though perseverance told in the end, trials and difficulties followed thick upon each other.

The camp-makers were ever at war with Nature, who, repellent and defiant, measured her strength with theirs. At first there was the densely growing screen of bamboo; then the rains, which caused the river to inundate the camp and wash away the works; finally, there was the jungle sickness, which spared neither man nor beast, and was most virulent where the virgin forest was being opened out. Beyond the immediate precincts of the camp, dangerous disease seemed to lurk in the slush of the decaying vegetation, in the giant nettles, and in the leaves of the palms.

Almost as soon as the coolies set out to cut a track they were found to be suffering from poisoned feet or inflamed legs from the bites of venomous insects, and were incapable for days. In the long run, of course, man was to triumph; though, as has been shown, the sweets of conquest were only secured after protracted struggling. Meanwhile nothing stopped the steady concentration. At rest in peace, the merest whisper of the wires had sufficed

SCENES IN KOBO CAMP. (2.)

Top left).—Sepoys of the Sappers and Miners building landing-stage; (right) Scotland Yard—Lines of the Lakhimpur Military Police, Bottom (left).—Sepoy on the edge of the jungle; (right) River steamers and "flats" at anchor off Kobo Camp.

SCENES IN KOBO CAMP. (3.)

Top (left).—Kobo Camp from mid-stream of the Brahmaputra River; (right) As the bank looked before it was cleared.
Bottom (left).—Sepoys of the 32nd Pioneers drawing tree-stumps; (right) As it appeared when cleared and complete.

for the several parts of the war machine to be slipped into place!

The early days at Kobo were full of the constant coming and going of troops. From near and far the gathering of the force proceeded, and but little was needed to set everything in motion. At first the trail of the coolies led only to Kobo. Later, it pushed beyond the camp, out into and through the jungle, to the advance post at Pasighat; stretching through the smoke of the burning undergrowth, through the closely matted thickets of bamboo, over river torrents and up and down the mountain gorges, in one unbroken line of men, patient and plodding, on occasions deviating, but never turning back.

Armies however great or small must march upon their stomachs and the question of supplies is the last, as it must be the first, consideration with the leaders of a force. Hence long before the troops moved out of Kobo, an endless train of coolies, burdened and uncomplaining, but heading always forward so that the force could feed to live and live to feed again, was on the road.

These coolies were to be present from the beginning to the end of the expedition, carrying supplies from the base at Kobo to the high cliffs above the falls of the Brahmaputra—if there are falls—and back again. Similarly, they were to serve as the supply train to the Miri and Mishmi columns, and it was felt that they would form the one perpetual, daily problem with which headquarters would be confronted.

Coolies in many thousands were required, and the supply was very limited until recourse was made to the men from the Manipur and Naga Hills. The Assamese were of no value, as for years they had lived in fear of the Abors. Bazaar "gup," too, speaking with the tongue of a lying jade on the eve of the expedition, had so added to the deadliness of the Abor reputation that one party of able-bodied men became panic-stricken when they realised the nature of the work before them, and disappeared in a night!

Prior to the present expedition, the terror of the border Assamese was a genuine fear far above the price of silver. Indeed, rupees heaped upon rupees were as dross beside it! It was found that nothing overcame it, though, happily, it was not shared in by the men from the Manipur and Naga Hills, who regarded it with amusement.

CHAPTER VIII

The Merry Naga—Manners and Customs—Head Hunters—The Ring of Love—Tea-cups as Ear Ornaments—Dainty Delicacies.

THE coolies employed on the Abor expedition were Nagas from the Naga Hills and from the Manipur Hills. In appearance they were sturdy fellows: dark brown of skin, with black eyes, tinged with yellow and very bloodshot from smoke. Their hair was blue-black, very coarse and with a tendency to curl; their features Mongoloid, though occasionally Aryan, while their physical development appeared to depend on their conditions of life.

Their height varied from four feet ten inches to five feet six inches. Coolies from villages to which no agricultural lands were attached seemed tall and slender, while the men, who had spent any time on their fields, were short, with magnificent chests and shoulders. Both sexes among the Nagas are adepts in the carriage of heavy packs, and will march quite steadily beneath a load of one hundred and twenty pounds. For the purposes of the expedition they were grouped in five corps, each seven hundred men strong, under the command of British officers.

Only men were employed, and all packs were limited to sixty pounds, which the coolies carried in kittas—conical-shaped baskets—slung from the shoulders and kept in position by a band of plaited cane round the forehead.

Living to the east of the Assam Valley the Nagas form a compact group and are by far the most interesting of the Mongoloid tribes, whose habitat is the northern hills of the Indian border. They number in all about 162,000 souls, and their country has been thoroughly explored by Colonel Woodthorpe, Mr. Damant and Mr. Davis, and well described by Mr. W. Crooke among many other writers. But few years ago the Nagas were in a state of savagery only to be compared with that of the wildest races in the Indian Empire—the Was of Upper Burma, and the Jarwas of the Andaman Islands. Bitter tribal feuds, complete disregard of the sanctity of human life, and the habit of raiding the settled villages on their borders in search of slaves or heads, illustrated the fiercer side of their character. On the other hand, they had attained considerable skill in agriculture and in the ruder arts of life.

The largest of the Naga tribes and that of which we possess the most complete knowledge is the Angami. Their culture is so far superior to that of the other members of the group that, while the latter raise their crops by periodically felling and burning a patch of forest, the Angamis grow their rice on terraces dug out from the hillsides with great skill and labour, and they water it by means of channels excavated for long distances along the contours. This art, according to Mr. Davis, is a link with Manipur, which the Angamis believe to have been their original home. The Angamis have practically no religion, beyond a vague belief in a Supreme Creator, with which is combined the animistic worship of the spirits of trees, rocks, and pools of water.

Their villages are designed to protect the inhabitants from the attacks of hostile tribes. Each is a stockaded fortress situated on an eminence, the houses being massed together without much attempt at arrangement, and the settlement guarded by an almost impenetrable fence of thorny shrubs and stinging nettles. Narrow sunken paths give entrance to the enclosure, the actual gateway being protected by a strong wooden door. At the present day this is seldom closed, an indication that British rule is gradually repressing inter-tribal warfare.

The better dwellings follow the type of the long house common to Eastern Asia. The chief's palace, if it may be so called, is often 250 or 300 feet in length, and occupies the centre and highest position in the village. Much trouble is expended in the decoration of a house. The approaches to the village are planted with trees, beneath which are the receptacles which contain or cover the remains of their dead. This habit of burial close to the house produces among them an attachment to their village sites which is unusual among the hill-tribes. Nothing short of the direst necessity will force them to abandon a place consecrated, as they believe, by the spirits of the departed. At the same time, the fact remains that the village is far from being a united community.

The unit of Naga society is the khel or sept, and each of these is in theory an exogamous group of brethren by blood at war with the rest of the world. Intense rivalry exists between the khels of the same village; and, though the feuds between each village and its neighbours, which in former times kept the whole country in a state of constant disturbance, have practically ceased since the British occupation, the quarrels between the khels not infrequently result in riots and free-fights at the great drinking festivals.

In this connection Mr. Crooke recalls the fact that the Nagas of North Kachar had a curious arrangement for mitigating the rancour caused by blood feuds. At stated times, once or twice a year, the whole village adjourned to a convenient spot and a general *mêlée* took place, every one fighting for his own hand. No weapons were used; and though severe bruises were inflicted, no ill-feeling resulted.

The Aos are even cruder than the Angami branch of the Nagas, for each of their villages is a small republic in which each man is as good as his neighbour. Indeed, it would be hard to find anywhere more democratic communities, and, though head-men do exist, their authority is small. Before they came under British rule the Aos were notorious for the kidnapping of slaves, a habit which has been now almost entirely repressed. In the old days slaves were, it is said, generally kindly treated, being considered almost as members of the family. If they were troublesome they were sold to more distant and more savage tribes, when not infrequently they were offered as sacrifice to evil spirits.

The ultimate end of slaves was always a little uncertain. Very often the unfortunate creatures were made over by one village to another as a means of healing a feud or in satisfaction for any heads which might have been taken. Slaves paid in this way, however, were invariably slaughtered by the village which received them as an offering to the spirits of the men on their side who had been killed.

The Semas, who are also included among the Nagas, are even more savage than the Aos, and were notorious for cruelty combined with treachery. It was considered by them praiseworthy to entertain a guest, and to slay him when he was off his guard. But all the Naga tribes are, on occasion, head-hunters, and shrink from no treachery in securing these ghastly trophies.

This practice exists in its most archaic form among the wilder tribes of Upper Burma, who are ethnically related to the hill-people of Assam. Their object in capturing the head of an enemy is to bring into subjection the spirit of the dead man, which is believed to accompany his skull to the home of the murderer. Hence, with a perfectly logical grasp of the situation, the skull of a stranger is preferred, because the spirit does not know its way in a strange land, and is less likely to wander.

Among the Nagas, on the contrary, the habit arose from the much less primitive desire of acquiring a trophy.

"Any head counts," says Mr. Davis, "be it that of a man, woman, or child, and entitles the man who takes it to wear certain ornaments according to the custom of the tribe or village. Most heads are taken, or rather used to be taken, not in fair fight, but by methods the most treacherous. As common a method as any was for a man to lurk about the water ghat of a hostile village, and kill the first woman or child who came to draw water. Sometimes expeditions on a large scale were made, several

SEMA NAGAS, WHO SERVED WITH THE MISHMI MISSION,

THE NAGA HAS SOLVED THE PROBLEM OF WHAT IS REALLY A SIMPLE COSTUME!

villages combining for the sake of making a large bag. Even then, if the village to be attacked was found prepared, the valiant warriors who had come against it would, as a rule, retire without striking a blow. If, however, it was found that the whole adult population was away in the fields, an attack would be delivered, and as many children and old people as could be killed would be killed, a retreat being effected before the men of the village attacked could have time to receive the news and return from their fields."

On account of their head-taking propensities the Nagas were more dreaded by the Abors than all the troops of the Field Force put together. The practice was prohibited by General Bower, though from that moment the Nagas, one and all, wore an air of unrelieved depression, which was terrible to witness. For a time they hoped that the Sirkar would relent, as indeed it should have done, since custom has made the acquisition of a head in battle the essential sign of a man's prowess. They abandoned their hopes when they were informed that, with the exception of the few who were employed as scouts, they would not be permitted to bear any active part in any fighting that might take place. When the coolies were in column of march they always moved in parties of six, in single file, with a sepoy, as protection, at the head and tail of each party. In addition a file of ten sepoys was allotted to every six units. On an alarm being sounded, the coolies were instructed to step quietly from the track, close up on their escorts, and crouch by them while the main body of troops doubled up the line of column.

The head-hunting and ruthless disregard of life which characterised the Nagas in the past, and still does so to some extent, has naturally checked the social intercourse of the tribes. Among the allied villages, it is true, communications were admirably maintained by improving the hill paths and bridging the streams. But in other places the roads, sufficiently dangerous in themselves, were further interrupted by the savagery of the people. Dr. Grierson calls them "a confused sample-bag of tribes," among whom the extraordinary divergences of speech—differences of language, not merely of dialect—clearly reflect the reign of terror which the people have endured for countless generations. Mr. Damant, a former Government officer of the region, writes: "Every tribe, almost every village, is at war with its neighbour, and no Naga of these parts dare leave the territory of his tribe without the probability that his life will be the penalty."

Within twenty miles of country five or six different dialects are often met with. Monosyllabic languages, like that of the Nagas, possessing no literature and uncertain rules of pronunciation, are bound to change very rapidly and quite independently of each other. This process has been facilitated here by the savage manners of the race. The tattoo marks, which each successful head-hunter is permitted to wear, differ in pattern with each tribe, and afford a means of recognising strangers. Without such marks and the use of gestures, communication between branches of the tribe, each speaking a different language, would be impossible.

The Bachelors' Hall, known among the Abors as the moshup, is also found among the Nagas, where it is called the dekha-chang or morang. Only very young children rest with their parents, the unmarried youths and girls sleeping in a separate house apart. The young men's hall is practically the village guard-room. It is built on a platform commanding an extensive view of all the approaches to the village. Here a sentry is always posted, who sounds the alarm by beating a hollow tree-trunk with a wooden mallet. This drum is often elaborately carved, like the figure-head of a ship, and usually represents the head of a buffalo which is curiously painted.

In this hall are preserved the skulls of enemies taken in battle, and the inmates are in charge of the arms of the tribe, which they carefully clean and polish. Along both sides are the sleeping-berths of the young men, and the central space, floored with massive planks, is left open to be used by the braves in their dances. Outside are seats where the greybeards assemble in the evening to watch the youths practising running and putting the stone, amusements in which they delight. In the girls' house the maidens sleep two or three together, and sometimes an old woman is posted there as chaperon. But these precautions do not prevent free intercourse between the sexes.

The laws of the Nagas regulating the Genna, or taboo, are most elaborate. These regulations enjoin the closing of the house or village, and are enforced on occasions of special manifestations of supernatural power, or when the gods are supposed to communicate directly with their worshippers. Thus a Genna is proclaimed in the event of an earthquake, eclipse, or the burning of a village. Such events are followed by an examination of the omens, and a special purgation is carried out in order to expel the evil spirits which are believed to be responsible for the occurrence. The village or house is then closed for two or three days, the inhabitants abstaining from all labour, and neither going out themselves nor permitting any stranger to enter during that period.

The object of the rite seems to be to prevent the return of the evil spirits which have been so carefully expelled by the priest, and as taboo is infectious, the people of the house are required to remain in seclusion. Genna is also declared at the annual ceremony of making new fire for the village. A general sacrifice is offered, and the fire, when produced by friction, is first used in burning down the jungle for the sowing of the crops. Genna is also observed at the birth of a child, or even of any domestic animal, such as a cow or dog. Mr. Damant was once refused a drink at a house because the dog had given birth to puppies. A similar taboo is enforced at the death of any important personage, the village being closed for two or three days, during which no one leaves or enters it.

When the anger of the gods is believed to be specially manifested against a family—if, for instance, a member of it is drowned, crushed by a tree, or killed by a tiger—the household is compelled to resort to a remarkable rite of purification. They abandon their house with all the property which it contains. Everything they possess is destroyed by fire, and, retaining only enough of clothing to cover their nakedness, they are compelled to wander in the jungle for a month, after which the anger of the gods is supposed to be appeased. The taboo extends even to the site of the house which they occupied, and a new place must be selected when it is rebuilt.

Though from the social point of view the Nagas are in a state of savagery, in other ways they have attained a fairly high state of culture. Their agricultural knowledge is higher than that of their neighbours, and their dress and arms exhibit some artistic taste and skill. They make a coarse cloth from the bark fibres of the nettle plant, and finer fabrics, curiously bordered and marked with triangular patches of red and black, are woven from the cotton which they grow. In this direction it is interesting to note among the Eastern Nagas the use of a kind of clan tartan. This cloth is made of cotton, dyed black with shades of red, blue, and green, arranged in stripes differing with different tribes. The pattern of the small apron worn by the Aos also differs from village to village. All their household vessels are of wood, which they carve elaborately, and they also make a rough kind of pottery, shaped by hand, without the use of the wheel.

Their spears and other arms are excellent specimens of metal-work. Their arms are a gleaming pole-axe with a short black handle, to which is hung a tuft of goat's hair dyed red; a broad-bladed spear, the shaft of which is covered with coloured hair like a brush; and a shield of buffalo hide. Their most important implement is the dhao, and they are adepts in laying out *panjees*. The helmet, made of wickerwork or plaited cane, is conical in shape, about a foot high, and is covered with a layer of fur and hair, black or red in colour. Sometimes it is decorated with singular coronals made of pieces cut out of large shells, and on the crown is a little periwinkle-shaped basket-work cap, coloured black, with a scarlet border, and ornamented with peacocks' feathers and bunches of dyed wool. In front is a disc of polished brass and a crescent-shaped piece of buffalo horn.

Warriors of distinction wear the hair of slain enemies hanging from the side ornaments of the helmet, and forming a fringe round the face. Women's tresses are preferred as being longer. The Eastern Naga warrior also wears a special collar on taking the first head. To this boar tusks are added to commemorate a second victim. After taking a third he may wear an apron covered with cowry shells arranged in a pattern which serves as a tally to mark the number of persons he has slain. He is also entitled to fix in his hair one feather of the Dhanesh, or hornbill, for every man killed, these signs of valour, with his other property, being placed on his grave.

Light-hearted and elemental, the Nagas have reduced their habits, together with their dress, to an inelegant simplicity. They eat dog, and, like some of the Tibetans, they "eat" tea by frying the leaves in ghee, a process which not infrequently sets up most violent indigestion when followed for the first time.

Up to the age of puberty Naga children wear no clothes. Afterwards, they exercise a choice between a small square of cotton cloth, suspended from the waist by a string, and a length of cloth, in the form of a dhotie, which they wear round the waist and tie in a knot in front in such a fashion that the end hangs down as a square of very limited dimensions. Costume varies, however, and in some septs the women, in others the men, use no clothing, while in many villages the women's costume consists of a few necklaces and an apron, though they usually manage to do without the apron. In North Kachar married women have a dress which distinguishes them from the maidens of the tribe. The former leave the bosom uncovered, while the latter wear a cloth tightly folded round the breast. The married women have their long hair plaited and knotted at the back, or sometimes flowing naturally over the shoulders. The unmarried girls have their hair cut square in front, and brushed down over the forehead nearly to the eyebrows.

In some Naga villages the men wear a penile ring of bone or of bamboo, about an eighth of an inch wide, which is known as The Ring of Love. At night, the man's wife wears it on her finger.

Its preservation at the present day is a link with the time when the tribal braves fought so much over women that it was necessary to devise some method of checking their robust spirits.

While there may be room for some few additions to the dress of the Nagas, their methods of hair-dressing leave nothing to be desired. It is at once complete and terrifying, though the style varies with the tribal division to which the man may belong. A wide difference exists for example between the mode of the men from the Naga Hills, and those from Manipur, while each differs from the coiffure favoured by the Rangpang Nagas. In the case of the former the head is shaved in a wide circle which passes above the ears, and allows the hair to fall mopwise over the crown of the skull. With the Nagas from Manipur a variety of patterns is followed, the most general taking the form of a broad shaven line which passes exactly down the centre of the head from the forehead to the nape of the neck. Among the Rangpang Nagas, the prevailing style is for the men to catch up the hair in a clump which is worn somewhat rakishly just above the brow. Naga women favour a knot which lies low down on the neck, in the manner once patronised by Mrs. Langtry.

In addition to their elegant methods of coiffure, the Nagas have a pretty taste in ornaments for the neck, arms, and ears. Bracelets of cowry beads, necklets of boar tusks and bangles of brass wire are much favoured, although, of all forms of ornamentation, the unsophisticated Naga savage prefers to pierce the lobes of his ears, and then distend the holes until they can carry an ornament some inches in circumference. An empty cartridge case was "the latest thing" in aural ornaments among the dudes of the Kobo lines; though it must be added that one enterprising Gam contrived to place himself upon the very pinnacle of fashion by fixing a small blue enamel tea-cup in his lobe-hole. Unhappily the effect on the feminine mind of such an ambitious scheme of decoration so angered his friends that it was a moral certainty that before many months had passed he would be "removed."

Another remarkable portion of the Naga wardrobe is a wooden tail, which, among the Sema tribe, is about eighteen inches long, and decorated with bunches of goat's hair dyed scarlet. According to Colonel Woodthorpe, all the Nagas' personal decorations have a defensive purpose in view, and are planned to ward off the spear and axe, while the long hair which is so profusely used, waving about with every movement of the wearer, distracts the eye of the foe levelling a spear at him, and disturbs his aim.

When Naga coolies are marching, they employ

a two-note chant—"He-hah," "He-hoh," which, in sound, repeats the tones of the Chinese language. All native races of the aboriginal order seem to find expression in song when on the move; but the Naga chant is singularly full-bodied and melodious. As the head of the column emerged from the depths of the jungle, the rumble of the notes rising from somewhere in the rear was not without a certain thrilling intensity. The coolies declared that it would put the fear of God into the Abor tribesmen as soon as they heard it.

The presence of the Nagas in camp and elsewhere was not altogether unattended by trials, and very genuine expressions of relief went up from Kobo, Sadiya, Saikhwa and Seajuli when, shouldering his pack-basket, the last of the porters fell in on his place in the column. Quiet and law-abiding, they exhibited a naturalness that was positively bewildering and impossible to check. Many of the coolies were untutored savages and knew no better, and one and all did everything in public in complete ignorance of the elements of decency. Accustomed to a style of dress that was curiously suited to their mode of life, and unrestrained in their manners, the gentle coolies soon rendered the atmosphere oppressive. If regulations were made in one direction, nuisances cropped up in another, until the unconscious misdemeanours of the Nagas became the joke of the messes, where they were christened "The Heavenly Terrors."

It was, of course, impossible for Colonel A. E. Woods, the Deputy Commissioner of the Naga Hills, who had procured the great bulk of the coolies, to be everywhere. Few men could have done more than he to facilitate the transport arrangements of the three "shows," for the general supervision of the corps of coolies, who were scattered over such widely separated places as Kobo, Sadiya, Saikhwa and Seajuli, was in his hands, and was more than enough for one man. Colonel Woods, however, took matters very unconcernedly, even when complaints about the mysterious disappearance of the village dogs came in from Assamese hamlets in the neighbourhood!

Of course the cheerful and utterly irresponsible Naga was the thief; but if only one-tenth of the reports had been true every man of those enlisted as coolies must have spent the whole of his working and sleeping hours in devouring hundreds of his favourite delicacy. As it happened, very few dogs were stolen, for a ration of meat was issued to the coolies so soon as it was realised that they regarded a prowling pariah as a dainty dish. This little fact, of course, was not known to the wily villagers who, never loth to squeeze the Sirkar, spent their time in presenting fictitious statements of non-existent losses among their dogs. Bills were in this form :—

"To wit—dogs damaged by spears	.	3 rupees.
„ „ —dogs eaten	. . .	5 rupees.
		8 rupees.

"Oh, Protector of the Poor, pay as above to thy Honour's Servant."

But his Honour never did !

For their own protection the Nagas were permitted to carry spears and dhaos, which were more than sufficient for their safety. As natural warriors they preferred their own weapons to any carried by the soldiers of the expedition. Altogether they were greatly impressed by the fine show which the force made on parade ; but, in their hearts, they undoubtedly looked with derision upon the elaborate character of the preparations. Feeling nothing but contempt for the Abors, they could not understand the large numbers of troops, the supplies of rifles, guns, elephants, etc., which were to be employed. Indeed, on one occasion the Naga head-men offered to "do" the job for General Bower in exchange for a gift of the country of the Abors, with which they had been greatly taken and openly coveted. No doubt, too, they would have "done" it very well: as expeditiously, perhaps, and much more cheaply, though of course the offer could not be accepted.

Rehearsals of the actual formation of the column on line of march, particularly if they themselves were included in the parade, tickled the Nagas vastly. In a way they seemed to think that these things were done for their own private entertainment; consequently they shouldered their loads and fell in on their appointed places to an accompaniment of roars of laughter, and a stream of excited chatter.

An elaborate system of signals by whistle was necessary for the safety of the column when marching through the bush, but the various calls were always a puzzle to the unsophisticated Naga. A long and short blast was intended to signify that the column was straggling; three blasts that the rear was closed up; one blast that the column was to halt. The Nagas were never quite sure what they had to do when the whistles sounded, and usually showed it—by doing nothing. In the end many of these little difficulties disappeared, though it is doubtful if the Nagas ever quite abandoned the idea that artillery tests, rocket practices, and emergency casualty drills with appliances improvised out of rifles and putties, or following the system designed by Captain O'Neill, Indian Medical Service, were not features of some extraordinary *puja* arranged for their especial edification. Fortunately for headquarters, the officers in command of the various Naga Carrier Corps, were

"THE UNSOPHISTICATED NAGA IS THE CHILD OF NATURE."

NAGAS REHEARSING A FORMATION OF THE COLUMN.

"WARRIORS OF DISTINCTION," WEARING THE SPECIAL COLLAR OF BOAR'S TUSKS WHICH DENOTES THAT THE WEARER HAS HEAD-HUNTED WITH SUCCESS.

"THEY—THE NAGAS—EAT DOG!" (See page 151.)

able to fall back upon Mr. Jack Needham, the son of the well-known Political Officer, who not only was highly respected by the Nagas themselves, but spoke their many dialects with a fluency that no ordinary European could ever hope to equal. His influence with the coolies in any time of crisis was indeed a pillar of strength.

CHAPTER IX

The Start of the Operations—Reconnaissance by Major Lindsay—Order of March—Sixty-Pound Kit—March to Ledum—First Blood.

WITH the arrival of headquarters at Kobo on October 7th, it only required a "let up" in the weather to allow the expedition to break camp. Unfortunately the white squall, which compelled the s.s. *Battani* to lay to off Kobo on the night of Major-General Bower's arrival and delayed his disembarkation, continued in another form, and for the first few days after the advent of the Staff the base camp was swept by rain-storms which effectually prevented any movement from being made. In spite of the prevailing deluge, which caused the streams to overflow until a part of the camp was under water and the rest of it a sea of mud, the General and his staff were always very much engaged. From reveille, which sounded at five o'clock in the morning, to retreat, at five o'clock in the evening, their duties varied from coolie inspection, the formation of the operating columns, to the testing of a couple of mortars which had been sent along with the force, and were designed by the Sappers and Miners on the pattern of those used in the Russo-Japanese war.

These guns promised to be very effective. At an angle of forty-five degrees they threw a bomb loaded with two pounds of dynamite about one hundred and fifty yards. The explosion, which was regulated by a time fuse, was very violent. It tore great holes in the ground and, when used in water, sent up a big column of water to a considerable height. It was thought that the two mortars and the Martin-Hale grenades would be more serviceable than the smooth-bore seven-pounders, which were so antiquated that they were only accurate up to four hundred yards. At the same time long-range guns were not required, the dense high-growing jungle making their use impracticable.

The principal task with which headquarters was occupied at this date was, of course, the formation of the two operating columns, one of which was to proceed *via* the village of Ledum while the other moved *via* Pasighat. As the Staff wrestled with this problem, apportioning the different details respectively to the Ledum Column or to the two divisions of the Main Column, a strong party under Major A. B. Lindsay, 2nd Gurkhas, was dispatched on October 9th on a path-cutting reconnaissance as far as Oniyuk on the road to Ledum. The little force was composed of one double company of the 2nd

Gurkhas, one company of the Sappers and Miners, one company of the 32nd Pioneers, a few hundred coolies, and three elephants. Oniyuk lay about ten miles down the Ledum road. Although so close to the base, the distance was more than sufficient to indicate the character of the work which would have to be carried out by the columns as they marched through the bush.

For the first mile and a half Lindsay's party followed the road to Pasighat, a wonderful ten-foot affair, which had been built during the July–October rainy season under the supervision of Mr. Watkins, of the Assam Public Works Department, out of a grant of thirteen thousand rupees furnished for the purpose by the Assam Government. The ten-foot gauge was continued for the first six miles of this road, and so imposing a thoroughfare 'mid the virgin wilderness surrounding it obviously merited a distinguished name.

It was christened with due ceremony and some degree of pride Rue de Kebang; but, when the sixth milestone had been passed and the dainty elegance of the Rue de Kebang was found to have degenerated into a rough-and-tumble track, some wag hung up the punning notice, "change here for the Rue of Watkins." At a later date the road was carried beyond Pasighat to Yambung, and not only bridged and drained but improved sufficiently to allow of its use by mule transport. Beyond Yambung it was continued as a superior jungle path as far as Simong and Riga. It was also given the flanking adornment of a military telegraph and telephone line, in which condition it existed until it was abandoned on the withdrawal of the expedition.

At the mile-and-half distance from Kobo camp there was open grassland, about nine square miles in extent, from where the first view of the frowning gorges of the Dihang, looming up on the north, was obtained. Here, as Major Lindsay pushed forward into the unknown, a forty-foot platform was erected from which Lieutenant Knight, as signalling officer, kept up communication with the little party.

Lindsay's march through the grasslands was stopped after a progress of four miles, by the waters of the Kemi River, a stream some ninety feet in breadth, six feet deep, flowing with a swift current over a sandy bottom. A narrow footbridge of bamboo poles, ricketty and on the point of collapse, linked the two banks, but gave way after a portion of the column had gingerly trodden its slippery surface. Abandoning the old bridge to the foaming waters of the Kemi, a working party of the Sappers and Miners was dropped at the river bank and, while the advance pressed on towards Oniyuk, a new bridge was put up two miles north of Mutke.

From the river bank to Oniyuk the direction

lay through dense jungle and over the Sikha River, a thirty-foot stream, two feet deep with a gravel bed. Though the distance to Oniyuk from the banks of the Kemi River was only six miles, the march occupied considerable time, as the jungle was so thick that in many places an impression could only be made upon it with the help of elephants. The order of march became "Elephants abreast" out of sheer necessity.

As the huge, willing and very useful beasts broke down the bamboo screen, the Gurkhas, by much cutting and chopping with their kukris, hacked out a track for the rest of the party. In addition to these difficulties, the heavy rains had caused the Kemi and Sikha Rivers to overflow, and much wading through waist-deep water was necessary before Oniyuk was reached. From Oniyuk the usual path to Ledum followed the bed of the Poba, but it was found to be impassable, one result of Major Lindsay's reconnaissance showing that it would be necessary for any column proceeding to Ledum to clear a way for itself through the jungle.

While the reconnaissance was proceeding to Oniyuk, headquarters had completed the task of organising the field columns, and by the time that Major Lindsay returned on October 18th everything was in readiness for a general start. The little interval, too, had given time for the various absent officers to rejoin, and for all units deficient in strength to be brought up to field state. Special service officers, regimental officers and additions to the original estimate of strength came to Kobo by every boat, General Bower remarking on one occasion that had he desired it he could have formed a force out of officers who had offered their services by letter, cable and telegram. Among others who reported arrival during these days were the details of the 2nd Gurkhas under Lieutenant-Colonel J. Fisher, who had the following officers with him :—

Major A. B. Lindsay.
Major E. H. Sweet.
Major J. Davidson (Indian Medical Service).
Captain H. C. Nicolay.
Lieutenant A. J. H. Chope.
Lieutenant A. H. R. Saunders.
Lieutenant H. F. F. Marsh.
Lieutenant G. M. McCleverty.

Similarly the full complement of the officers of the 32nd Sikh Pioneers was now present, the list being as follows :—

Lieutenant-Colonel F. H. Peterson, D.S.O.
Major E. H. S. Cullen.
Captain G. C. Hodgson, D.S.O.
Captain H. B. Drake (Indian Medical Service).
Captain J. E. H. Wilson, 34th Sikh Pioneers (attached).
Captain H. S. Mitchell.
Lieutenant and Adjutant the Hon. M. de Courcy.

Lieutenant W. M. Ommaney.
Lieutenant N. S. Taylor.
Lieutenant A. T. G. Beckham.
Lieutenant C. T. Daly.
Lieutenant B. Christie.
Lieutenant I. Burn Murdoch.
Lieutenant and Quartermaster H. W. Andrews.

Other officers who came up were four members of the Survey section of the Royal Engineers: Captain C. P. Gunter, R.E., Captain O. H. B. Trenchard, R.E., Lieutenant J. R. Oakes, R.E., and Lieutenant H. T. Moorshead, R.E.; Captain F. Bailey, of the Indian Political Department, Captain R. L. Bignell, 41st Dogras, officiating A.D.C. to the General Officer commanding 8th Lucknow Division, as Treasure officer, Captain Stewart and Captain O'Neill, Indian Field Ambulance, Lieutenant R. L. Gamlen and Lieutenant Evans, Indian Medical Service, Mr. de Smidt as Telegraph officer in charge of the field operations, and the following non-commissioned officers of the Ordnance Corps: Conductor F. Williams, Sub-conductor H. Ward; Store-Sergeant E. W. Guest, Armour-Staff-Sergeant W. Smithson.

As designed by headquarters after careful consideration, the order of march for the columns in the jungle was, in normal circumstances, to be as follows :—

"THE INVALUABLE ADJUNCT TO THE MEN OF THE 32ND PIONEERS AND OF THE SAPPERS AND MINERS WAS THE ELEPHANT."

BY CART TO THE FALLS ——!

THE TROOPS CARRIED MUCH ON THEIR OWN SHOULDERS.

"AS THE COOLIES FELL IN——" (See p. 171.)

(1) Naga Scouts; Sepoys.
(2) Advance Guards.
(3) Headquarters.
(4) Infantry.
(5) Sappers and Miners; Pioneers according to circumstances.
(6) Guns with escort.
(7) Infantry.
(8) Sappers and Miners; Pioneers.
(9) Ammunition.
(10) Signalling.
(11) Hospital.
(12) Officers' baggage.
(13) Baggage of troops in order of march.
(14) Supplies.
(15) Rearguard.

In view of the difficulties of transport and the necessity for marching "light," to which Field Force orders constantly referred, the individual private was compelled to carry much on his person if he wished to supplement the weight allowed to him by Orders. As it was, the dead weight borne per man, including two days' rations, ammunition, accoutrements, rain-sheet, etc., was not far short of sixty pounds, though this amount expressly excluded the ten pounds of baggage allowed to the men and carried by coolies. It may be added that a ten-pound scale just allowed the men to carry one complete change. It took effect from Kobo.

As far as Pasighat the baggage allowance for officers was restricted to sixty pounds. Beyond the advanced base, this scale was reduced by half. As a sixty-pounds' scale admits only bare necessities, when orders were issued that officers were to carry but thirty pounds of kit into the zone of actual operations, a shiver passed down the force. At the moment the weather was both wet and cold. There was, too, no immediate prospect of an improvement in it by the time that the columns marched out of Pasighat, so the decision practically promised a succession of wet, chilly and cheerless bivouacs, with scanty rations and no opportunity for drying rain-sodden clothes.

There was no alternative to the reduction. Major Lindsay's reconnaissance had clearly shown the difficulties which were to be expected when the troops entered the jungle. Although the scale imposed, therefore, was by no means popular, its justice was at once admitted, since any increase in the weight of baggage meant a longer coolie train, which in turn was an invitation to disaster, the dense undergrowth making any form of movement save in single file quite impossible.

Few people who have not made the experiment can realise the limitations of a sixty-pound kit. Although individual tastes may differ in the selection of the absolute necessities, some taking, for example, a Crooks' valise, which can be converted into a shelter tent and be of incalculable use in rainy weather, in place of the Wolseley valise, which is lighter and does not lend itself so well to the same purpose, others discarding the pillow for a suit of Burberry's indispensable Gabardine, or some non-essential, in order to include the quite essential Kodak, the articles included in kit on a sixty-pounds' scale are usually as follows :—

1 Crooks' or Wolseley valise in Willesden canvas.	1 canvas bucket.
2 blankets.	1 medicine case.
1 pair pyjamas.	3 pairs socks.
1 khaki tunic.	1 pair boots.
1 pair breeches.	1 pair native shoes.
1 mosquito net.	1 writing-case.
1 khaki shirt.	6 handkerchiefs.
1 vest.	1 cap.
1 set washing materials.	1 regulation overcoat.
1 towel.	1 pillow, or suit of Burberry's Gabardine.
	1 box Bromo paper.

Kodak camera and films.

In addition to actual clothing worn, officers of the expedition carried on their persons as a rule all the following things :—

Sam Browne belt.	Map.
Sword or kukri or shot-gun.	Compass.
Field-glasses.	Emergency ration.
Revolver and Ammunition.	First-Aid Field Dressing.
	Brandy flask.

Haversack.	Rations for two days.
Water-bottle.	Whistle.
Regulation waterproof.	Knife.

Notebook.

Those who had a finger on the pulse of the expedition knew that the reference by Force Orders to the baggage allowance indicated the speedy departure of the field columns. In point of fact headquarters was only waiting a cessation of the rains to effect a start. After nine days of torrential downpour a break occurred on October 16th. Although time was required for the force, as well as for the jungle, to dry after such incessant drenching as each had received, every one "knew" when Major Lindsay returned two days later that the hour of departure was imminent. Happily general conjecture proved for once to be correct. At half-past five on the morning of October 20th a column of one thousand men under Lieutenant-Colonel J. Fisher, 2nd Gurkhas, accompanied by Mr. Scott, Indian Civil Service, as Assistant Political Officer, marched from Kobo camp *en route* for Ledum, where a number of stockaded villages belonging to the Minyong Abors was known to be situated. The details of this little force comprised two companies of the 2nd Gurkhas with seven-pounder, 300 Lakhimpur Military Police with maxim, a party of 32nd Pioneers, a hospital unit under Dr. J. M. Falkner, fourteen elephants and a corps of Naga coolies.

Long before dawn the camp was aroused by the sounds of departure, which, as there had been some return of stormy weather during the night, was not altogether expected. Tents were quickly rolled and the transport baskets soon filled. As the coolies fell in, the salmon-pink tints of a wonderful sunrise suffused the heavens. The glow increased; night faded away, the risen sun banishing the last traces of the rain-clouds. As the sun mounted its eastern horizon the line of waiting Gurkhas and Naga scouts forming the vanguard broke into movement. The march had begun. One by one the details of the column approached and were swallowed up by the mysteries of the jungle, each section stiffening to the salute as it trailed past the base where the General Officer commanding was taking a silent, though sympathetically interested, farewell of every man. In a little the last salute had been given; the last sepoy had filed by and disappeared, and the forest of nature had enveloped without effort a forest of steel.

In spite of the length of the column and its numbers not a sound came from the jungle. There was no sign of any force; no indication of the scouts on whose watchfulness depended the safety of the column; of the coolies, burdened yet full of song; of the Military Police, who had been giving yeoman service since the previous April; of gunners, signallers, or of hospital bearers carrying network doolies; of elephants bearing the heavy equipment of the column and embodying in every stately movement strength, dignity, and docility. The bush was still; the silence was impressive, the extreme ease with which the jungle could absorb the passing of a thousand men being demonstrated quite uncannily. It seemed incredible that less than a quarter of a mile away a large force should have had its being, and the jungle not betray the sound.

The progress of the column, necessarily, was slow. Though the track had been cleared for the first few miles men had to pick their way, step by step, over bamboo stumps and through a ruck of trailing creepers, wide-eyed and alert the while against man's, as well as nature's, insidious attack. The first halt of any purpose was at Oniyuk, to which the reconnaissance under Major Lindsay had penetrated, and where camp was pitched for the night. From Oniyuk the difficulties of the march began, and very soon there was work for all.

As soon as camp was reached the Naga coolies set to work to build a stockade, while fatigues from the 32nd Pioneers started cutting a track for the next day's march. Before nightfall this path reached very nearly to Dorak, where the second camp was to be established. Work was not unaccompanied with misfortune, for the undergrowth swarmed with leeches which became an even greater nuisance than the wet. In spite of all precautions these jungle pests contrived to find a way through every article of clothing. In a few hours several score would be picked off a man's body. Nothing really checked their ravages; it required the lighted tip of a cigarette or a dab of carbolic acid to make the beggars drop off. Even then relief was only momentary, as, where one dropped off, two dropped in —and stayed!

In spite of leeches the path-cutting parties arrived at Dorak early on October 21st. Much to the relief of the little column, who had experienced so very early a foretaste of future hardships, it was found that Dorak and the immediate region was fairly clear of jungle, while a good path was reported to run from Dorak *via* Mangnang, Mekong and Bamung, to Ledum. Abor paths, however, were regarded with suspicion, so the advance continued through the jungle by a road specially cleared, and camp was pitched at Mangnang for the night of October 21st.

On the following day Colonel Fisher moved upon Mekong, where small bodies of the enemy's scouts were reported to be lurking. Progress now slowed to a snail's pace, though camp was reached without any actual incident occurring. Resuming the march on October 23rd, the advance guard sighted two small parties of the enemy, and exchanged the courtesies of the occasion with the effect of bagging one Abor. Later in the day the column was engaged by a body of sixty archers, who beat a hasty retreat when their flights of arrows were returned by a volley of—bullets.

In view of the fact that the enemy's arrows were poisonous it was rather fortunate that the column suffered no casualties. At the same time it was a pity that circumstances did not permit Colonel Fisher to ascertain the results of the men's fire. At a later date, however, it appeared, from statements of prisoners who were captured by one of Colonel Fisher's patrols, that two Abors were killed outright and at least a dozen badly wounded on this occasion. The operations of the first day, therefore, may be said to have been blooded very nicely.

After this little skirmish Colonel Fisher pushed on to Ledum, sending as messengers to the tribesmen the Gams of Mangnang district with a request for a palaver. From the fact that the Ledum Gams curtly refused all overtures, and that an early crop had been cut, it was obvious that the temper of the place was hostile. Colonel Fisher halted, built a strongly fortified post, and decided to await at Ledum the arrival of a convoy of stores from Kobo. Meanwhile he began an examination of the country towards Mishing.

WITH THE LEDUM COLUMN.
The camp below Ledum after the jungle had been cleared.

WITH THE LEDUM COLUMN.
The lines of the 2nd Gurkha Rifles at Mishing after the jungle had been cleared.

RIVER CONVOY PREPARING TO START.

CHAPTER X

Start of Major-General Bower and Main Column—The March from Kobo to Pasighat—Land and River Convoys—Wayside Experiments—The Question of Communications—First Glimpse of the Dihang.

While Colonel Fisher was picking a laborious way through the depths of a virgin jungle to Ledum, the last touches were being put to the column which Major-General Bower himself was to lead to Pasighat. As the General had an eye for everything, and Major Hutchinson, the Chief Staff Officer of the force, had the energy of a hundred men, it was but a very few hours after the departure of the Ledum Column before the main body was ready to move. Early on the morning of October 22nd the men of the first division of the Main Column, as the headquarters command was described to distinguish it from Colonel Fisher's party, fell in. The force parading comprised five companies of the 8th Gurkhas with one seven-pounder gun, two companies of the 32nd Pioneers, half a company of Sappers and Miners with two grenade guns, one hospital section, one telegraph party, one carrier corps and half-a-dozen elephants. In addition to Major-General Bower and Major

Hutchinson, the headquarters staff included Mr. Bentinck as Assistant Political Officer, Captain Smithers as Orderly Officer, and Captain Hore as Intelligence Officer.

Inspired by the knowledge that they were starting at last on the actual work of the expedition, a note of triumphant light-heartedness animated the troops. Cheer after cheer was flung up as the various sections of the force filed off to their appointed places in the column; overwhelming enthusiasm, emphasised by the shrill trumpetings of a number of elephants, greeting the appearance of the General himself. Asiatics are seldom deficient in the qualities of imagination; but on this occasion there was unusual warmth in the vociferous spontaneity with which every man participating in the march-out realised for himself the significance of the event. All arms were bearing themselves magnificently, the brave fellows of the 8th Gurkhas and the fine stalwarts of the 32nd Pioneers, who formed the chief strength of the force, sweeping out of camp into column of march with a suggestion in their movements of strength, sturdiness and martial pride that was most impressive. Indeed, it is safe to say that not for a long time has the north-east frontier of India formed the background to so stirring a spectacle! Perhaps, too, the opinion may be hazarded that, if "little wars" produce so true a spirit, there need be no fear of what would happen were a "set piece" to fill the theatre of the Indian borderland.

It was no "child's work," as dear friends in Germany suggested, to which the troops were about to turn their hands. Deep snows capped the mountain crests; dense jungles blocked the way; there was in the matutinal and nocturnal hours the nip which bespoke the rigours of the coming marches, and the need for hardy constitutions. Where there was no waste of upland snows the frowning faces of the distant mountains were seared with yellow where giant landslides had torn their monstrous way from icy pinnacle to jungle-covered base. Arctic snows; flooded jungles and raging torrents; avalanches of God; booby traps and poisoned arrows of Man! These things seem to set out a fairly arresting list of the unconsidered, yet perpetual, difficulties which attended the daily progress of the troops!

Before the first division of the headquarters command could leave Kobo camp various small duties remained to be done. In the first case a ration convoy, with two companies of the 2nd Gurkhas as escort, had to be sent out to Colonel Fisher at Ledum, and a boat convoy of forty-six dug-outs, under the command of Lieutenant Hay Webb, to be dispatched to Pasighat. Known to many as "Captain Kettle," and to others as "The Pirate," out of compliment to his astuteness in rounding up boats and boats' crews, Lieutenant Webb, in taking over direction of the water convoys, had a task which left him in that state of glorious suspension which describes Mahomet's coffin. Rapids, whirlpools, rocks and sand-banks so disfigured the course of the river between Kobo and Pasighat that it was never possible to say when any particular dug-out would arrive ; or—even if it would arrive at all. No one knew this better than Lieutenant Webb, who, though he abandoned calculations to the winds of high heaven, kept on smiling.

As it happened very few accidents attended the start, voyage or arrival of the river columns, though the long list of coincidences—which began by the way with Abor prayers for exceptional floods—associated with the Field Force, received an ill-timed addition in connection with the departure of the first convoy through the death of its principal boatman during the initial voyage from Kobo to Pasighat.

Of more interest to the men of the Main Column than the minor activities of ration and boat convoys was the departure, on October 21st, of Major Wilson and a couple of companies of the 8th Gurkhas to prepare the site on the bank of the Kemi River which had been chosen as the first halting-place out of Kobo on the road to Pasighat for the main force. Accompanying Major Wilson were the two war dogs that had been presented to the expedition by the wife of one of the officers of the 8th Gurkhas, and were found on one or two occasions to be very useful.

A pleasant camp was laid out by the gallant Major's merry men; and, when the first division arrived at a little after ten o'clock on the following morning, its details found that there was little for them to do beyond putting up some shelters for their own convenience. The march from the base to the Kemi River was exactly six miles and a half. The morning was cool; the road level; the going delightful. In one section it ran through the wide belt of grasslands that has been mentioned in a previous chapter; in another it gave a charming vista of jungle and snow-capped mountains. Above all, again, was the hum of the serried column and the roar of rushing waters.

During the march a partial eclipse of the sun occurred. It was hailed by natives, soldiers and coolies alike as a good omen. As it coincided with the chief day of the Hindu festival held in honour of the Lakshmi, the goddess of luck, and as her satellite the moon was seen by day in conjunction with the sun, a double stroke of fortune was prophesied to the expedition by soothsayers. As Dame Fortune, however, is notoriously a fickle jade, and the success of the "show" depended upon the perfection of its organisation, no opportunity of improving the working arrangements was to be lost.

When camp was reached the Sappers and Miners engaged on some river-crossing experiments with rafts made of waterproof bags filled with straw. The device was the invention of Captain Wheatley, of the 6th Cavalry, Indian Army, and was unusually novel and interesting. In indication of the weight-supporting character of bags filled on the Wheatley system, it was shown that six bags lashed together and bound with bamboo would support the weight of six men. If the bags were in couples, six pairs lashed together would bear the weight of a light field-piece.

Another interesting feature of the first camp out of Kobo was that long before the troops had turned in for the night a telephone office was opened by the men of the signal unit from which telephonic communication with Kobo and Dibrugarh could be secured. This little feat was but one of many triumphs earned by Lieutenant Knight and his signallers, whose work with field telephones was of special interest since the Abor operations were the first in India in which field telephones had been put to serious use, supplanting field telegraphs and flags.

Simultaneously with the departure, on the morning of October 23rd, of the first division of the Main Column from "Six Miles Camp" for Pilong Camp, the second division of the headquarters command left Kobo for Six Miles Camp. The little force arrived without incident under the command of Lieutenant-Colonel Peterson, D.S.O., 32nd Pioneers. Everything had been left quite snug and shipshape at Six Miles Camp by the men of the first division, General Bower's plan of dividing the headquarters command into two parties, the first of which should proceed one day ahead of the second, the formation to be continued as far as Pasighat, appearing to promise an easy passage for Colonel Peterson's column.

In all the second division numbered with the coolies and hospital followers about two thousand men. It was composed of four companies of the 8th Gurkhas, two companies of the 32nd Pioneers, half a company of Sappers and Miners and Signallers, the detachment of the Assam Valley Light Horse with a maxim, and one coolie corps. Two additional companies of the 32nd Pioneers were to join the second column a little later. While the presence of two more companies of Pioneers strengthened the working parties, the actual value of the fighting force, the bulk of which was supplied by the 8th Gurkhas—the 32nd Pioneers and the Sappers and Miners furnishing construction parties, and the Military Police the details for garrisoning route posts—remained a little weak. With the junction between the two halves of the Main Column once effected, the striking capacity of the headquarters force would be improved, though not by very much if the character of the future operations were to call for any large number of field columns. Under a united condition the total strength of the Main Column was returned as:—

Headquarters; Maxim detachment, Assam Valley Light Horse; 10 companies, one seven-pounder, 8th Gurkhas; 2 corps of coolies; 6 companies 32nd Pioneers; 1 company Sappers and Miners; 2 grenade guns; 1 section Field Hospital.

With the departure of the second division from Kobo the base camp dropped out of the active sphere of General Bower's operations. Concerned only with the forwarding of the supply convoys, whose requirements were very admirably looked after by Major Brooke, its change from the bustle of its early days to the torpidity of its middle period was a sore point with those whose duties tied them to the wrong end of the line of communications. Nevertheless, much was done to improve Kobo, and the two companies of the 2nd Gurkhas and the two companies of the 32nd Pioneers, who were left behind as garrison, were never weary of artistic effort!

The road to Pilong lay through the heart of the jungle, and the route gave the column its first real taste of the difficulties attending bush-marching. There was no gainsaying the fact that the difficulties were real—"a damned sight too real," some one said—for eighty per cent. of the insects seemed to sting and the remaining twenty per cent. to stink. When squashed on the face, arms or neck, they passed out of existence with insistent effect ! While insects were everywhere, not a sight or smell of Master Abor was obtained in these first marches. His aloofness, perhaps, was not without its advantages to the column for the track was a veritable road of suffering, and, though the Sappers and Miners bridged streams with astonishing rapidity, and the Pioneers tunnelled their way through the bush, progress remained slow, daily proving more difficult and damnable than dangerous.

Pilong Camp was situated on the right bank of the Mora Lalli, about seven miles beyond Six Miles Camp. As the march was short, the troops again were able to enjoy an early rest, though there was no repose for the men of the Sappers and Miners, or for those of the 32nd Pioneers, for both were turned on to the task of bridging the Mora Lalli as soon as they had finished with the jungle ! Hours of ease, however, were to be but sweet recollections, for with the advance on October 24th the jungle grew worse, numerous small streams and a naturally heavy "going" made heavier by drenching rains operating against the troops. As an example in point it required, on October 24th, nine hours' hard marching to cover the nine miles between Pilong and Lokhpur where the column passed the night. No one, of course, minded the bad "going"; what was better no one fell out, officers and men keeping fit and remaining cheery, and as keen as school-boys.

Unfortunately the bloodless character of the march of the headquarters column was broken at Lokhpur by two casualties: Conductor Williams of the Ordnance Department being badly contused by the fall of a tree, and a sepoy of the 32nd Pioneers being wounded in the hand by the contents of a comrade's rifle that was accidentally discharged. Considering that the march had passed through country that was unknown and covered with virgin jungle as heavy as it is possible to conceive, the immunity from accidents of all descriptions that the column enjoyed paid a high compliment to the skill with which the movements of the force were planned.

Jungle-marching always imposes an exacting strain on troops and calls for the highest qualities of generalship. In Aborland, particularly, the jungle was a perpetual difficulty, for not only was it quite beyond the recorded experience of other operations, but it offered no comparison with the conditions that are usually met with in India and Africa. As the rainfall of Aborland, with the exception of the Arracan coast, is the heaviest in India arboreal growth in the jungles assumes most massive proportions, the girth of one tree which Mr. I. H. Burkhill, F.L.S., the botanist to the expedition, measured being no less than forty-two feet, though only one hundred and thirty feet in height. Leaves, too, attain a huge size, and specimens were secured with surfaces ranging from 140 square centimetres to 609 square centimetres. Such dimensions defy the ordinary methods of man, though they succumb before the deadly insidiousness of creepers that poison where they do not smother. Little wonder, therefore, that the Abors regard their haunts as inviolable, for dark, mysterious and rising like some evil enchantment before the traveller, the forest presents an impregnable rampart of trees and undergrowth, impassably entangled.

So far as the efforts of the expedition were concerned, the jungle, unmoved by frontal attack and impervious to flank attack, was conquered only after long and sustained sapping of its foundations with dhaos, picks and shovels and, on occasion, dynamite! Under such circumstances it is not surprising that the headquarters column only moved at a snail's pace. Here and there, as if the protecting spirits had been over-confident, or blessed with a merciful hand, there were patches where the growth was less dense or altogether absent, and movement was freer. Such places were few and very, very far between; though, by rare good fortune, such a patch did mark the last stage of the march to Pasighat.

From Lokhpur the march to Pasighat on October 25th was only six and a half miles, which, as the "going" was good, were soon accomplished. Camp was pitched on high ground amid beautiful surroundings. Every one was housed in huts, with walls and roofs of giant plantain and magnolia leaves. The soil was sandy, and a fresh wind from the snowy uplands of Asia blew through the gorges of the Dihang, the spectacle of which, after the gloom of the forest, was greeted with delight. The view, indeed, was splendid and offered ample compensation for the many trials of the march. At once inspiriting and awe-inspiring, the river held the attention and wrapped the mind within the mantle of its mystery.

Whatever the secret in the character of the upper reaches of the Dihang, whatever the river's twists and turns or influence over the singular peoples who know and yet withhold the riddle of its course, there was no doubt at all of its power of fascination. Flowing with torrential strength, it swept down a course five hundred yards in width with the glissading swiftness of a mill-stream. Where rocks broke the smoothness of its surface, a swirl of water fell in foaming cataracts, while lofty-browed gorges intensified the clamour of the stream until the place hummed with the thunder of a hundred avalanches. Below the rocks the swiftly-flowing cascade of tumbling waters formed a giant maelstrom, which would have dashed a boat to pieces as easily and quickly as it battered the decaying trunks of the fallen trees that gyrated helplessly in its heart.

CHAPTER XI

The Start of the Political Missions—Mr. Kerwood's Mission to the Miris—Mr. W. C. M. Dundas's Mission to the Mishmis.

WHILE the field columns of the Expeditionary Force were hewing their way through the jungle to Pasighat, Mr. Kerwood and Mr. W. C. M. Dundas, the Political officers of the Missions which were to visit the Miris and the Mishmis, were hurrying forward the completion of the hundred-and-one little details that were hindering their departure. Differing in all essential particulars from the Mishmi Mission, which was invested with an importance to which the situation in the Lohit Valley was expected to give a grave turn, the Miri Mission was intended to occupy itself with a survey of the Kamla-Subansiri region, and was, therefore, scientific rather than political in its composition. For this purpose a survey party of seventeen members had been detailed to accompany Mr. Kerwood, whose progress was expected to be peaceful, and whose strength indeed was calculated with the idea of providing sufficient numbers to repel an attack but not to allow of an advance against opposition, or the protection of a long line of communications, should the Miris prove

GURKHA SEPOYS OF THE MILITARY POLICE CROSSING BY AN IMPROVISED BRIDGE.

CAPTAIN GRAHAM.
The Military Chief of the Miri Mission.

hostile. In addition to Mr. Kerwood, the composition of the Mission was :—

Commanding: Captain A. M. Graham, 5th Gurkha Rifles, with seventy-five men, whose numbers were afterwards increased to one hundred and fifty, of the Lakhimpur Military Police Battalion ; Mr. Kerwood as Political Officer ; Captain Nevill of the Assam Police as Supply and Transport Officer ; Lieutenant Lewis, R.E., commanding the Survey party ; Lieutenant Wahab, Indian Army, with Survey Party and Captain Beauchamp Duff, 1st Gurkha Rifles as Military Intelligence Officer.

It had been arranged that the Miri Mission should take the field before the Mishmi Mission. From the beginning of October, Mr. Kerwood and Captain Graham had been collecting stores at Dibrugarh and consigning them to Lakhimpur, from where the start was to take place at the end of the month. As October drew to its close, an end came to the work which had so closely engaged Mr. Kerwood and Captain Graham. On October 28th, three days after the arrival of Major-General Bower and the Main Column at Pasighat, the first stores began to move out from Lakhimpur to Seajuli, a tea-garden in the district and one march distant from Lakhimpur, being followed on November 8th by Captain Graham, Mr. Kerwood and an escort of fifty rifles and a transport train of three hundred coolies. It was proposed at first that the party should move direct from Seajuli to Chimir, which is situated just below the junction of the Po and Kamla Rivers, where the advanced base was to be established, and that Captain Duff, Lieutenant Lewis and Lieutenant Wahab together with the Survey party and a small escort should follow after. When the two parties had effected a meeting at Chimir all the coolies were to go back to Captain Nevill at Seajuli and bring up under that officer's direction to the advanced base whatever stores were required for the needs of the force during its stay among the Miris.

Unfortunately difficulties were numerous. Chimir was not to be reached for many weeks and the plans that had been made so confidently had to be re-cast. From the outset the rain-clouds had hung low over the waters of the Subansiri and when, in the grey dawn of November 10th, Captain Graham and Mr. Kerwood together with their little party paraded in marching order, there was an element of ill-omen in the scene. Two days later, however, Captain Duff, Lieutenant Lewis, Lieutenant Wahab and the Survey party also moved out. By this time the difficulties which confronted the advance party had shown that a direct march upon Chimir was impracticable and, accordingly, fresh arrangements were made. While the Chimir road was abandoned Captain Graham struck north to Gochum on the Kamla River, Mr.

Kerwood marched through Beni to the junction of the Siplu and Subansiri Rivers, and Captain Duff returned to Seajuli, from whence all men and stores were removed to Dulungmukh on the Subansiri, thus establishing a new line of communications—Dulungmukh, Siplumukh, Beni, Gochum, Chimir—which remained in use until the whole system was rolled up.

The work of the Mission was divisible into four parts, the primary objectives of the field parties being the unmapped water-shed and sources of the Subansiri and Kamla Rivers. At the same time, as the surveys which the Miri Mission had to make embraced an extensive area, and the visit was limited to two months, afterwards increased to five months, the days to be employed in any direction were very limited. After careful consideration, it was planned that fifteen days should be spent on the Subansiri water-shed, on conclusion of which, after returning to Chimir to replenish, a shift should be made early in November to the neighbouring course of the Kamla River, a tributary of the Subansiri, with which it runs almost parallel for the greater part of its length.

On completion of the Kamla survey and the re-assembling of all units at Chimir, the third part of the Mission's work was to be found away to the west on the Apa Tanang Plateau, where more fresh ground was to be broken. Under this arrangement the posts on the line of communications from Chimir to the plains were to be closed up, while the main body of the Mission marched as one party from Chimir to Hong on the Ranga River and passed ten days in surveying the Apa Tanang Valley before taking up the fourth and final phase of its task by returning to Lakhimpur down the Ranga River.

Unlike the Miri Mission, Mr. Dundas's Mission to the Mishmis was concerned almost wholly with the political issues, set afoot by the activity of Chinese on the Mishmi marches. Before dealing with the work of the Mishmi Mission, however, it is necessary to make clear the character of our position in regard to the Mishmi people. Unlike our association with the Abor tribesmen, the course of our relations with the Mishmis has been consistently progressive. At the time when we assumed the protection of Assam, the Mishmis were subordinate to the Kamptis as also to the Singphos, and paid tribute at Sadiya to the Khawa Gohains. The authority of the Kamptis over the Mishmis was not altogether unquestioned, and, wherever the lands of the one people approached those of the other, there was constant strife. Similarly, there was incessant inter-tribal fighting between the Chulikattas, the Bebejiyas, the Digarus and the Mejus, the four great divisions into which the Mishmis fall.

These conditions confronted Captain Bedford

MISHMI CHIEFTAINS FROM THE LOHIT VALLEY WHO ACCOMPANIED MR. DUNDAS.

MR. W. C. M. DUNDAS, WHO HAD CHARGE OF THE MISHMI MISSION.

A YOUNG MISHMI WOMAN.

AN OLD MISHMI WOMAN.

when, after visiting Aborland in 1826, he proceeded along the southern bank of the Brahmaputra to Diling in the country of the Digarus with the intention of crossing from the areas of the Digarus into those of the Chulikattas. Not only were the Digarus and Chulikattas engaged in a feud, but war was raging between the Kamptis of the Sadiya district and the Chulikattas. Under such circumstances, it is not surprising that travelling in the Lohit Valley should have been considered unsafe; or that Captain Bedford should have been regarded with suspicion alike by the Kamptis as by the Chulikattas, who blocked his way. The Digarus, responsive from the beginning to our advances, gave him a cordial reception, just as in the following year, they also extended a hearty welcome to Captain Wilcox, though Rajah Jingsha, the supreme chief of the Mejus, who was embroiled with the Digarus, turned him back when he had reached within a few miles of the embouchure of the Lu Ti.

In the next five years so much inter-tribal fighting occurred among the Mishmis, that their lands remained unvisited by Europeans. In 1836 the Mejus, being defeated by the Digarus, allied themselves with the Tibetans of the Zayul Valley, at the north-eastern extremity of the Lohit River, who provided a contingent of seventy matchlock men and contrived to turn the tables on the Digarus with crushing effect. Regarding themselves as the watch dogs of Tibet, the Mejus now sought the favour of their new allies by preventing travellers from entering the Meju territories. Accordingly they turned back Dr. Griffith, who had journeyed along the southern bank of the Brahmaputra to the Meju border. While this traveller failed in his efforts, the prolonged bout of inter-tribal fighting which occupied at intervals the next nine years prevented any other explorers from copying his example.

As is usual with tribal warfare, success in the various fights seems to have favoured each contestant by turn; for, although in 1839 certain of the Mishmi tribes joined the Kamptis in an attack on Sadiya and, on being repulsed, murdered the Kampti chief who had conducted the operations, by 1842 the Kamptis had taken such effective reprisals against the Mishmis that for some time to come the Mishmis were regarded as being subject to them. From this date, for several seasons peace reigned up and down the marches. When it had remained unbroken for nearly two years, Lieutenant E. A. Rowlatt set forth in the winter of 1844–45 on a journey of exploration along the northern bank of the Brahmaputra. Reaching without difficulty the Du River in the country of the Digarus, he ascended this stream as far as Tuppang, but retraced his steps when within sixty miles of the Tibetan border on being informed by the Digarus that the intervening country was destitute of supplies. Six years later, however, Père Krick, a French missionary, following the same route, succeeded in reaching Rima, the largest village of the Zayul Valley and the seat of the Tibetan Governor of the region, and in returning safely to Sadiya.

In 1854 the Mishmi peoples being still at peace, Père Krick, accompanied by Père Boury, again attempted the Rima journey. Passing safely through the country of the Digarus, the two missionaries were pursued by a band of Mejus under a chief called Kaisha and murdered at Same, a Tibetan village only six miles from Rima. For this offence Kaisha's village was attacked in February 1855, when a force of twenty sepoys of the 1st Assam Light Infantry under Lieutenant Eden, assisted by forty Kamptis and some Mejus, captured the chief and took him prisoner to Dibrugarh, where he was subsequently hanged.

For many years from this date, the Kaisha affair became one of the burning questions of the border; for, in his operations against Kaisha's village, Lieutenant Eden had been assisted by the supporters of a Meju chieftain by the name of Lumling. This circumstance not unnaturally roused the ire of Kaisha's people, and when the news of Kaisha's execution was received by his son, that youth enlisted the help of the Chulikattas and immediately attacked the renegade village. Lumling, who had received both money and gifts for his services, appealed for aid to the British authorities at Sadiya, but was refused, with the result that he and his people were massacred. A little later, Chulikattas contrived the seizure of three of Lieutenant Eden's servants, while in 1856 and 1857 the same tribesmen carried out some successful raids on the Kampti villages near Sadiya. During the next few years, in part by way of avenging themselves on the Kamptis for their share in the Kaisha expedition, one or other of the Mishmi tribes constantly harried the Kamptis in the region about the Kundil and Deopani Rivers. So serious did the resulting situation become that in 1866, the British authorities, as the only means in their power, issued firearms to the Sadiya Kamptis, when the raids at once ceased. Two years later, moreover, peace had been so far restored that a large party of Chulikattas, as a special concession, was allowed to settle in the Kundil Valley.

Unfortunately for the general condition of the border, the act of grace shown to the Chulikattas had little immediate effect, for Mr. J. T. Cooper was turned back by the Meju chiefs at Prun, a few miles west of the point reached by Wilcox in 1827, when he attempted in the winter of 1869–70 to travel along the southern bank of the Brahmaputra to Tibet. Mr. Cooper's visit was not entirely fruitless, however, as it was due to the courageous and tactful resource of this gallant traveller that the seeds of the present cordial understanding with the Mejus were sown. Mr. Cooper at once agreed to return to Sadiya, when ordered to do so by the Mejus, but before leaving asked to be permitted to talk over the reasons of the hostility of the chiefs. As so often happens when dealing with native tribes, discussion soon showed that the grievances of the Mejus needed only explanation to be settled. After long and anxious deliberation all the points were adjusted, the immediate outcome of the talk with Mr. Cooper being that the Mejus agreed to pay a visit of ceremony to the Sadiya Durbar.

The tact of Mr. Cooper at his meeting with the Meju chiefs, assisted by the good-will of the Chulikattas, was sufficient to keep the peace for the next few years, and matters progressed favourably up and down the border. In 1878 a survey party under Captain Woodthorpe broke entirely fresh country by visiting Kaladoi, one of the leading chiefs of the Chulikattas who lived on the water-shed of the Dibong and Deopani Rivers. Unfortunately, within a few months of this visit, the Bebejiyas, who were near neighbours of Kaladoi, raided some Assamese and Kampti villages on the Assam plains, as well as carried off some prisoners from a village only twenty miles from Sadiya. As a precaution against any recrudescence of this pleasantry, Major Beresford, in

February 1879, with a detachment of the 43rd Assam Light Infantry marched up the Diphu River, and established frontier stockades at Bishemnagar and Nizamghat, returning to Sadiya by the valley of the Deopani. While the peace of the frontier marches was being attended to in this direction, Chowsa, the chief of the Kamptis, was persuaded by the British authorities to pay a friendly visit to the Digaru and Meju tribesmen along the Lohit Valley. Chowsa, with an eye to the possibilities of the occasion, was quite willing to fall in with the suggestion, and following the footsteps of Lieut. E. A. Rowlatt he travelled as far as the Zayul Valley, where his further progress was stopped by the Tibetans. Received by the Digarus and by the Mejus with cordiality, the old chief brought back to Sadiya so many expressions of good-will from the tribes he had visited that the success of his Mission was never doubted.

Although the task of establishing friendly relations with the various tribes on the north-eastern section of the frontier of India had progressed but slowly in the century that had passed, the results of Chowsa's visit plainly showed that the policy of forbearance and non-interference with the frontier peoples, which had been rigidly observed, was reaping its reward. By the concessions of land to the Chulikatta in the Kundil Valley in 1868 and the cordial reception extended to the Meju chiefs in

1870, important steps towards overcoming the habitual reserve and almost ineradicable suspicion of these tribes, had been taken. In the ten years that had slipped away since those events were enacted, new forces had sprung up along the Lohit Valley, the nature of which was indicated by the reception which had been extended to Chowsa, as an Envoy Extraordinary. At the moment the one tribe whose distrust was adamantine, were the Bebejiyas. With a view to removing their ill-feeling, and at the same time fostering the understanding growing up between the other tribes and ourselves, it was arranged in 1880 that the principal chiefs of the frontier should be received in a Durbar at Sadiya, during the Annual Fair. From this Durbar much was anticipated ; but, all expectations were surpassed, when, led by Kaladoi, first one and then another of the chiefs of Chulikattas, who long since had displaced the Digarus from their predominant position in the Councils of the Mishmis, professed allegiance to the British *raj*.

Save for minor disturbances in 1884 and 1885 by the Bebejiyas, who showed no inclination to adapt themselves to the changed conditions of the border, the peace of the north-eastern frontier was now established on fairly firm foundations, and there remained only the precise direction of the Tibeto-Mishmi boundary to be determined before those areas of the border could be considered as inalienably belonging to the Indian Empire. Early in the winter of 1885–86, therefore, Mr. J. F. Needham, as Assistant Political Officer at Sadiya, accompanied by Captain Molesworth, commanding the Lakhimpur Military Police, and a small party which included Chowsa, the Kampti chief, left Sadiya and moved along the northern bank of the Brahmaputra, ultimately arriving within a mile or so of Rima, when they were compelled to return by the marked hostility of the Tibetans. In so far as it went Mr. Needham's journey was a triumphant success; for, not only did he receive every assistance from the Mejus, but it established with approximate accuracy the Tibeto-Mishmi boundary as falling near Menilkrai, and solved the geographical problems concerning the identity of the Sanpo, the Dihang and the Irrawaddy. From now onward, as was previously believed by many, the Sanpo was known to have nothing whatever in common with the Irrawaddy.

Upon returning to Sadiya in January 1886, from his easterly trip, Mr. Needham found that the tribes had preserved unbroken the peace of the border. Accordingly, as a mark of the good-will of the Government of India, Mr. Needham was permitted to invite the principal chiefs of the Mishmis to visit the Exhibition which was to be held later in the same year at Calcutta. When the time came, Kaladoi and Lakho of the Chulikattas, Chowsa of the Kamptis, Nassi of the Bebejiyas, with their sons, attended at Sadiya, and were duly introduced to the capital of India by their protective sponsor. In spite of all that was then done, and continued to be done to win over the Bebejiyas as the years passed, this people continued to maintain an attitude of defiance and detestation of our wishes and of ourselves.

From attacking their neighbours, which had been a recurring pastime since 1884, they turned their attention in 1893 to the sepoys of the Military Police, and on November 27th cut to pieces a patrol near Bamjur on the Dibong River, carrying off the men's rifles, which were subsequently recovered through the kindly intervention of the Chulikattas. For this offence a blockade was instituted against the tribesmen but withdrawn five years later, in 1898, as it was found that the Chulikattas rather than the actual culprits, the Bebejiyas, were suffering by it. Within a few months the Bebejiyas were again offending, for, as an act of reprisal for the murder of a relative by Kamptis many years before, a party of Bebejiyas from the village of Abrangon visited, on May 4th, 1899, the Kampti village of Mitaigaon and butchered two men and two women, besides carrying off a number of guns and a few prisoners.

After this signal illustration of the tribal temper the Government of India decided to send an expedition against the recalcitrant tribesmen. The column, which was under the command of Lieutenant-Colonel Molesworth and was accompanied by Mr. Needham as Political Officer, mobilised on the 23rd of the November following. It was composed as follows :—

1 Company Bengal Sappers and Miners.
2 Companies 10th Bengal Infantry.
3 Companies 42nd Gurkha Rifles.
1 Company 43rd Gurkha Rifles.
2 Companies 44th Gurkha Rifles.
200 Rifles Military Police.
Signallers from 3rd and 10th Bengal Infantry, 42nd, 43rd, and 44th Gurkha Rifles.
Survey Party.
No. 48 Native Field Hospital, Nos. C and D Sections; No. 56 Native Field Hospital.
2 Mountain Guns from Shillong.

The officer commanding and his staff were as follows :—

Officer Commanding : Lieutenant-Colonel Molesworth, 44th Gurkha Rifles.

Staff Officer: Major Anderson, 3rd Bengal Infantry.

Field Intelligence Officer : Lieutenant Ward, 44th Gurkha Rifles.

S.M.O. : Major Daly, I.M.S.

Commissariat-Transport Officer : Captain Rynd, D.A.C.G., Lucknow.

Signalling Officer : Captain Robson, 10th Bengal Infantry.

Officer in charge of coolie corps: Captain Stanton, 3rd Bengal Infantry.

Officer in charge of guns: Lieutenant Thatcher, No. 9 Native Mountain Battery.

Survey Officer: Captain Robertson, R.E.

Political Officer: Mr. J. F. Needham, C.I.E.

In addition to recovering the captives and punishing the Bebejiyas for the outrage at Mitaigaon, as also for their previous offences, it was intended to make a survey of the country and to establish whatever posts might be necessary to secure the peace of the border. The operations lasted for three months and were eminently successful, though conducted in the face of numerous obstacles arising from the nature of the country and from the character of the weather. In spite of these mishaps, however, all the objects of the operations were secured, for the guilty village was destroyed, one of the murderers hanged and over eight hundred miles of new country were surveyed. Returning to Sadiya on February 8th, the demobilising of the force was commenced at once, and was completely concluded by February 15th.

From these operations in 1900 to the present day, some twelve years later, there have been no great troubles on the Mishmi border. The late Mr. Williamson followed in the footsteps of Mr. Needham, and now Mr. W. C. M. Dundas has succeeded Mr. Williamson, and the peace of the border continues. Moreover, although no treaties bind the Mishmis to us and no allowances are paid to secure their good behaviour, peace is assured because the good relations between the tribes and ourselves are based on mutual respect. The tribes both trust and honour the men whom we send to them as the representatives of the great Sirkar, and are content to accept their word that no ill shall befall them.

Before passing to an examination of the problems that awaited Mr. Dundas's arrival in the Lohit Valley it is necessary to co-ordinate the results of observations by previous travellers in the region. They have not been numerous. From the day when Captain Bedford tried his luck in 1826 down to the effort of the late Mr. Williamson in our own time, the list is far short of a dozen, as will have been seen by any one who has run through the previous paragraphs on our relations with the Mishmis. The existence of a route into Tibet by the upper waters of the Brahmaputra has been known to the Government of India, of course, ever since the occupation of Assam. It has been as a closed book to travellers, however, for reasons that are in part due to the prohibition issued by the Government of India, and in part to the action of the Tibetans and the tribesmen themselves.

Enough is now known, nevertheless, to enable a

NAGA HEADMEN WHO SERVED WITH THE MISHMI MISSION.
Middle row.—Lotha Nagas. Bottom row.—Angami Nagas.

THE HEADMAN OF KROLING.

THE HEADMAN'S WIFE.

general description of the route to be given, for most of those who essayed the journey left a few notes behind them, while each of them pushed the limit of penetration further and further eastwards until Rima itself was reached.

The distance from Sadiya to Rima by the northern bank of the Brahmaputra is about 187 miles, and the best idea of the journey is to be obtained by dividing the route into five sections, according to the natural characteristics of the country traversed. The northern bank was that favoured by Lieutenant Rowlatt in 1844–45 and Mr. Needham in 1885–86. The first section, one of 46 miles, extends from Sadiya to Temeimukh, and lies entirely through the plains. The first stage, Chunpura, so called from the lime (*chun*) which is collected here from boulders rolled down by the stream of the Lohit, which is the name of the Brahmaputra above Sadiya, 18 miles from Sadiya, is the easternmost outpost held by the frontier police upon the Inner line, and is connected with Sadiya by a patrol-path cut through the jungle. In the next four marches, the Digaru, Dora, and Temei Rivers, affluents of the Brahmaputra from the northern hills, are successively crossed. Here the route passes partly among the boulders in the bed of the Brahmaputra, and partly through the dense jungle of the bank; and, while a good cold weather track the whole way to Temeimukh could probably be cleared without much difficulty, Temeimukh is the last stage of travelling in the plain country, and the farthest point which can be reached by elephants. Similarly, boats can ascend the Lohit as far as the mouth of the Dora, but the current beyond that point is too strong for navigation in ordinary circumstances.

The next section is one of 24 miles, from Temeimukh to a Digaru village—Chose's—beyond the River Tedeng. This contains the only piece of high mountain marching on the whole route. The country traversed is a lofty spur which runs down to the Brahmaputra from the great mass of the northern mountains, and forms the water-shed between the Dora and Temei on the west and the Tedeng on the east. The first march from Temeimukh ascends the hills by the gorge of an affluent of that river, and leads to a camping place at an elevation of 3200 feet. The next march ascends 1300 feet in the first four miles, crosses the ridge at 4500 feet, and descends again to a Digaru village—Hai-imsong's—at a height of 1800 feet, overlooking the Tedeng Valley. The third march descends to and crosses the Tedeng at an elevation of 600 feet, and then ascends 1000 feet to the first-mentioned Digaru village. This section of the route, therefore, includes the greatest ascents and descents met with in the whole journey, and attains the highest elevation, *viz.* 4500 feet, at the point where the ridge is crossed. This track was precisely that which was followed by Lieut. Rowlatt in 1844–45, and by Mr. Needham in 1885–86, and Hai-imsong's village appears to have been in the same situation on each occasion. Lieut. Rowlatt calls the place Salumgum, a name which Mr. Needham mentions as the local title of its site. The name of the gam or headman in 1844–45 was Abasong. The Tedeng is a considerable river, and its valley is occupied by Digaru villages to the distance of several days' journey above Hai-imsong's. After leaving the Tedeng, the route continues in the immediate vicinity of the Brahmaputra, until it ascends to Chose's village. This village, or one near it, seems to have been one of Lieut. Rowlatt's stages also, the name of the chief then being Heasong. He is probably the Keasong who was one of Lieut. Eden's allies. In 1836 Dr. Griffith found a chief called Premsong living near the site.

The third section of the route comprises the country traversed between Chose's village and the Dalei. This river is the largest affluent which the Brahmaputra receives on its right bank eastwards of the Digaru. This part of the route presents much difficult marching, with sharp ascents and declivities. There is a descent of 900 feet to the Paini (which was visited by Griffith on a botanising excursion during his journey in 1836), and a corresponding ascent of 800 feet on the other side ; the path then descends gradually to the bed of the Brahmaputra, crossing the Talua stream, and follows the bank of the river to the mouth of a larger stream called Um, which joins the Brahmaputra at an elevation of 950 feet. From this point there is a steep ascent of 650 feet to a village at a height of 1600 feet. On leaving this village the path taken by Mr. Needham and Captain Molesworth passed along the face of a precipice rising immediately from the bed of the Brahmaputra, though the servants and Khamtis of the party followed a cattle-path higher up. The next step is a descent of 700 feet, succeeded by an ascent to a village at an altitude of 1300 feet. The path then improves until the last part of the descent to the Dalei, which is difficult by reason of its steepness.

Lieutenant Rowlatt seems to have made a single march of this section of the route, from Chose's village, or its vicinity, to Lumling's village near the Dalei. He mentions the crossing of the Talua River, as well as the dangerous piece of road along the face of the precipice, "from which," he says, "had any one fallen, he would have been precipitated some thousand feet into the boiling stream, the noise of whose waters was just audible from the height we were passing."

"The Dalei River," says Lieutenant Rowlatt, in another passage, "is a stream of considerable size, having its rise in the snowy range bordering the Lama-Tibet-country, along whose banks a path to that country exists." The Mishmi chief Premsong offered to take Dr. Griffith into Tibet by this route in November 1836. These facts corresponded with the information gathered by Mr. Needham. He was told that the Dalei had its source in "the snowy mountains bordering on Tibet," that Mishmi villages were numerous in its valley, and that the most northerly of them was situated within a short distance of the Tibetan border.

The fourth section of the route comprises the country traversed between the Dalei and the frontier of Zayul. The first three marches include some considerable ascents and descents, which are generally steep and difficult. The path first ascends 200 feet from the Dalei, and then descends 300 feet to the Du, rising as high again on the opposite side ; farther on, it descends abruptly to the Brahmaputra, rises 200 feet again, passes a hill-stream called the Tini, and ultimately comes down to a halting-place upon a sand-bank in the bed of the Brahmaputra. The next march crosses the Oi River at an elevation of 1250 feet, and continues along a winding and uneven path, sometimes descending into the bed of the Brahmaputra, and rising at one point to 1700 feet. In the third stage the changes of elevation are considerably greater. After passing along the face of a dangerous precipice, the path descends gradually 700 feet, and rises again 900 feet; then descends 900 feet to the Halai River, which is crossed at an elevation of 1300 feet; the path then climbs 800 feet up a spur, crosses the Nam Ti, and reaches a camping-place at the height of 1800 feet.

In the next two marches the average elevation gradually rises; the Sa rivulet is crossed at 1850 feet, and subsequently the Chua, and the altitude of the bed of the Brahmaputra is now 1700 feet. The sixth stage crosses the hill-stream Ma Ti, passes the embouchure of the Lu Ti on the left bank of the Brahmaputra, and subsequently that of the Ghalum or Kalang Ti, crosses the hill-stream Chura, and ends at an elevation of 2200 feet. The seventh stage crosses the hill-streams Kam Ti and Chung Ti, and ends in Krongdong's village, at 2600 feet. The eighth stage, from Krongdong's to a camping-place in the jungle adjoining the Tibetan border, attains an elevation of 2800 feet at one point, and includes a dangerous piece of road across the face of a precipitous spur. The hill-stream Sa Ti is crossed in this stage, and the road is generally uneven and difficult, occasionally descending among the boulders of the Brahmaputra from elevations of 1800, 2000, and latterly 2500 feet.

In general, throughout this section of the route, the path traverses steep stony undulations, or passes under over-arching jungle, where progress must be made in a stooping posture. Mr. Needham reiterates Dr. Griffith's complaint that "it is one of the characteristics of Mishmis that they would sooner risk their necks than take the trouble of cutting down the jungle." Another feature of this section of the route is the alternation of these difficult places with level terraces which are under cultivation, or bear traces of having been cultivated. Between the Dalei and the Lu Ti, the valley of the Brahmaputra up to 1886 was apparently pretty thickly settled. Wilcox in 1827 found well-built villages, with abundance of cattle, covering the open and undulating country upon the southern side of the Brahmaputra, above the embouchure of the Halai. Cooper in 1870 mentions the fact that the lower hills on the southern side are "dotted with Mishmi dwellings, surrounded by patches of cultivated land," and Mr. Needham's diary bears witness to the frequency of cultivation on both sides of the river along this part of the route.

The valley of the Brahmaputra is here half a mile wide, and the breadth of the stream does not exceed 20 yards in the narrowest places; it is impetuous and full of rapids, and flood-marks show 20 feet above the cold-weather level. It is crossed by numerous cane bridges. Another feature of this section of the route is the change in the character of the vegetation which is observed after crossing the Halai. Pines here begin to clothe the hill-sides, and oak forests also occur, while in places peach-trees were found. These changes in the scenery and vegetation of the valley were remarked upon by Wilcox, who says that beyond the Halai River was "a new succession of hills of a totally different character. These green grass-covered hills have many firs growing singly, even near the level of the water, and they are striped sometimes from the summit to the base with fir forest."

Going farther eastwards, the information which Wilcox has left on record about the Ghalum or Kalang Ti was confirmed by the particulars collected by Mr. Needham. The Kalang Ti takes its rise in the snowy mountains which give birth to the western sources of the Irrawaddy, and appears to be the most considerable affluent of the Brahmaputra on its southern side, eastward of the Tengapani. Its valley, where it joins the Brahmaputra, is nearly as wide as that of the great river itself, and is occupied by Meju villages, which carry on a trade with the Bor Khamti country. Beyond the Ghalum Ti, the route along the southern bank of the Brahmaputra comes to an end, and travellers bound for Tibet have to cross to the right or northern bank. This fact is alluded to by Wilcox, who mentions that if he had insisted on advancing, the hostile Meju chiefs were prepared to attack him upon the division of his party "at the crossing-place of the great river."

Wilcox's farthest point was a few miles short of the embouchure of the Lu Ti, and would correspond to a point about 57 miles short of Rima, and 130 miles from Sadiya along the right bank of the Brahmaputra. Cooper also turned back at about the same point. The village of the Prun clan, which Cooper mentions, was pointed out to Mr. Needham while he was still to the westward of the embouchure of the Lu Ti. The position of Prun—Cooper's farthest—is wrongly marked on all the maps, being shown a long way to the eastward of the Ghalum Ti, and much nearer to the frontier of Tibet than it really is. Cooper never crossed the Lu Ti or the Ghalum Ti, and indeed does not mention either of them, though Wilcox does. Lieut. Rowlatt's farthest point along the right bank of the Brahmaputra was a village which he calls Tuppang, situated on "the Dagoom range of mountains," which forms the eastern boundary of the valley of River Du. Lieut. Rowlatt was informed that the "Lama country" could be reached from Tuppang in three days, and in fact he met some Tibetans there, who "had come across the snowy range for the purpose of trading with the Mishmis." M. Krick's servant who was carried off by Kaisha, told Lieutenant Eden that the journey from Same in Zayul to Kaisha's village, by the head-waters of the Du, across the snow, occupied five days.

For the fifth and last section of the route to Rima it is necessary to follow the route taken by Mr. Needham, as the notes of this traveller are our only index to the region. The section consists of a march of twenty-six miles within Tibetan territory. There are no physical difficulties to encounter, the path being generally good, though steep and slippery in some places, and the altitude gradually rises from 2600 to 3600 feet. The first stage, after passing the Tibeto-Mishmi border-line on a piece of open grassy country called Menilkrai, crosses the hill-stream Yepuk, and passes the embouchure of a considerable stream called Ding Ti, which comes from the mountains of Bor Khamti, and falls into the Brahmaputra on its left bank. Two villages, and the deserted sites of others, are passed on this stage. One of these latter is the village Walong, in which M. Krick found shelter in 1851, before its inhabitants fled from Tibetan oppression. In 1886 there was, too, a large solitary stone near this spot, upon which could be seen, standing upright, two stone slabs, about two feet high, reputed to have been placed in such position by the two French Fathers Krick and Boury to commemorate their journey. The next stage crosses the hill-streams Krup Ti and Kuchu, and passes the villages of

Kande and Kanau, while the final stage, one of six miles, leads past the village of Same, where the two French priests were murdered by Kaisha in 1880, across the stream Sa-chu, and through the lands of the village Sang-gu, up to Rima.

CHAPTER XII

The Mishmi Mission—Mr. W. C. M. Dundas—Where two Empires Meet—Chinese Intrigues—A Delicate Situation—Suggestions for a Frontier.

THE Mishmi Mission was, of course, a peaceful one; but, from the complex character of the task which it had been set, it was, at the same time, the most important that had ever passed through the Lohit Valley. The chief political officer of the Mission, Mr. W. C. M. Dundas, had been specially appointed to it and was a man of wide experience in frontier matters, of high position in his Service, and an officer in whose tact and skill the Government of India felt absolute reliance.

Although but little more than thirty, Mr. Dundas is an unrivalled expert on the languages and tribes of the north-eastern border of India, and is deservedly held in high esteem by the frontier chiefs. A recognised successor of the men whose names have been handed down to posterity in the annals of the Indian frontier, Mr. Dundas seems destined to wear the laurels of a great career. While his name is rapidly becoming a household word among the

Mishmi people, the lines upon which he conducts the duties which make his office so important reflect at once the honesty of his methods and the innate secret of our policy. Nothing is more interesting, nor so instructive in its revelation of cause and effect than the spectacle of his reception of the press of people who daily throng the Residency. From early morning until the small hours of the night his time is spent in the closest communion with his charges, and it is quite impossible to be blind to the great influence exercised by the magnetism of his personality.

On the eve of the departure of the Mission there was of course a more striking attendance, and Mr. Dundas seemed for ever to be granting audiences to the representatives of rajahs, through whose districts the Mission would pass, or receiving in Durbar the chiefs themselves. The grounds of the Residency became for the time a meeting-place for all sorts and conditions of people belonging to the border, for the fact that Mr. Dundas was to visit the tribal lands had aroused the greatest enthusiasm, and head-men from far and near tumbled over each other to make their salaams to the Burra sahib.

When he was not conferring honours, redressing wrongs, or awarding the Sirkar's penalties, he would be eliciting information from natives who had been sent in by the gam of a village to descant upon some aspect of the march. Many valuable items of news were gathered on such occasions by Mr. Dundas, for to a well of sympathy and a fount of quiet humour he added the qualities of a good and tactful listener. While his visitors talked he reclined in a low chair, his guests squatting in a circle at his feet all happily puffing at cheroots, or finding restoration after a trying march in tumblers of sweet rum.

With Mr. Dundas, as the lawyers say, was Major Charles Bliss, 1st Battalion 2nd Gurkhas, a keen-hearted officer, whose experiences of active service on the Assam border had been gained almost yearly since he was wounded and mentioned in the Dispatches (medal and clasp) of the Tibet Expedition of 1903–04. Two years of inactivity followed on the Lhassa business and then, with a rush, there came Kehomi, 1907 ; Ranpang Naga, 1908 ; Mozungjami, 1909 ; Aishan Kuki, 1910 ; Makware, 1911 ; and the Mishmi in the present year of grace. The mere list of Major Bliss's post-Tibet " shows " has a tinge of romance in it, for it brings up echoes of " Little Wars," of which the majority of the public has never even heard. Major Bliss commanded in all ; and though each was concerned with the north-east frontier of India they were so much a part of the life of the border soldier that the expeditions carried neither medal nor clasp for officer or man.

The military strength of the Mishmi Mission was 750 troops, made up of 350 Naga Hills Military

THE POLITICAL AND MILITARY CHIEFS OF THE MISHMI MISSION.
Left.—Major Charles Bliss. Right.—Mr. W. C. M. Dundas.

CAPTAIN F. M. BAILEY, OF THE MISHMI MISSION, AND HIS TIBETAN SERVANT, PO-LUN-DO.

THE TIBETAN INTERPRETERS OF THE MISHMI MISSION.

Police, with Captain Hardcastle and under Major Bliss; 150 Dacca Military Police, with Captain Robertson and under Captain Bally; 200 of the 1st King George's Own Sappers and Miners, with Lieutenant Chesney, R.E., Lieutenant Martin, R.E., and under Lieutenant Le Bretton, R.E.; 50 Survey, with Lieutenant Morshead, R.E., and under Captain Gunter, R.E. Captain Jeffery, 69th Carnatic Infantry, who knows more Chinese dialects than any other officer in the British Army, acted as Intelligence Officer, while Captain F. M. Bailey, of the Indian Political Department, who just prior to the start of the Mission had made a venturesome journey from China into India, traversing the Chino-Tibetan border and the heart of the Mishmi country in doing so, was Assistant Political Officer. Captain MacDonald, I.M.S., with four Indian hospital assistants, had charge of the medical arrangements, while Conductor Lyttle, of the Indian Supply and Transport Corps, was responsible for the supply train, and the direction of the 1200 Naga coolies who acted as its porters.

The route which the Mission was to follow threaded the course of the Lohit Valley, which, it will be remembered, had never before been entered by so large a party of Europeans. Unless Mr. Dundas was invited by the Chinese to visit Rima, however, the Mission was not to advance into

Tibetan territory, the frontier of which was supposed to fall near Menilkrai. From Sadiya to Menilkrai the distance by the northern bank of the Brahmaputra was 172 miles; and, as there were neither supplies nor villages in the tract of country intervening between the two places capable of supplying the requirements of a force as large as the Mishmi Mission, Mr. Dundas proposed to establish in advance a string of posts which would serve as the main supply depôts of the column. These posts were to be placed at intervals of fifty miles; and, between them, were to be erected small stockades which would serve as camps at the conclusion of the day's march.

Even in this one detail it will be seen how elaborate was the character of the preliminary work which had to be put in hand before the Mishmi Mission could make a start. As a matter of fact, too, almost every part of the preparations entailed equal labour, for, before the posts could be built, the sites had to be selected and surveys to be made. Before the stores could be transported from the base to the selected positions on the line of march, a track had to be cut through the jungles or blasted across the mountain slopes. In many cases, also, the rivers had to be bridged. While Mr. Dundas wrestled with the political part of the preliminaries, Major Bliss, assisted by Captain Jeffery,

Captain Gunter, R.E., and Lieutenant Chesney, R.E., took in hand the general organisation in which many parts of India were concerned.

In the first place coolies had to be brought to Sadiya from the Naga Hills and at once formed into road and river corps; winter clothing and stores had to be requisitioned from Calcutta, military supplies from Shillong, and provisions from Dibrugarh. When these duties were completed, a system of transport, so elastic that it was adapted equally to railway train, bullock cart, or river steamer, had to be evolved for the conveyance of the stores to Sadiya, and from Sadiya to the supply depôts in the interior. As a part of the practical economy of these schemes, mathematically correct tables of weights had to be worked out in regard to the loads of stores that a coolie convoy could carry, the length of time that such stores would last, and the number of men the gross amount would feed.

Broadly speaking, convoys were divided into columns of 250 coolies; and, as each coolie would carry a load of fifty pounds per day, a single train of 250 coolies moved 12,500 pounds per day. Unfortunately, 250 coolies consumed 500 pounds of stores per day, so that a day's delay on the march, or even longer, very seriously affected the margin of stores that would arrive at the depôt. As the weather was bad, and a certain proportion of the coolies was always a little under condition, the anxieties attaching to the apparently simple task of shifting a given quantity of stores a fixed distance in a definite space of time brought many grey hairs to the officers associated with the work. Greater expedition, of course, was secured when the river could be turned to account; even then there was the risk, when the water in the upper reaches dropped sufficiently to allow rafts and country boats to be sent up, that the merry Naga, ever a better head-hunter than a boatman, would knock out the bottom of the boat on a submerged branch or totally capsize it in one of the innumerable rapids.

In spite of the fact that every one associated with the Mishmi Mission worked day and night to perfect the arrangements for a start, the actual date of departure had constantly to be postponed. Sadiya, unfortunately, is inaccessible by land, and is not readily approached by water. Situated on the right bank of the Lohit on a high plateau opposite Saikhwaghat, the terminus on the left bank of the Dibrugarh-Sadiya Railway, the only means of communication between Sadiya and the outer world in normal times is a ferry that plies from a point on the north bank of the river, some four miles below the Sadiya settlement, to a point about a mile out on the river bed on the left bank, opposite Saikhwa. Although the place is the headquarters of Mr.

MR. DUNDAS'S TANDEM.

THE RESIDENCY AT SADIYA.
Mr. W. C. M. Dundas's official headquarters.

WITH THE MISHMI MISSION.

1. Hauling up the cataracts on the Kundil River. 2. Bridge over the Kundil River.
3. Halting on the Dibong River.

Dundas, as Assistant Political Officer, it is merely a small, though picturesque, riverside village, with a score or more of shops mostly belonging to the enterprising Marwaris who, under strict supervision, trade with the Abor, Mishmi and Khampti tribesmen who come down for barter during the cold season.

It is garrisoned by a detachment of the 114th Mahratta Infantry, a native regiment with headquarters at Dibrugarh, and by a small force of the Lakhimpur Military Police Battalion—a Gurkha regiment of armed police having three European military commissioned officers specially selected for this duty—which in the cold season is distributed in stockades along the northern frontier of Assam from the Darrang district to Margherita and the coal-mining settlement of Ledo, in the south-east of the district of Lakhimpur. These, with the support of the highly-efficient members of the Assam Valley and Surma Valley Light Horse, are the local forces on which the Government relies to meet disorders on the frontier of Upper Assam. There is besides at Shillong, in the Khassi Hills, three to four days' march from the railway and river at Gauhatti, the 1st battalion of the 8th Gurkha Rifles, a regular native infantry regiment of the best class of fighting Gurkhas, 800 strong and officered by twelve to fourteen Europeans.

When the state of the river permits them to do so, steam "floats" come up from Dibrugarh to the Sadiya ferry landing-stage; but, as they are considered very fortunate if they do not ground on a shoal on their way up-stream, they do not often make the journey, so that the ferry becomes really the sole link between Sadiya and the outer world on most days in the year. Owing to the pressure that the work of pushing up the supplies intended for the Mission had put upon the service, the Sadiya ferry was supplemented by a fleet of country boats, with a capacity varying from seven hundredweights to one ton. These boats loaded the stores for the Mishmi Mission from an improvised jetty on the Saikhwa bank, and paddled or poled across to a similar contrivance on the Sadiya bank, where the cargoes were landed and portered by coolies over the four miles intervening between the ferry and the camp. Such a system of communication naturally was neither expeditious nor dependable; and, in the circumstances, it was really remarkable that anything at all was accomplished.

As the work approached completion, Mr. Dundas and Major Bliss left Sadiya on a flying reconnaissance of the first fifty-mile stage of the coming march. On that occasion the capacity of both the road and river routes was tested; for, while two hundred men of the 1st King George's Own Sappers and Miners, accompanied by one hundred and fifty Naga Hills and Dacca Military Police moved by land, Mr. Dundas, Major Bliss, and a party of Gurkhas proceeded by water. The order of march provided for an early start, and at sunrise on October 30th, Lieutenant Le Bretton, R.E., Lieutenant Chesney, R.E., and Lieutenant Martin, R.E., moved out by road with the detachment of Sappers and Miners. A little later the headquarters flotilla, carrying Mr. Dundas and Major Bliss, pushed off, Captain Gunter's map-making party, with Lieutenant Morshead, R.E., not leaving until the following day.

The first camp of the water party was at Diphu, which was reached after a venturesome journey, and where a stockaded post was erected. The second camp was at Sanpara, which was found to be the extreme limit of possible progress by boat, and was the point where the river and land columns united. The journey by water was not without its dangers; and, on the whole, the results only too plainly showed the insuperable difficulties presented by the current and the rapids. Subsequently the worst of the rapids will have to be removed, for so long as they remain they must be regarded as offering a definite bar to navigation on this section of the river.

From Sanpara Mr. Dundas and Major Bliss pressed on to inspect Temeimukh, the first of the future chain of main depôts which were to be set up along the route, after which they returned to Sadiya to put the finishing touches to their work. During their absence the several sections of the force had taken up their allotted duties, and only the final arrangements for the departure of the two—political and military—headquarters awaited completion. The Sappers and Miners were constructing the advanced posts; the Pioneers were busy with road-making and bridge-building, while the Military Police were acting as escorts to supplies and as guards to standing camps. Everywhere there was the sign of the finishing touch, when of a sudden, as it were, everything seemed ready. The final orders were issued; the bugles sounded the "fall-in"; and, while Mr. Dundas, Major Bliss, and the few others still remaining turned their heads to the east, the gates of the Residency rolled together with a clang, and vigilant, determined-looking sentries took stand before them.

The posts selected as the fifty-mile depôts of the Mishmi Mission in its march through the Lohit Valley were Temeimukh, where three months' provisions for the entire force were held in reserve; Kupa, where only two months' reserve supplies were stocked; and Mingszan, where supplies for six weeks were kept. When the British Government resolved that the Mishmi Mission should not proceed to Rima unless it received from the Chinese Government a special invitation to do so, it was decided to make Mingszan the last of the supply posts of the force. With this purpose in view, it was arranged that Mr. Dundas should pay merely a flying reconnaissance to Menilkrai, carrying such stores with him as would be necessary for the maintenance of a small party there for a few days.

As Chinese flags had been reported to be at Walong, it was thought that the representatives of the Chinese authorities in Rima might be encountered somewhere on the border. If this were to prove the case, and matters threatened to become protracted, further supplies could be brought up very easily from Mingszan, as that camp would be only fifteen miles away. If, on the other hand, it should turn out that they were not there, Mr. Dundas had received orders from the Secretary of State for India to erect a cairn at the spot where the Dragon flag was flying, with a view to marking the Tibeto-Mishmi boundary.

Meanwhile we were proposing to make clear our interests in the trans-border area in an emphatic manner, for, although none of the supply depôts of the Mission were to be carried beyond Mingszan, that place was to become the terminus of a new trans-frontier road, which was to be projected from Sadiya. If nothing else came of the work of the

P 2

Mishmi Mission, therefore, the Sadiya road at least would remain to offer its conclusive, though silent, testimony of our interest in the region. Moreover, it would be the first time that any such facilities had been given to the tribes on this face of the frontier, and it could hardly fail to carry its own special significance to their Chinese neighbours, or to promote the future traffic between the bazaars of India and the Mishmi marches. Where practicable the road was to be of the breadth of nine feet, which dimensions it was hoped it would be possible to continue at least as far as Kupa, if not all the way to Mingszan. Owing to the fall of the mountains about Mingszan it was just possible that it would not be feasible to carry so wide a road so far, whereupon a coolie track was to be cut, and the widening left to a future day.

So far I have dealt only with the "incidentals" of the Mishmi Mission. In a measure the duties entrusted to the Mission were of a threefold character. While cutting a road through the Lohit Valley, laying down the correct boundary-line between Tibet and the Abor marches in a northerly direction, and between Tibet and the Mishmi border on the east, were important tasks, the main object of the Mission was, of course, to ascertain the precise extent of Chinese activity on the Tibeto-Mishmi, Tibeto-Abor borders. At the moment when the

Mishmi Mission left Sadiya there were several points of contact between the territories of the Chinese and Indian Empires which, it may be safely averred, have not in the interval grown any fewer.

From the nature of the work confronting it the Mishmi Mission was in close relation with the position of the Burma Boundary Commission in respect of the Burma border. Dating from the appointment of a Chinese High Commissioner for Frontier Affairs, an officer whose powers are both civil and military, the Chinese have been steadily increasing their influence in the wild and desolate region which defines the marches of Assam and Burma, and hitherto has been considered within British jurisdiction. They have already subdued the tribes, including the very savage Lolos, lying between Sechuan, Yunan and Tibet, while the reports which have been received of Chinese activity, at least in respect of the Burma border, were proved to rest on ample foundation, when it was discovered, in September of 1910, that the Chinese had established themselves at Pien-ma.

While there is not the slightest doubt that Pien-ma stands on the Burmese side of the Indian watershed, the moving spirit behind the occupation of Pien-ma, as, also, behind the situation generally created by Chinese activity on these marches of north-east India, was that of the late Chao-Ehr-

Feng. The seizure of Pien-ma, of course, was but a move in a game of which at the moment only the preliminaries were disclosed. Although it was countered by moving a strong column of Police from Myitkyina to the border to prevent further encroachment, the mistake was made of leaving the Chinese troops in possession of the town, for, undoubtedly, an entirely different complexion would have been put upon the situation if they had been summarily ejected in the first instance.

While the columns of Burmese Police were watching the border, the Chinese shifted their ground and, keeping possession of Pien-ma, marched a battalion of troops, 400 strong, into Chikung, the official capital of the Zayul Valley, though most of the Government buildings are situated at Rima. Having dispossessed the Tibetans of their independence, China was within her rights in putting a garrison into Chikung, but the men had had hardly time to settle in the derelict spot before half a company was dispatched to Rima and a movement made which was mistakenly considered by the great majority of newspapers in England and India to be an actual infringement of the Mishmi border.

In regard to Rima it is of interest to recall that the late Dr. Gregorson, in the last letter that was received from him before his untimely end, mentioned that he was on the eve of starting into the

Abor country, and was only waiting the return of Mr. Noel Williamson, "who was then at Rima, making history." Dr. Gregorson went on to speak of interviews between Mr. Williamson and the "Chinese Governor" of Rima. This was the first that the public had heard of a "Chinese Governor" of Rima, the governing authorities hitherto having been Tibetan: a *jong pen*, or military governor, and a *shian-u*, or civil magistrate. In regard to Mr. Williamson's presence in Rima, we must presume that the Government of India, having heard about the Chinese activity on the Mishmi border, had sent him to see exactly what it was the Chinese were doing.

From Rima, early in the spring of 1911, fresh activities were announced, for in April twenty men were withdrawn from the Rima post and moved to Rongdo, five miles away, where a second outpost was established. With the receipt of this news, it became apparent that the Chinese were seeking to build up a strong position on the Mishmi border from which to influence tribes that have long been accustomed to regard the Indian Government as their protecting power. Moreover, signs were not long in coming that showed that the general situation on the Mishmi border was becoming graver, for rumours of strange flags and foreign-drilled troops having been seen in the Lohit Valley were very frequent. Inquiries were made and confirmation obtained when

Captain F. M. Bailey, of the Indian Political Department, arrived in Sadiya, on August 7th, from the east, and reported having seen Chinese flags and Chinese troops both at Menilkrai and Walong.

While this evidence concerned matters on the Chinese side of the Tibeto-Mishmi border, it was suddenly discovered that the chief of the Singphos of the Hukong Valley had been presented with the robes of a Chinese Civil Mandarin of the first class, although both the chief and his people had long acknowledged British jurisdiction. There was, too, a situation on the borders of the Pomed Abors that required watching. The crux of the whole position came, however, when it was reported that Rajah Chowna, Chief of the Kampti peoples who have rendered such invaluable help to us in the past and are protected by the Indian Government, while, in a measure, they are overlords of the Digarus and Mejus, had been informed by the Chinese Governor of Rima that the Kampti areas had been annexed two years previously by the Imperial Government of China and that he was now a subject of The Son of Heaven. In support of this wholly ridiculous and utterly unwarranted claim, a number of mining and timber concessions, issued from Pekin and bearing dates that were two years old, were flourished before the astounded eyes of the old ruler.

From the recital of these details it will be seen

CAPTAIN F. M. BAILEY, INDIAN POLITICAL DEPARTMENT, ASSISTANT POLITICAL OFFICER MISHMI MISSION, INTERVIEWING MISHMI TRIBESMEN AT NIZAMGHAT.

NUMEROUS SMALL STREAMS HAD TO BE FORDED.

NAGA TRANSPORT.
The column at ease.

that the regulation of the British and Chinese frontiers in the snow-clad fastnesses where the two empires meet, does call for immediate settlement. Though there is no reason to expect that any unfortunate contretemps will arise, the delicate nature of the problem is undeniable. In its way, too, it is as significant as the task which engaged the Pamirs Boundary Commission in 1896, for, now that Tibet can no longer be regarded as independent of China, India and China become *vis-à-vis* in a country where the line of frontier runs almost as it lists.

No less authorities than two ex-Viceroys of India, Lord Curzon and Lord Minto, have expressed the opinion that the centre of possible trouble on the Indian frontier has shifted from the north-west to the north-east. Unfortunately it is not only a case of an advance by Chinese soldiers, but of an efflux of Chinese settlers, who are swarming in all along the frontier from Tibet to Yunnan, and are settling as much in the Shan states as on the Mishmi borders. In one or two instances, moreover, the tribesmen have objected and have massacred the settlers, while Chinese troops, with intolerable presumption, have effected reprisals.

It is to be feared that the British Government has delayed too long in dealing with the north-east frontier. Where it has taken the question in hand it has treated the issues as if the problems of the north-eastern border were similar to those of the north-west, and has left between India and China accordingly a long tract of non-administered territory in the hope of forming a buffer State. But on the north-west, Afghanistan is a true buffer State because it holds Russia in check without interfering with the frontier tribes. There is no buffer State on the north-east; though, if the frontier line has been vague, it has never fallen short of the Mishmi lands. Rima, of course, is a Tibetan possession no less than Menilkrai and Walong, but there is no question of Pien-ma, or of the lands of the Singphos and of the Kamptis being within our jurisdiction. As the Chinese have penetrated so far, there can be no doubt that they are advancing, just as the Russians would have done had there been no Afghanistan and had we not taken possession of Chitral, and they must certainly be kept back.

The position created by these movements, if set up by our neglect of obvious precautions, is very delicate, though not alarming. Moreover, it is not incapable of adjustment, for, as the Burma frontier embraces the whole of the water-shed of the Irrawaddy, the corresponding corollary of that line along the Mishmi and further western tribal borders should provide a solution of the Tibeto-Mishmi difficulty in a natural frontier that could not be "turned." Though a large part of the country through which the surveys for such a line would have to pass is unexplored, a natural frontier is believed to exist in a range of unsurveyed snow mountains of vast height and without passes that is reputed to run from north-west to south-east across the north of the Mishmi border. It is true that the adoption of such a line means an advance of the Indian frontier some distance beyond Lord Crewe's cairn between Menilkrai and Walong. Against this there can be placed the fact that the intervening country on the north is no loss to any one, for it is desolate, barren, and unproductive, and only really fit for utilising as a containing barrier against the peoples on its either side.

Beginning roughly at Tawang on the Tawang Chu in the western Miri country, the suggested line of frontier would run in a north-eastern direction to latitude 29, which it would follow to longitude 96, whence it would proceed along the crests of the range of lofty snow mountains which has been mentioned and run from north-west to south-east to the ridge of the Lohit Valley. Proceeding to the Lohit River, and crossing it, the direction of the line would continue to the Rima Valley, which it would traverse between Rima and Same, where boundary cairns could be established. From these pillars the frontier should follow a little east of north as far as the Nam Kiu range, whence it should travel along the water-shed of the Irrawaddy by the crests of the Rirap Phasi range to a junction on the Burmese border with the line adopted by the Burmese Boundary Commission.

Such a line gives a very good ethnic and physical division between China on the north and the British Indian tribal possessions on the south, and there is nothing inherently objectionable in its adoption. In the opinion of all who know north-east India, moreover, it is believed that its recognition would achieve a fair and business-like adjustment of mutual differences on the Tibeto-Mishmi border, since the range marked as a "snow range" on all maps, and employed here as the main border line, has always been regarded by the Mishmis as defining and running parallel with the northern border of their lands.

CHAPTER XIII

Pasighat abandoned—Major-General Bower at Jonakmukh—"Heaven," "Hell," and "Purgatory"—The Fascination of the Jungle—The Ledum Column—The Fight at Dorsing—Advance to Old Rengging.

WITH the arrival of the Main Column at Pasighat on October 25th General Bower's force had reached the limits of the country held by the outposts of the Lakhimpur Battalion of the Military Police. For the future every step of the forward movement had to be gained at the expense of heroic exertions by the Sappers and Miners and by the Pioneers, whose previous labours with jungle-cutting, bridge-building, and blasting paths out of the precipitous slopes of the mountains were to be eclipsed.

Though others had trod the jungle which lay ahead and climbed through the rocky gorges, the strength of these earlier parties was smaller and their position different, while the lapse of years had obliterated all traces of their footsteps. Moreover, so large a force as that which General Bower was leading forward was more dependent than a smaller body on its lines of communication; and, though the rate of road construction was on occasion little more than a mile or two a day, nothing could be done until the way was cleared. At the same time, from the uncompromising character of the barrier of dense forest and containing rampart of grim, inaccessible heights which held the way, it was easy to understand the reluctance of the Indian Government about raising Nature's purdah on the mysteries of Aborland. However, the process had to be done; and, as the failure of former attempts had been due to the difficulty of keeping open the lines of communication, General Bower saw to it that an absence of success at the present time would not be attributable to any similar cause.

No movement was to be made until the track had been prepared and no step was to be taken that was unaccompanied by infinite precaution. For the nonce Lieutenant Knight, with his corps of merry signallers, became a band of peripatetic spirits upon whom every one relied, for the helio or the telephone was in hourly use and never lacking where the one or other could possibly be needed. In particular was the telephone in evidence. It accompanied the column as it advanced until the number of yards of cable paid out could be counted by the thousand. It kept the General and his headquarters in touch with the men on road and bridge construction; it linked up the rear guard with the advance guard; it trailed after every party going out on reconnaissance and brought a sense of security to isolated picquets on remote heights by giving them an easy method of communication with the camp. The signalling corps, in short, was everywhere at once, and Lieutenant Knight's enterprise in rising superior to the vagaries of the mist which screened alike hill-top and valley bottom drew well-merited compliments from all quarters.

Pasighat, where the Main Column was now established, was one of the chief villages of the Pasi Abors who, just prior to the start of the Abor expedition, were associated with an ingenious plot against Balek, a neighbouring police post, where a garrison of one hundred and fifty men of the Lakhimpur Military Police and a section of artillery kept watch over the Pasi tribesmen. Report showed that, a few weeks before the column left Kobo, one thousand Kebang and Komsing Abors had appeared at a village about fifteen miles north of Balek and proposed to the Pasis that on a given date the Pasi fighting men should join the northerners at a secret rendezvous near Balek. The force was then to be divided into two bodies, one of which was to be placed in ambush while a sham attack on one of the Pasi villages was made by twenty men who were to draw after them whatever detachment of police was sent in pursuit. While the party of pursuing police was cut up by the men who were in ambush, the main body of the Abors was to rush the stockade from an unexpected direction.

The Pasis are said to have expressed full approval of the scheme and to have agreed with the Kebang and Komsing gams that it would be a success. At the same time they pointed out that the Indian Government held them responsible for keeping the peace in their villages and they explained that, if the Balek stockade were captured, their position would be a dangerous one for, while the Kebang and Komsing men could retreat in safety beyond the hills, the Pasi villages inevitably would be destroyed. The Kebang and Komsing men thereupon denounced the Pasis as cowards and withdrew threatening to raid the Pasi lands. In the meantime the Pasis informed the police at Balek who at once took the necessary steps to safeguard their charges and themselves.

The wisdom of the Pasi Abors in refusing to entertain the proposals of the northern tribesmen was shown when, a few weeks later, Pasighat became the base camp of the Main Column. Situated on the right bank of the Dihang against a singularly impressive background of cliffs and jungle, the place offered an ideal situation for a supply depôt and very quickly rivalled Kobo in importance. Laid out on a site six hundred yards square that had previously been virgin jungle, it was protected with a five foot seven inch ditch and a three foot parapet, while many thousands of *panjees* were set in the ditch. A couple of strong stockaded works were put up on the corners and a pretty frieze of barbed wire imparted a decorative and defensive touch to its approaches.

From Pasighat the force was to proceed to Jonakmukh, similarly situated on the right bank of the river and a distance of seven miles. After resting on October 26th half a company of Sappers and Miners, the detachment of the Assam Valley and Surma Valley Light Horse and three hundred Naga coolies, escorted by six companies of the 8th Gurkhas, set to work at sunrise on the following day to cut the path. The direction lay along the bank of the Dihang through a forest of giant bamboos, wild plantains, screw pines, poisonous nettles, wild orchids, thorns and water creepers. By nightfall the working party had tunnelled through some five miles of vegetation, the Gurkhas in advance with kukries cutting a narrow track which Nagas, coming up behind, widened to eight feet, while the Pioneers and the Sappers and Miners graded the work in bad places and made the bridges. No special difficulties were encountered; but, at the conclusion of the fifth mile, there were indications of the presence of rocks ahead. Thus, for the next day, there was still the burden of the road, the force not taking up the advance on Jonakmukh until daybreak on October 29th.

Early as the working parties were on the road just as early was headquarters on the move reconnoitring the country. On October 27th Major-General Bower, Major Hutchinson, Lieutenant Knight and the remainder of the headquarters staff, escorted by one company of the 8th Gurkhas under Captain J. D. Coleridge, swarmed up some spurs on the right bank of the Dihang and had a look at Rammi Dambang in the north-east; on October 28th a second reconnaissance by headquarters succeeded in penetrating to within three-quarters of a mile of Jonakmukh without encountering an enemy. This effort was not without incident, however, as Captain Molesworth of the 8th Gurkhas came into such violent disagreement with a poisonous creeper that he was *hors de combat* for some little time to come.

Although the Sappers and Miners had contrived to lay out an admirable road, the time occupied by the column in accomplishing the little journey was some nine hours. Accordingly, it was long past noon before the vanguard made its appearance in Jonakmukh and nearly three o'clock before the last of the rearguard had reported. Slow movement is of necessity fatiguing and the crawl down the Rue de Kebang became almost as wearisome as a promenade down Piccadilly. Once the place was reached, however, it was seen to possess natural ad-

BRIDGE-BUILDING BY THE 5TH COMPANY BENGAL SAPPERS AND MINERS.

WOUNDED NAGA COOLIE.

vantages, Major-General Bower quickly deciding to transfer the supply depôt from Pasighat to Jonakmukh as the latter camp not only could be reached quite as easily by the boat convoys, but was a stage farther ahead.

Jonakmukh lay on the bank of the river in a hollow of the hills. As the camping ground was a mass of rock and rubble in the densest jungle, another two hours' labour had to be added to the nine hours spent on the march before sleeping places could be cleared and chappars—shelters of leaves and grass—erected. From the dizzy crests near at hand a fine, all-round view could be caught: of fields which lay like aprons of patchwork on the knees of the mountains near Rammi; of the snows of the Chinese frontier on the east; of Saikhwaghat and Sadiya on the south. Kobo stood behind a ridge and was invisible in a land where, as a matter of fact, nothing could be seen without a climb up the sheer face of the hill-side and a crawl along some razor edge to a lofty eminence, where a slip spelt perdition. Even when the peak was crowned, the tree tops usually had to be cleared before any signal station could be established, as it is one of Nature's little ironies in this part of the world that the steepest and most knife-like acclivities invariably carry the thickest jungles.

In these reconnaissances General Bower was easily

first for he was as nimble and indefatigable on the hills as the Gurkhas themselves. If such exertions were somewhat appalling it must be remembered that they produced, nevertheless, much valuable information for the signallers and for the surveyors —then again, there was the view! For the purposes of the survey, the hills round Jonakmukh were numbered No. 1, No. 2, No. 3: they were also not unknown as "Heaven," "Hell," and "Purgatory." Rising sheer from the Dihang, the three hills dominated the reaches of the river for many miles up and down stream and were promptly supplied with helios and telephones, and utilised as signal stations.

From the rugged crests of Hell, Gurkha picquets, holding solitary station, watched the working parties of Sappers and Miners and Pioneers on the river's edge far below them slowly eat their way with dynamite and pick across the granite cliffs *en route* to Rengging. For at least a mile at this point the advance was blocked by massive mountains which buttressed the river; while, for more than a mile, a right of way was secured only by blasting a track out of the solid rock. After prodigious effort two miles were cleared in three days; yet, as the days passed, each difficulty surmounted was something gained. Though the rate of advance was dispiriting, and every one would have preferred by travelling light and fast to have had a "butt in" at Kebang and road made afterwards, the crawling pace at which the forward movement was conducted was really unavoidable. It was not until half-past six on the morning of November 2nd that the column moved out. At first the "going" was a pleasant climb across the bare shoulder of the slope along a path which, in some places, was slung by galleries from the face of hill, while, in others, it climbed over flights of steps cut out of fallen trunks of trees laid zigzag-wise up the cliff until some obstacle was turned. Here the road dipped to a ragged nullah; there it hung suspended in mid-air, and so progressed, until, at the head of construction, there was once again the dank, dark forest rising stiffly ridge on ridge in verdant splendour, waiting to be cut.

It was necessary now to proceed with even greater caution than had been already observed for the column was entering the country of the Minyongs, whose implacable hostility was one of the influences inciting the resistance of other tribesmen. In view of their activities, and as a safeguard against ambuscades, all advance road-making parties of Pioneers and of Sappers and Miners were withdrawn, the line of march being cleared by the troops themselves as they moved along. Progress was consequently very slow; a yard or two and then a halt; and then, perhaps, another forward step. For all its drawbacks nevertheless there was an impressive majesty in the luxuriant verdure of the jungle. There was, too, not a little mystery in the almost total stillness and the dim half-lights of the dark glades. From their moist recesses Nature defied herself, for, while every form of tropical growth preyed upon its neighbour, one and all combined to suspend the curtain of their entanglements before the sun. Gigantic trees towered skyward blocking out the sunshine, their very life sapped by the interlacing ropes of creepers which, twisting and twining around their victims, garlanded them with the trappings of decay.

The luxuriance and fertility of these insidious parasites which, like gigantic octopods, threw out their deadly tentacles in fantastic festoons of pot-hooks and hangers, was as phenomenal as the active forces of destruction were overwhelming. Presented in the guise of some rare orchid, as the frailest of tree ferns, feathery thorny "bet" or water creeper, these agents of ill-omen battened upon the trunks of the more vigorous monarchs of the glade until the time came when, as the effect of their work of destruction, the leaves withered and fell, and the sapless trunks sank to the ground to lose themselves for ever in the carpet of the jungle.

Happily there were signs here that the long

"THERE WAS AN IMPRESSIVE MAJESTY IN THE LUXURIANT VERDURE OF THE JUNGLE."

WITH THE LEDUM COLUMN.
View over the Sireng Valley from Mishing Hill.

stretches of primeval forest, with their myriad vicious insects, their poisonous undergrowth, their obnoxious fumes as, also, their almost total exclusion of light and air, through which the expedition had been steadily forcing a way, were soon to be left behind. For the moment at all events there was a marked change. The jungle was growing less dense; the trees were smaller; the air drier. Of a sudden, too, the road passed out of the forest and fell away to low hills and open cultivation; where, amid a profusion of pink, yellow and blue flowers, camp was established. The place was Rammi Dambang.

Well situated and swept by river breezes, the camp was a happy one and offered a series of splendid views. From some hills on the north-west Lieutenant Knight opened up helio communication with Pasighat and Jonakmukh, while in the camp itself the field telephone worked with Jonakmukh and Kobo. After halting three days at Rammi Dambang, during which the Sappers and Miners and the Pioneers, escorted by Lieutenant Buckland and strong parties of the 8th Gurkhas, prepared the road, Major-General Bower moved, on November 6th, to the Sirpo River, a tributary of the Dihang River, which he had reconnoitred two days previously.

The road from Rammi Dambang rose over a steep acclivity and then fell by a long, almost sudden, descent some eight hundred feet until it came to a rest in a hollow of the hills on the banks of the stream. Bold cliffs towered loftily above the camp, which by reason of its position was rocky, uncomfortable and cramped, though not lacking an element of the grim as of the romantic. There was grimness in the rugged setting of the river gorge with its beetling brows and nestling chutes; picturesqueness in the masses of driftwood that were piled high about the stones of the river bed; much beauty in the riot of natural colours that distinguished the variegated hues of rocks and jungle. The march was uneventful. It passed the practice ground of some Abor bowmen and disclosed many camping-places of the enemy, whose carefully laid traps on the hill-side overlooking the river had been taken in the rear by the direction in which the Sappers and Miners had laid their road.

During the progress of the march, the General and his Staff climbed a very steep hill on the right flank of the advance. From the top patches of cultivation on the side of the Sirpo River could be seen, while across the Dihang and Yamne Rivers the village of Pongging, numbering some forty huts and apparently situated on a cliff looking on to the river and connected by a narrow neck with the hill behind, could be distinguished. This village was inhabited by Panggi Abors whose attitude was as yet uncertain. From the glimpse of the prospect that headquarters had obtained, there was nothing at all uncertain about the difficulties that lay ahead.

While the advance of the Main Column was delayed by the difficulties of the road, the best of fortune was attending the operations of the Ledum Column. After the successful occupation of Ledum on October 24th, Colonel Fisher, whose presence was intended as a check upon the Minyongs and the Galongs on the left flank of the theatre of war while it also served to prevent so far as possible any combination of the forces of these two tribes, entered upon a systematic reconnaissance of the Ledum region.

The movement opened in the best of form on October 27th, when an advance party of the 2nd Gurkhas was attacked in jungle near Mishing, two days from Ledum, by a party of archers with poisoned arrows. After a brisk encounter, in which the enemy's bolts fell in showers about the sepoys, the attack was repulsed without loss to our own side though two Abors were killed and three wounded by the good shooting of the Gurkhas. On October 29th Mishing itself was occupied by the same party of Gurkhas when, since it was evident that the tribesmen hotly resented the presence of the little force, the remainder of the Ledum force was hurriedly pushed forward. Four days later, November 2nd, Colonel Fisher was able to report to Major-General Bower that the concentration of the Ledum Column on Mishing had been completed.

The inhabitants of Mishing were but recent arrivals from Kebang and were as hostile as other Minyongs. Similarly there was no doubt that the Galongs, with the possible exception of the Dobang division, were equally in arms against us. By securing Mishing, Colonel Fisher had placed himself in some degree between the Galongs on the west and the Minyongs on the north. As his force was too small to hold out against any concerted tribal movement, there was an element of refreshing boldness in his act. At the same time his position called for wariness. Booby traps were plentiful; the roads in all directions barricaded and set with *panjees*. These precautions, however, were not enough to prevent a party of the 2nd Gurkhas from surprising one of the enemy's picquets in the bed of the Sireng River, when an ammunition runner, carrying two hundred and fifty poisoned arrows from Kebang to the Galong tribesmen, was laid out.

Colonel Fisher read into this piece of good fortune evidence of tribal plans for a possible combination against his column. Believing that the best method of dealing with such an eventuality was to destroy at once the tribesmen's power of unity, he dispatched, on November 6th, a force of two hundred Lakhimpur Military Police under Captain Sir George Duff-

Sutherland-Dunbar, Bart., to reconnoitre the Kebang road beyond the Sireng River. At the same time, Major Lindsay and one hundred of the 2nd Gurkhas proceeded towards Kaking. Few difficulties attended the movement under Captain Dunbar who, though the road to Kebang was blocked, was able to clear away without opposition many of the barricades which had been constructed across it.

The task set Major Lindsay did not prove so easy. After marching six hours over a roadless country that was covered with dense jungle and was very steep, the party reached the Sidong River and entered Galong territory. The Galongs, in part because of pressure by Kebang and in part because they regarded us with hostility, had made common cause with the Minyongs, so that, although their villages were isolated, they could be regarded nevertheless as outposts on the fringe of the area of hostilities. In any case they made independent arrangements for their defence ; and, by setting up barricades, laying down *panjees* and stockading their villages, had done what they could.

It was this scheme of resistance which confronted Major Lindsay on his advance into the Galong country for the purpose of his reconnaissance towards Kaking. Barricades and *panjees*, which happily were safely negotiated, held the road which one mile to the east of Dorsing, a village of forty houses with a population of two hundred and fifty, emerged suddenly at a distance of ten yards upon an invisible stockade that was strongly posted on the crest of the precipitous paths by which the troops were proceeding. Delay was fatal; and, as the track was completely blocked and the stockade defended by arrowmen and stone chutes, the troops, led by their officers, attempted to rush the position, only to be repelled again and again by the stone chutes which swept the face of the path with the thunder and effect of landslides. Arrow fire, well sustained and cleverly directed, followed upon the descending rocks, which of themselves brought bad bruises to several of the attacking party, the enemy precipitately retiring when the last collection of boulders had been released. The check at this stockade was not sufficient to deflect the advance of the little column. Only one rifleman had suffered seriously, though many bruises could be counted on the heads, legs and bodies of others. Accordingly, a party of forty men pushed on to Dorsing village, which had already been deserted, and destroyed it. A few days later the position became the site of an outpost of the Military Police and, in this capacity, continued to be held throughout the operations.

From Dorsing the position of a number of villages was located. Kaking, the real objective of the Lindsay party, lay off about seven miles to the south.

Another village, Kharan, was situated south-west of Dorsing, across the direct road between Ledum and Kaking. These villages were active and important centres ; and, at daybreak on November 9th, while fifty rifles of the 2nd Gurkhas proceeded to Kharan, which numbered some twenty houses, a party of Military Police advanced against Kaking. Both operations were successful, though differing in results, for, while the party that attacked Kharan killed one Abor and wounded others, the Military Police had one follower killed by a gunshot in the head as the detachment was moving through the jungle.

While reconnoitring parties from the Ledum Column were clearing the left flank of Major-General Bower's area of operations, the Main Column at the moment could do but little more than continue its work of looking for a way over, a way through, or a way round the myriad obstacles that each reconnaissance revealed to be lying ahead. The dreary monotony of the process went against the grain for all ranks were anxious for a scrap, and there was nothing doing. In spite of everything the days were passed and energies were sapped in no more exciting pastime than road-making and reconnoitring for a road alignment. Fine views, of course, were offered by the marches up and down the mountain-side ; but they were views of the snow-capped water-shed, of the racing river, of the Assam plains, veiled in the haze of the distance. They were seldom views of the enemy.

The reflections of an evening from the setting sun, however, were superb. The troops, looking on the plains of Assam through the deep-throated gorges of the Dihang, saw the distant undulations of that vast acreage of busy tea-gardens shown up as a blue, inchoate mass set amid the faint shimmer of glistening silver. The sparkle of the water in the course of the Brahmaputra led on to where the light grey of the horizon formed into support of the darker canopy of the heavens. Delicate clouds, snow-white and fleecy, lit up by the rays of the sun with fires of rare gold, of puce, and of the palest pink, hovered o'er the middle distance, dreamily drifting beneath the breath of the zephyrs. Farther across, towering in stately gloom against the splendour of the vespers, could be distinguished the shadowy outline of the mountains of the Naga border, while, nearer at hand, the serrated peaks of other ranges fashioned a line of ghostly spires athwart the sky. It was always beautiful; yet ever impressed with the glamour of the unreal until the glow died out in the clouds, the pale tints faded from the west and a uniform drabness spread everywhere. In that moment the fugitive hands of the fairies touched the scene for the last time; in that moment, too, came disillusionment and the reality of regret. Beauty had gone: all trace of its presence vanishing as the pall of night brought in place of the delicate fabric of God's handiwork the fitful gleaming of camp fires.

As the slow progress of the Main Column was unavoidable the best complexion was put by every one upon the extremely disagreeable position in which the natural difficulties of the road had placed the force. Everything in the meantime was done to turn to account the orology of the route, and hill after hill above the respective camps was climbed by Lieutenant Knight and his signallers, as also by the surveyors, in search of advantageous positions from which to carry out their work. Sirpo camp, of course, was no exception. Telephonic communication with Kobo was set up by Lieutenant Knight within an hour or two of Major-General Bower's arrival on November 6th, and maintained until the force moved on again. For the three days, however, there was no move, hill-climbing and road-making becoming routine duties. Three reconnoitring columns moved out on November 7th. One of these, composed of two companies of the 8th Gurkhas, rounded up and burnt a newly built, strongly barricaded village which proved to be New Rengging; while another came across the case of Mr. Williamson's fishing-rod, much cut about by dhaos. Each of the columns discovered and released numerous rock chutes. On the next day the promenade was more in the nature of a "set piece," for Major-General Bower and his Staff, with thirty rifles of the Gurkhas and the detachment of the Assam Valley and Surma Valley Light Horse, made a reconnaissance in force in a north-westerly direction.

Crossing the Sirpo River, which had been bridged by the Sappers and Miners, the column proceeded towards the site of Old Rengging. The track led up and down very steep gradients, but was shorn of many of its hardships by the careful work of the road-makers, who had contrived a number of zigzag paths across the cliffs. The march was without incident; though, as the column was returning and was about three miles from camp, the barking of dogs and the voices of Minyongs in the valley below could be clearly heard. No encounter, however, took place. From the crests of the hills the position of Pongging, some four miles distant, was again made out, as well as the big area of cultivation in its neighbourhood. With the exception of Balek this was the first big village in the Abor country that had been seen. In addition to being composed of some forty substantially built huts, it seemed to possess about as many granaries. No human beings moved in the village, though, no doubt, they watched from the jungle the movements of the force.

From Sirpo River, Major-General Bower shifted early on the morning of November 9th to Old

Rengging, where camp was established on the steep hill-side in a wilderness of thick and prickly jungle, fallen trees and rocks. From the reports of spies, the character of the difficulties ahead were common knowledge. As they indicated even longer halts than any that had yet been made, the troops prepared for it by terracing the slopes to secure an even surface for their weary bones.

CHAPTER XIV

A Gruesome Discovery—Abor Jungle Craft—A Second Deluge—Visitors from Damro—Mr. Dundas's Durbar—Signs of the Times—"The Last shall be First"—The Fight at Egar Stockade—Major General Bower wounded—Advance to Rotung.

Although the halt at Old Rengging was to prove protracted it would not have been quite so long if the weather had been better. As it was, in spite of a modified edition of the Deluge, the days were fully occupied with the dual penances of road-making and occasional reconnaissance, one of the latter accomplishing only two thousand yards in five hours. Each span brought of course its own little quota of interest, humorous and tragic, an incident of the latter kind associated with November 10th leaving an indelible impression on the troops. Late in the afternoon, as the working parties were extending the perimeter of the camp, they came upon four skulls, undoubtedly of a Mongoloid type, and some bones all bearing upon them the marks of dhaos. Round about the scene were the debris of baskets, scattered loads, including a gun case, fishing-rod case, a plane table together with a few fragments of letters and diaries. Some of the latter pieced together were just decipherable and established beyond doubt that what had been found were the remains of the Nepalese carriers and the Miri runners who had been sent back by Mr. Williamson. The story of their fate has been related on a previous page, but the discovery brought back to the mind the underlying motive of the Abor Expedition, filling every one with an even keener wish to have a slap at his elusive foe than he had before.

While the recovery of such relics threw into relief the tragedy of past months, intelligence, which came from Sirpo River camp two days later, gave prominence to an incident of more immediate reference to the portion of the Main Column. From time to time Orders notified "all concerned" that escorts must accompany field working parties. In spite of this, and apparently trusting to Providence for a safe conduct, a party of telegraph coolies had ventured out on duty with the almost inevitable result that they were cut up. These little encounters were not usually fatal, but they were of frequent occurrence as the Abors were past masters in the difficult art of "lying low" until the crucial moment arrived. They seemed then to enjoy drawing a bow at a venture and diving to cover as the bolt flew to its mark. The episode was regrettable but, nevertheless, it was impossible to deny that the spirit of orders on this point was most emphatic.

Although construction of the road absorbed the energies of many people, progress was slow for difficulties were many and there was much to be done. With the exception of November 11th, which was spent by every one as a period of well-earned rest and recuperation, from the time when the column arrived at Old Rengging every day was devoted to the road construction problem. The labour expended had been stupendous yet, for it all, the column was still hemmed in by the twin barriers of semi-unsurmountable ranges and dense jungle—and, seemingly, would continue to be hemmed in in the best of circumstances for several days. Unfortunately, where the Goddess of Fortune was wanted to smile most beatifically she smiled not at all for, on November 13th, the weather broke. Rain fell in a manner which churned the ground into mud and made the task of the road-makers both damp and disagreeable. Beginning with a few hours' preliminary downpour on the previous day, it streamed steadily from the early morning of the thirteenth until the night of the sixteenth, by which time it had penetrated everything and clothes, blankets and chappars were absolutely sodden. For three days and three nights all ranks worked, lived, and slept in sopping things, the force being engaged, as it was picturesquely reported at the time, in fighting a rearguard action with General Rain and General Damp.

Before the deluge started it had been announced from Sadiya that Mr. W. T. Ballantine, the Assistant Political Officer at Sadiya in the absence of Mr. W. C. M. Dundas, was *en route* for Army headquarters with three Padam gams who had come down from Damro on an urgent visit to Mr. Dundas. Two of the chiefs were representatives of the Damro tribe while the third came from the Dambuk tribe, the three being preceded by a courier who had been entrusted with a message of peace to Mr. Dundas. This message took the form of a sword and a spearhead, bent double, which was the symbol of peace among the Padams. A Mr. Dundas, in his capacity as Political Officer in charge of the Mishmi Mission, was paying a flying visit of inspection to Temeimukh, one of the route posts on the line of march up the Lohit Valley, it had been necessary to recall him post-haste to Sadiya, where, on the day after his return, accompanied by Major Bliss, Mr. Ballantine, many officers of the Mishmi Mission and the Residency escort, he had received in Durbar the Abor emissaries.

In a scene that was at once impressive and inspired by much historic significance the three chiefs, standing boldly defiant before Mr. Dundas, emphasised the sincerity of their message of peace, and declaimed their tribes' guiltlessness of any participation in the massacre of Mr. Noel Williamson, Dr. Gregorson and their party. The principal spokesman of the group, who was over six feet in height and cut a magnificent figure, was one of the Damro chiefs and a man from whom it was impossible to withhold a meed of sympathy. Fierce, passionate and fearless he harangued the Durbar with fiery eloquence, appealing to the spirits of Earth, Sky and Water for corroboration of his words. At one moment his voice rose to the gamut of ill-restrained anger; at another it fell, and he beat his breast, picking up and throwing down his bow and dhao. For nearly half an hour he poured out a torrent of words and then desisted while one of the others took up the story. All the time his companions were speaking, however, he was the prompter and, in the end, he concluded with a fine denunciatory outburst which reached its climax in one last appeal, alike for quarter as for peace, as one by one the three chiefs cut the strings of their bows, broke in twain their poisoned arrows, doubled in two the blades of their dhaos and blunted the points of their spears, flinging each article as it was rendered useless at the feet of the Sirkar's representatives. The effect of such an action was intensely appealing for, looking from the magnificent simplicity of the men, veritable untutored children of nature that they were, to the little litter of broken weapons at their feet, it was obvious that they had given what they conceived to be a demonstration of sincerity that would be overwhelming.

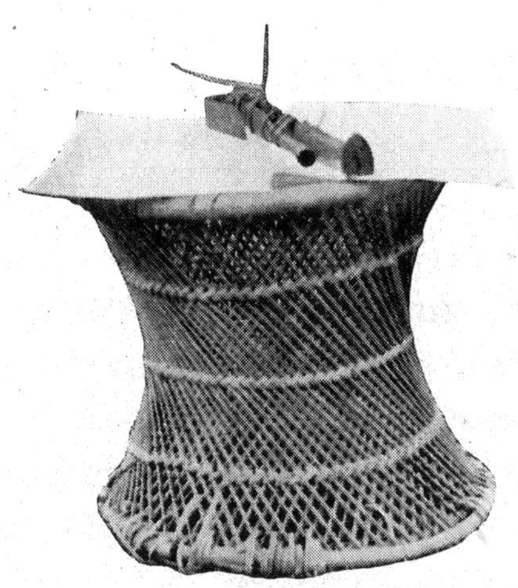

THE SYMBOL OF PEACE EMPLOYED BY THE THREE GAMS OF THE PADAMS WHO CAME FROM DAMRO TO SADIYA TO SEE MR. DUNDAS.

Photo] [*Colonel Lumsden.*

THE GAM OF KEBANG.

THE PADAM GAMS FROM DAMRO WHO VISITED MR. DUNDAS AT SADIYA.
The central figure is the leading gam of this section of the Abors.

The overtures for peace from the northern tribesmen were the sequel to a visit paid to Damro in September of last year by the chiefs of four lesser groups of the Padam Abors, who had been informed that representations at Sadiya would pass unheeded unless they were made through Damro, as that centre, which, hitherto, had maintained a defiant attitude, was the principal sept of the tribe. The value of the plea made in the existing circumstances therefore was very questionable. After giving a patient hearing to the three gams, Mr. Dundas explained that if the Padams were innocent of any complicity in the murders they had nothing to fear; while, if they wished their asseverations of good faith to prove acceptable to him, they must be accompanied by a manifestation of the tribes' readiness to pay taxes, and to provide working parties for road-making—two duties which up to the present they had declined to carry out. Mr. Dundas's words were weighty; but their justness struck home on the three gams, eliciting their prompt and entire agreement.

From this audience the gams, accompanied by Mr. W. T. Ballantine and a suitable escort of military police, as has been mentioned, had set out by canoe to Jonakmukh to pay their respects to Major-General Bower. Arriving at headquarters on November 14th the men repeated to Major-General

Bower and Mr. Bentinck, the Political Officer attached to the Main Column, the statements that they had made to Mr. Dundas. In reply they were told that the column would pay a friendly visit to Damro, and that the Padams would be expected to have the road open and in readiness for the occasion.

In this direction it may be of interest to explain the symbols employed by these hill-people. A stone signifies the gravity of any matter ; a chili means anger ; a piece of coal or burnt clay implies extreme urgency ; a piece of burnt wood indicates incendiarism if the opportunity should occur ; a sharpened dhao reveals the intentions of the sender ; a dhao with blunted edge shows that the quarrel has been made up and peace restored ; an unsharpened dhao and a piece of aconite carries the warning that the sender's feelings are very much upset ; anything pretty such as a white flower or a piece of white cotton denotes good-will. Messages are usually sent in very diminutive cane baskets ; if a native should find in his field or in his house a basket containing a scrap of aconite, a chili, and a bit of burnt stick, it is usually wise for him to prepare for trouble.

A curious instance of the comprehensive character of messages sent by these means came to light on the way to Pongging. A miniature stockade with a small trench in front of it was discovered across the path. Two broken arrows and a gateway made of the boughs of a particular tree were in the stockade. The Abor who was responsible for the erection of this symbol explained that the smallness of the stockade signified weakness; that the trench represented the frontier line of the village in regard to the men of hostile Kebang; that the broken arrows showed that the village did not desire war, while the leaves on the bough of the tree, which was called "Fang," indicated peace. Somewhat similar to this is the practice when the villagers are expecting attack, of placing a dismembered pig across the path by which the enemy must come to show that the invaders will be cut to pieces if they give the chance. Of these signs of the times enough, perhaps, has been written to show how grave would have been the significance of the different colours of the envelopes to the villagers of Rotung when the Miri runner flourished them before them.

With the cessation of the rains on the sixteenth, it required only a touch of sun to charge the vale of the Dihang with heavy, impalpable mist that rolled up alike from plain, forest and river gorge in great volume. The jungle, of course, was drenched and only the echo of a thousand little waters where they dripped from the trees and raced down the hill-side at first was heard. Still there was the problem of the road; and, again, there were reconnaissances so, early on the morning of November 17th, Major-General Bower and the headquarters staff, accompanied by three companies of the 8th Gurkhas, explored the gorge of the Lelek River, that cut across the immediate line of advance, and generally reconnoitred the country towards Rotung. A four-foot path which wound round the head of a couple of deep nullahs and ended in a kotal some three thousand feet high had been cleared by the Sappers and Miners for four miles in the direction of the Lelek. From the kotal descent to the Lelek valley was gained by a native track that registered a declivity of nearly one foot in three in a sudden drop of over thirteen hundred feet. The way down ran through a belt of thick bamboo forest, but the rise from the Lelek River to the summit of the next ridge was a sheer "hanging-on-by-thumbnails" climb. At the top the road-makers were negotiating a difficult passage, though beyond again to Rotung the country was open and under cultivation. Nearer to hand, however, the sounds of falling stones showed that the Abors were keeping watch upon their dauntless enemy, signs of their presence which, as the reconnaissance returned, were to assume more definite shape, having been supplied a little previously through the discovery of a machan in a tree near the Lelek stream.

The incident in question occurred where a party

of Rotung men, concealed in ambush a little below the line of march, had fired into the "brown" as the column was checked in crossing a makeshift bridge of logs over the gorge. With rare luck the bowmen managed to bag an officer, no less than Captain J. R. Hutchison, the plucky adjutant of the Assam Valley and Surma Valley Light Horse, and to escape with the loss of only one man killed though many rifles were emptied after them. Captain Hutchison, by reason of his stature, which is rather over six feet, offered too good a mark to the elusive archers. While one bolt hummed past his shoulders, another passed through his thigh ; though, as became an adjutant of Light Horse, the wounded officer proceeded to give a striking example of coolness and resource. Borrowing the kukri of the nearest Gurkha and without removing his pipe, he sliced off the poisoned head of the arrow, withdrew its shaft, and was applying his own first aid when the doolie came up to carry him off. Thanks to clever nursing, a brave heart and a sound constitution, Captain Hutchison rallied to complete recovery, though there were days in the period of getting well when things looked very black for the fate of the leg which had been so seriously wounded.

As the result of the casualty to Captain Hutchison, the last officer to join us as he was the first to get wounded, and universally liked for his keenness and good spirits, a further reconnaissance swept through the region on the eighteenth. Beyond discharging a few chutes from the crests of their hills, the enemy gave no chance and the columns returned to camp to prepare for the march to Rotung which was to begin at an early hour on the following day. The march was on bivouac scale, every one carrying two days' rations on his person. Transport was restricted to one hundred and seventy coolies who carried the kits which were reduced to one warm coat and blanket per man.

Marching in light order, the column left at a quarter past six on November 19th, and followed for the first few miles the four-foot track to which allusion has already been made. Swinging round the face of the gorge, the force passed over the bridge which had been the scene of Captain Hutchison's wound. Descending to the bank of the Lelek stream the column halted while Gurkha picquets and a telephone party of Lieutenant Knight's went forward to crown some hills in front. Information to hand tended to show that the enemy was in force between the existing position of the column on the banks of the Lelek River and Rotung. Caution was essential, and the Gurkha picquets on the heights and the screen of Gurkha and Naga scouts in advance were reinforced. With the Gurkha scouts were the war dogs, and it was one of these that first gave warning that there was a serpent in this Eden of dense forest, verdant-clad cliffs and singing river. The discovery of a small barricade on the other side of the stream, of another post of observation in a tree with a litter of arrow shavings below it and a newly-cut path behind it, read a moral and adorned a tale—but the enemy had bolted. Meanwhile, as the column rested by the river, Lieutenant Knight's telephone party had clambered to the crest of the opposing range and reported that the advance could proceed.

Leaving the baggage under guard by the Lelek River, the column began to swing itself up the face of some five hundred feet of precipice to which adhesion was obtained as much by will power as by any other means. The climb led to a ridge, razor-edged and dropping on the far side nearly perpendicularly to the valley of the Egar River. Once again there was a halt, while the advance scouts slipped down the khud to the Egar stream, and the telephone linked up the baggage train by the banks of the Lelek River with the force on the ridge. When communication was established the main column followed the van down the khud, and the baggage closed up on the ridge. Arriving at the Egar River, Major-General Bower decided to halt for the night where he had then arrived, as the spot, though little more than a mass of boulders, was large enough to contain the force and near enough to enable the coolies on the ridge and by the Lelek River to reach him before darkness set in.

While Major Hutchinson was directing the arrangement for the night's camp and Lieutenant Knight had halted on the ridge to repair a fault in the telephone cable, Major-General Bower, accompanied by his Orderly Officer Captain Smithers, the Intelligence Officer Captain Hore, the Provost Marshal Captain Becher, together with some twenty men of the 8th Gurkhas including Lieutenant Kennedy and Subadar Jaichand Thakur, and commanded by Lieutenant Buckland, had moved forward up the steep face of a neighbouring hill with a view to locating the position of a stockade, the presence of which was reported while it was believed to be unoccupied. The party had climbed some two hundred yards up the hill-side and were within fifty yards of their objective which apparently rested on the edge of a skeer precipice. It did prove, too, to be unoccupied and, as later circumstances showed, to have been built as an advanced stockade, specially designed so as to hold any attacking force beneath the arrow fire and rock chutes of a larger one in juxtaposition with it.

The larger stockade was built with its right flank resting on an inaccessible height, and was most cunningly contrived in a commanding position, where every advantage had been taken of the fold of the ground. A cross-flanking, enfilading and a frontal fire could be directed from it on any advancing force; while some forty yards away a flanking bastion was furnished with rock chutes—formidable and expressive! Both stockades had been built by the Rotung people immediately after the massacre of the three coolies who were returning from Mr. Williamson's camp. They were shown afterwards to have been held at this time by Rotung men who somehow always seemed to provide the enemy's firing line with the most courageous and stubborn fighters.

The character of the position confronting the reconnoitring party was being examined by Major-General Bower when, as if to remove any possible doubt as to its true nature, a gun-shot rang out and Lal Bahadur, the survivor from the attack on Doctor Gregorson at Panggi and now acting as guide to the column, staggered and collapsed, while blood gushed from a jagged hole in his breast. A second later the contents of an enormous rock chute clattered down the gorge, missing only by a few inches the whole of Major-General Bower's party.

With the first report of the firing from the hill-side every one in the camp on the Egar River had dashed for stations. A few minutes later Lieutenant Knight and his party, with the greatest energy, had run up a telephone cable to the position occupied by Major-General Bower who, with those with him, was receiving in the fullest Abor measure the honours of war. As the arrows fell in showers about the headquarters group, and the music of the Gurkhas' rifles blended with the more sonorous crashes of half a dozen rock chutes, which swept in savage succession down the precipitous approach, a tiny trickle of casualties showed itself among the expeditionary party. Major-General Bower himself had an arrow wound in the hand ; Lal Bahadur a bullet in the chest while, in sublime disregard for the importance of his office, Captain Becher, Provost Marshal was struck on the head by a boulder, the force of which sent him spinning down the hill. Moreover, the fusillade was getting hotter every minute ; and, as the position was close, the enemy defiant and both their bullets and their bolts were falling about the troops in the camp, a clearing process was imperative.

Dividing his little party Major-General Bower, who had been joined by Major Hutchinson, chief staff officer, Captain Melville, principal medical officer, and Captain Poole, D.S.O., the official press-correspondent, ordered Lieutenant Buckland, Lieutenant Kennedy with Subadar Jaichand Thakur and a few men to climb the hill in an attempt to outflank the stockade. Obeying the order with alacrity, the flanking party worked its way up the cliff in full view of the defenders of the stockade and in the face of continued arrow fire, supplemented by the contents of several rock chutes. Separating after a little into two bodies, Lieutenant Buckland, Lieutenant Kennedy and four men made for the advanced stockade, while Subadar Jaichand Thakur with six men swarmed up the high hill which held the right flank of the main stockade, and, at the same time, commanded the line of advance. During this climb, which similarly was within eyeshot of the enemy in the stockade, the Subadar's party became the target for flight after flight of arrows. It was also only by the rarest good fortune that they escaped being crushed by the masses of rock which were tumbled upon them, the contents of one chute actually sweeping right over the gallant native officer who was leading the attempt. Undeterred by the warmth of their reception the Subadar and his party manfully persevered, finally winning their way to a point from which the whole position of the enemy was outflanked and over-reached.

Meanwhile, as Subadar Jaichand Thakur swarmed up the right flank of the big stockade, Lieutenant Buckland and Lieutenant Kennedy, brushing aside the few difficulties presented by the advanced post, turned their attention to the left flank of the main stronghold. The task was hazardous, the more so as one after another the contents of the chutes came tumbling upon them, one, indeed, carrying away a Gurkha sepoy though happily inflicting on him only a few bad bruises. Menaced on each flank, and by Major-General Bower's party in front as they were, the enemy clung with splendid obstinacy to their position, though, as they did so, the flanking parties gradually, and in circumstances requiring no small degree of coolness and courage, were achieving their purpose. Just at the moment of triumph, with a view to facilitating the out-flanking parties, a request was telephoned to camp for the two seven-pounders, Castor and Pollux, a maxim and additional Gurkhas, though before any troops could arrive the tenacity of the Subadar and his men, coupled with the steadiness of the movement executed by Lieutenant Buckland and Lieutenant Kennedy, had carried the day. The stockade had fallen, being reached, rushed and captured in a fierce spasm of desperate fighting. Lieutenant Buckland was the first to drop across the rampart of tree trunks and rocks which formed the front of the position; the coolness and determination of Subadar Jaichand Thakur being rewarded by the bestowal upon him of the Third Class of the Military Division of the Indian Order of Merit.

Beyond the stockade, the defences of which were a network of pitfalls, where several chutes still waited to be sprung and eight Abors lay dead, the foe were in full flight up the hill. Gathering his party together Lieutenant Buckland scrambled after them as rapidly as the dense jungle and the precipitous slopes of the hill permitted, eventually coming up with a number of them. Two who were clad in khaki coats, which were supposed to have been taken from the followers who were murdered near Rotung, and were mistaken for sepoys, escaped. Two others were killed: one being shot by Lieutenant Kennedy with his revolver as he wrestled with Subadar Jaichand Thakur. With the fight over, attention was given to the surrounding heights where a dozen undischarged chutes were destroyed and a few additional bodies were found. Other dead must have been removed for the enemy admitted, at a later date, a loss of eighteen killed and many wounded as the result of the fight. When the scouting parties returned a chain of picquets was posted, one of the seven-pounder guns and a telephone being mounted on the stockade. By nightfall all precautions were completed; and the force dropped back, tired, hungry and very happy, to its bivouac by the river.

The fight at Egar stockade was only a temporary check in the advance to Rotung whither, early on November 20th, the move was resumed. On the hills beyond the scene of the fight the scouting parties reported the presence of more stockades, booby traps and fugitive bands of the enemy. Nothing happened, however, to disturb the peaceful progress of the column. The booby traps were released by the scouts; the stockades proved to be empty and the enemy held discretion to be the better part of valour—and disappeared. From the crests of the hills a view as far as Kebang was obtained, for the jungle had been cleared and the hills were under cultivation. In the middle distance, less than two miles away, there was what remained of Rotung. Overnight it had been burnt and it was now merely charred and smouldering ashes; a pillar of smoke to the country-side before the face of God. Curiously enough Rotung's punishment had come from the Abors themselves for, when the day had been lost at the Egar stockade, the village had been burnt by the men of Panggi in retribution for the troubles Rotung's misconduct had brought on the land.

In a measure it was kind of the men of Panggi to burn Rotung. It saved the expedition the trouble of doing it. At the same time, it placed a well disinfected area at the disposal of the troops. The site was ideal, being both large and spacious as the village had contained some forty houses and held some three hundred people at the time of its destruction. Well sheltered from the wind, with excellent views south, west and north, and standing some eleven hundred feet on a slight slope, it was quickly converted to the needs of a camp.

CHAPTER XV

Crossing the Dihang—Fight at Kekar Monying—Burning of Sissin and Babuk—Side River—Puak Post—Towards Kebang—Burning of Kebang—Advance to Yambung.

WITH the arrival of the column at Rotung, a very cursory examination of the country ahead was sufficient to show that it would be eminently injudicious for the force to advance any farther before the line of communications between Rotung and Renging was in working order. It was also necessary to replenish stores and to issue additional warm clothing to the troops, for the light scale on which all ranks were existing was causing considerable discomfort. Up to the present the sepoys were in possession of one blanket, one great-coat, one waterproof sheet, and a single pair of boots. The heavy going, the rains and the daily use of the same articles had worked havoc with them. In many cases—though the official span of life allotted to a pair of ammunition boots in a campaign is four months—the footgear had given out, and the men were marching bare-footed.

While the energies of the Sappers and Miners and of the Pioneers were concentrated on the road,

Major-General Bower pushed out reconnaissances in all directions, achieving some very satisfactory results. The first of these scouting trips occurred on November 21st, when a small party of the 1st Battalion of the 8th Gurkhas managed to kill six Abors in a brief encounter, bringing back as trophies of the little fight a muzzle-loading musket, a quantity of Mr. Williamson's cartridges, and a large stock of poisoned arrows. On the same day, too, another party came across two stockades which had been abandoned and a number of chutes, all of which were destroyed.

On the following day, Captain Molesworth and a party of the 8th Gurkhas, accompanied by Captain Hore as Intelligence Officer, reconnoitred the Kalek road, returning with the news that the enemy were gathering in strength about a position which lay a few miles to the front of the column. From the distance it seemed a huge outcrop of rock, bold and formidable, that rose sheer up from the side of the Dihang. It was called Kekar Monying, which meant in the native language, Black Bad Place, for it possessed the reputation of being the worst bit of country in Aborland. The rock lay on the right bank of the river, and, as the valley narrowed to a gorge just beyond where the mass loomed up, completely dominated the line of approach from the south. On the left bank, nearly opposite the enemy's position, rose Sissin Hill, which offered an admirable coign of advantage to any attacking force. More remote and on the left rear flank of the Kekar Monying itself were the Babuk ridges.

Acting on Captain Molesworth's information, Major-General Bower, Major Hutchinson and the rest of the headquarters staff, escorted by a company of the 8th Gurkhas, moved out a short distance along the Kalek path on November 23rd, in order to get a view of Kekar Monying. Two days later, a force under Lieutenant-Colonel Murray again visited Kalek region, marching to Kalek itself, which lay some five miles off. Except for a mere handful of the enemy, who retreated as the troops arrived, the village was found to be deserted. The place numbered some fifty-five houses, all of which were burnt.

While the enemy were assembling at Kekar Monying, they were neglecting at the same time no opportunity of attacking any unprotected parties of road-makers, surveyors or signallers that offered a possible target for their arrows, much as they were missing no chance of carrying off large sections of the telephone and telegraph cables when the occasion presented itself. These forays were beaten off, but they served to show that, though the Main Column was forging forward and the enemy falling back, the Abors were still a grave menace to the lines of communication. Accordingly it was decided to strengthen the road posts as opportunity offered. The chance of doing this came almost immediately, for intelligence was suddenly received that the gams of the Galongs were in treaty with Colonel Fisher, and that an end of the fighting in that region had been reached. When the terms of peace were settled, and the tranquillity of the Ledum region was assured, the Ledum Column was withdrawn to the main line of advance.

Under the arrangement which ordained the break-up of Colonel Fisher's force, one hundred and fifty of the Lakhimpur Military Police were left as garrison at Mishing and a similar number posted to Balek. Colonel Fisher, with two companies of the 1st Battalion of the 2nd Gurkha Rifles and all the Pioneers, who had been serving with the Ledum Column, joined the lines of communication, while Major Lindsay, Lieutenant McCleverty and Dr. Falkner, with two companies of the 1st Battalion of the 2nd Gurkhas, one seven-pounder gun and one maxim, proceeded to Rotung. The march of Major Lindsay's party was entirely unopposed. The force accomplished some thirty miles in three days over country that, at the moment, was quite unknown and presented the usual obstacles of dense jungle and steep hills. On the first day the little column covered eight miles; on the second day it advanced an additional eighteen miles, when many sharp ascents and steep declivities were negotiated ; while, on the third day, it had to turn a strong position on a hill-top and to destroy a number of rock chutes before the march could be resumed. In the end the force arrived at Rotung on December 2nd, as preparations for the attack on the enemy's position at Kekar Monying were being pushed to completion.

While the work proceeded, Major-General Bower assembled the officers at headquarters and explained to them the plan of the forthcoming attack. It appeared that there was to be a force operating on the left bank or right flank, which was of course a trans-river force, a second force on the right bank or left flank, and a supporting body which was to deliver the main attack. So far as was possible, the two flanking parties were to seize the hills on the left and right of the enemy's position, while the main column slowly advanced along the edge of the right bank of the river. As the river flowed between the two bodies operating on the right and left flanks respectively, the plan was bold, and depended for its result on the success of the inter-communications. Each column, therefore, was accompanied by several thousand yards of telephone cable and helios—some fifteen miles of cable being used altogether.

To give effect to this plan, the river had to be crossed and, as it flowed at this point with great velocity and was broken up by many rapids and whirlpools, the difficulties in the way of a successful attack were very great. The breadth of the stream was one hundred and seventy-five yards at its narrowest point; and the only possible landing-place on the left bank was a patch of sand, invisible from the enemy's stockade and lying between rugged cliffs which towered two hundred feet above the water. The approach to the riverside on the right bank was by a path that was nowhere more than twelve inches wide and overhung a precipice three hundred feet deep.

It was hoped that the crossing would present no trouble, and a party of Lieutenant Knight's signallers and three companies of the 8th Gurkhas assembled on the afternoon of November 30th at the water's edge to make the passage. As it happened, however, no cable was put across on this day, as the line attached to a Berthon boat, which was towing the cable, broke just as the Berthon boat, with Lieutenant Cave-Brown and four Sappers and Miners aboard, reached the opposite bank. All efforts to re-establish communication failed for the time and, though work went on during the night, the attempts continued to be unavailing. A heavy fog on the morning of December 1st enabled the work to be renewed; but when, at noon, the mist dispersed and no definite success had been achieved, it was decided to abandon all ideas of secrecy and to proceed with the work throughout the day. In spite of everything that could be done, the varying nature of the current proved insuperable, and a second day passed without the party who were stranded on the far bank either being relieved or reinforced. All through the ensuing night, too, the work was unabating, success coming at last when a light wire was got across as dusk fell on December 2nd. For the moment nothing more could be done.

The crossing of the Dihang commenced at a few minutes after five o'clock on December 3rd, when Captain Coleridge and three hundred men, consisting of three companies of the 8th Gurkhas, sixty men of the 2nd Gurkhas, the Assam Valley and the Surma Valley Light Horse detachment, a telephone party and two maxims, embarked in parties of fifteen on rafts, made out of waterproof ration bags which had been stuffed with straw. Each journey took about a quarter of an hour to accomplish ; and, as the night was clear and the moon bright, the details of the right flank party were safely transported by a quarter to eleven.

Though no attempt was made by the Abors to check the landing of the right flank party, they very quickly made their presence felt. Quite suddenly—at a little before three in the morning—as the troops were climbing to their positions, the enemy made a desperate sortie from two directions against the force. Advancing to the attack with loud war-cries, they charged with the utmost gallantry, using both swords and guns in their attempt. Owing to the rapidity and dash of the enemy's movement, two sepoys of the 2nd Gurkhas were killed, while two others were slashed with swords, the one on his rifle and the other on his great-coat, before any one could realize what was happening. Short and sharp though it may have been, the attack was admirably delivered, and was pressed well home by an enemy who took every advantage of the rocks and trees, and of the shadows of the hills, while showing to advantage as a courageous fighter. In the end, of course, after a brief rifle fire, by way of return for the flights of hissing arrows which seemed to come at the moment from anywhere and everywhere, the foe was repulsed; the bodies of three Abors being found afterwards on the field. With the retirement of the attackers peace closed in on the scene, and half-an-hour later Captain Coleridge's little force reached its assigned position on the crest of Sissin Hill, where it lay, awaiting the dawn that was to be so pregnant with interest for the column.

As Captain Coleridge was scrambling to his position, preparations were afoot in Rotung camp for the dispatch of the left flank party and of the main body. At dawn, Captain Giffard with the left flank party, composed of three companies of the 8th Gurkhas and a party of Lieutenant Knight's signallers, marched off, while shortly afterwards headquarters and the details of the main body dropped down to within a few hundred yards of the big rock. By sunrise the main body and the right flank were in position ; but, owing to the difficulties in its way, the left flank party had not yet reported its arrival. Communication was proceeding by telephone, however, between the three forces ; and, as a dense mist obscured the whole valley, it was decided to await the arrival of Captain Giffard's party at its appointed station before delivering the assault. Unfortunately by mid-morning the mist cleared from the river and rolled back from the hill-tops, when, as the mantle of the fog drew off, the enemy's position and the presence of the attacking forces were revealed at one and the same time. Although the left flank party was not yet quite in position, further delay was impossible, and the engagement opened with a salvo of artillery and rifle fire from the main body, and of maxims from the right flank.

Under cover of the saluting guns the main body advanced slowly, when it was seen that the position before the troops was somewhat singular. The rock was precipitous ; its flanks were dominated by steep hills, which offered untold opportunity for the discharge of chutes. The outlines of a large stockade could be seen on the crest of the main position, while other works were adjacent, one and all being held in great force. Altogether the prospect in front of the column was hopeful, for, if the place were a "bad" one, it at least had the promise of returning the good bag for which every one so devoutedly prayed. The actual pivot of the position, the Kekar Monying itself, rose some three hundred feet in the air and was some three hundred feet in length. Broadly speaking, it was just a natural fortress of vast strength, crowned on the crest of the hill by a stockade which communicated with a nullah in the rear which, in turn, afforded a line of retreat to the jungle. The enemy, who swarmed behind the defences, were drawn in the main from Rotung and Kebang. They seemed fierce and eager, and were full of confidence, as the only means of direct approach to their position was by a path barely six inches in width that passed below a line of fifty rock chutes that could be seen but a very few yards above it.

From the frontal view of the position it seemed that there was the promise of a fight, and it was hoped that the opportunity for inflicting a severe lesson on the foe had really, and at last, arrived. The spirits of the attacking force not unnaturally rose in anticipation of the fight, but the enemy decided to retreat, and retire they did, leaving three dead behind them as hostages to fortune. At a later date it was discovered that no less than thirty had been killed, eighteen being Kebang men and twelve Rotung men, the majority falling to the maxim fire of the detachment from the Assam Valley and Surma Valley Light Horse, who belonged to Captain Coleridge's party on the right flank. Curiously enough, the shell fire was almost ineffectual, the fire of the maxims being more telling, since from the position which the right flank force had taken up it had been able to cover both the rear of the stockade as well as the line of retreat.

With the fall of the stockade, which took place within an hour and a half of the opening of the bombardment, an immediate pursuit of the enemy was decided upon. Four companies of the 8th Gurkhas under Lieutenant-Colonel Murray, D.S.O., accompanied by Captain Hore, Intelligence Officer, proceeded along the right bank of the river to Babuk, which they burnt. At the same time Captain Coleridge and a party from the right flank force moved along the left bank as far as the hostile village of Sissin, which was also burnt, the remainder of the force advancing meanwhile to a bivouac on the banks of the Side River. From the Side River, Major-General Bower moved on December 6th to Puak, some three miles farther on, where the formation of the hills offered facilities for the establishment of a post that would serve as a half-way house between Rotung and Kebang. Puak camp was not established without some objection from the Abors, however, who, on the night of December 7th, again essayed to rush the lines under cover of the darkness. Their attempt was driven off, while the traces of blood left behind showed that it had not been without its tally of casualties.

As Major-General Bower moved to Puak, Lieutenant-Colonel Murray returned from Babuk, and Captain Coleridge recrossed the Dihang from Sissin, after his successful foray along the left bank, ample evidence of the complete rout of the enemy being forthcoming from the reports of these two officers. Signs of flight had been noticed in all directions. Weapons, food-bags and innumerable rock chutes had been abandoned ; tree-posts, stockades and villages had been deserted ; and, though it was obvious that the country had been very carefully prepared, it was none the less evident that, at the last moment, the Abors had lacked the courage to stand by their original intentions. Moreover, it seemed that they were taking to heart the punishment which Major-General Bower was inflicting on them, a curious instance in this connection being afforded as the column was preparing to move from Rotung, by the release from Pongging, a Minyong village on the left bank of the Dihang, of Narin Singh Thapa,

PUAK POST.

VIEW OF THE DIHANG RIVER FROM SIGNAL HILL TWO MILES WEST OF YAMBUNG HILL, LOOKING NORTH.

one of the survivors of the massacre and the servant of Dr. Gregorson. After the murder of his master, he had hidden in the jungle until he was captured by the people of Pongging, who had kept him in captivity until events proved that the tribesmen were unable to oppose the advance of the columns.

In spite of the successful issue of the operations against Kekar Monying, the general rejoicing was tempered by the receipt of unexpected news of the death of Captain Alan M. Hutchins, an officer who had performed very distinguished services in connection with the Ledum Column. Captain Hutchins, who was Assistant Commandant of the Lakhimpur Military Police, died at the base hospital at Dibrugarh on December 3rd from pneumonia, which he had contracted at Mishing. Belonging to the 3rd Queen Alexandra's Own Gurkha Rifles, the deceased officer was attached to the Eastern Bengal and Assam Military Police. He joined the service in 1903, and reached the rank of Captain in August 1910. From the beginning he had taken his work very seriously, and was transferred at his own request to the Military Police for the love of his profession. He had done much work in connection with the earlier phases of the Abor expedition, and in May, after the assassination of Mr. Williamson and Doctor Gregorson, he moved up to Pasighat and kept watch over the border. He was acting with the Ledum Column when he contracted the chill from which he subsequently succumbed.

Captain Hutchins was the only British officer to die from the vicissitudes of the campaign, though Lieutenant-Colonel MacIntyre; Major Wilson; Mr. Scott, Political Officer of the Ledum Column; Lieutenant Marsh of the 2nd Gurkhas; Lieutenant Ross of the 8th Gurkhas; Captain Hutchison and Trooper Henning of the Assam Valley and Surma Valley Light Horse, all became, from one cause or another, unwilling inmates of the base hospital. The rank and file also suffered somewhat severely from fevers, mumps, and chills, on one occasion eighty-two men out of a detachment of one hundred and eighty being down with mumps at the same time.

With the capture of Kekar Monying the Abor Field Force was within appreciable distance of its objective, and so soon as the road had been carried across the face of the rock and brought up from the Side River to Puak, it was intended to start. Every effort was made by the road-makers to press on with the work of construction. While the Sappers and Miners and the Pioneers improved and removed, various small columns reconnoitred the country through which the advance was to pass. Numerous stockades were discovered and destroyed on these occasions, one measuring no less than forty yards in length, while innumerable rock chutes were released. Similarly giant barricades, entanglements of trees and rocks, foot-pits and panjeed paths were cleared away. Unhappily there was no enemy ; and, though there were many signs of recent occupation, no resistance was offered.

Three roads led to Kebang ; an upper track which was circuitous and wound inland past many villages to the Abor citadel, a middle track that was steep and narrow and gave barely a foothold in many places, and a lower road which clung to the river bank, and required a great deal of attention before it could be converted to the needs of the column. Choice was made of the upper and middle tracks ; and when, at dawn on December 9th, the striking force marched off, it advanced in two columns moving parallel so far as circumstances permitted.

One column, consisting of three companies of the 8th Gurkhas under Lieutenant-Colonel Murray, proceeded by the upper route, climbing in doing so a long series of steep hills on the left flank, the larger force, under Major-General Bower, keeping to the middle line and maintaining touch by means of telephonic communication. All went well with the columns ; and though the customary signs of the times were found on all sides, the stockades were untenanted and the rock chutes deserted. Where any of the enemy were noticed, they were either out of range or in actual flight. Such discretion was depressing. Nevertheless it happened that no incident of any kind occurred to mar the peaceful advance of the force and, accordingly, Kebang was reached a little after noon in a march of six hours.

Kebang lay on a plateau some 3000 feet up from the Dihang in a position that was invisible until the village was almost within touch. It was large and dirty ; numerously inhabited and holding about one hundred houses, which meant a population of about seven hundred souls. The huts were well built, and there were two large moshups for the unmarried fighting-men, where a large quantity of bows and arrows were discovered. Much of the ground about it had been laid out with patches of plantains and chilies.

Although the village was defended by a monster stockade, and all the paths leading to it had been prepared with *panjees*, man-traps and any obstacle which the wily Abor could devise, the place was surrendered without an effort being made to defend it, though the departing villagers certainly laid it in waste. The stockade alone was worthy of a better fate. It was fifty yards long, fourteen feet high, four feet thick, with a moat which was about twelve feet deep on the outside, the whole forming a singularly unique rallying-point for a final stand. Yet, in spite of its undoubted strength, of the vaunted might of Kebang, and of the trouble which the adoption of guerrilla tactics would have caused to the advancing column, the Abors melted away and could be seen in groups in the village of Panggi, on the far side of the river.

The arrival of the British column at Kebang established something of a record, for it was the first time that any force, large or small, had entered the place in the sixty years of its existence. As its inhabitants had already vanished, all that it was necessary for the column to do was to apply a torch, which was done as quickly as possible. The village made a good bonfire, and was swept clean by the flames and rendered sweet in the process. There was no alternative to the course adopted, for only by the capture and ultimate destruction of their chief stronghold could the recalcitrant Abors be given a lasting lesson. When the whole place had been destroyed, Major-General Bower moved from the plateau to a temporary bivouac on its jungle-clad slope. From this camp, on the following day, December 10th, he proceeded to the banks of the Yambung River, some two miles and a half farther on. Beyond, on the far side of the river, lay Komsing, Panggi and other centres to which punishment had to be meted out; and, accordingly, headquarters halted, while the force settled down to the life of a permanent camp, and was pleasantly satisfied with the suggested prospect of a long rest.

CHAPTER XVI

Advance to Komsing—Minor Operations—Peace Overtures—His Majesty's Christmas Greeting—Dihang River Column—Yamne River Column—Unveiling of Memorials to Mr. Williamson and Doctor Gregorson.

WITH the arrival of the Abor Field Force at Kebang, Major-General Bower may be said to have attained successfully the principal object of his expedition. At the same time, though the columns were organised with the idea of punishing the murderers of Mr. Noel Williamson, Dr. Gregorson and their party, the operations had certain supplementary reasons for their existence which had now to be considered. In the first case the Government of India wished to establish friendly relations with those villages that were not concerned in the massacre; in the second case it was anxious to open up a country which, hitherto, had been a sealed book to every one; and, finally, it desired to demarcate a line of frontier between China and India. As matters stood, no white man had ever previously visited the country north of Kebang; and though it must be necessarily a labour of years before our knowledge of the region is complete, and we can feel we possess the confidence of the savage peoples frequenting it, the expedition was in a position to reap the first fruits.

Before anything could be done to establish a cordial understanding with the tribesmen there still remained a certain amount of " rounding-up " to be carried out by punitive parties. Consequently, as soon as the camp at Yambung had been put in order, several small columns took the field. The first force to start off on its pilgrimage of awarding penance and adjusting peace was one commanded by Lieutenant-Colonel Murray, who had with him five companies of the 8th Gurkhas. The objective of this column, which left on December 13th, was Yemsing, which village, with that of Kebang already destroyed, had stimulated the resistance of the Ledum tribesmen. With the destruction of Kebang the principal malefactor on the right bank of the river was eliminated from the situation, but a clean sweep of the warring centres had to be made ; and, accordingly, Yemsing, like Rengging, Rotung, Sissin, Babuk and Kalek, was given over to the flames.

Yemsing lay about nine miles distant from Yambung. Though the enemy did not oppose Colonel Murray's advance, they were careful to cut and carry off several sections of his telephone cable, so that no communication between the column and army headquarters was possible for three days. The village was found to be deserted with the exception of a handful of fighting-men, four of whom were killed and three wounded in the ensuing skirmish. Larger than Kebang, and more straggling, it was defended by a strong stockade and might easily have become the scene of an interesting encounter if the inhabitants had only had the heart to make a stand. From Yemsing Colonel Murray reconnoitred the surrounding country; when, after impressing his presence upon a few isolated groups of fugitive tribesmen with eminently satisfactory testimony to the good shooting of the sepoys, he retraced his steps to Yambung.

While Colonel Murray was attending to Yemsing, a column of three hundred of the 8th Gurkhas under Captain Coleridge was sent in pursuit of the Kebang tribesmen, who were reported to have retired in a westerly direction after the capture of their village. Elsewhere, too, the operations of the field columns were continued, and preparations of a somewhat similar process against Panggi and other villages on the left bank of the river were put in hand. Before anything could be done it was necessary to establish a means of crossing the Dihang. After several days of effort this work was successfully accomplished by Lieutenant Cave-Brown and Lieutenant Chater on December 17th, when, accompanied by a sepoy and a flying cable, these two officers negotiated the stream in a Berthon collapsible boat under cover of the rifles of a party of thirty men of the 8th Gurkhas and two maxims. As it happened little difficulty and no opposition attended the attempt; and, so soon as the cable was properly secured, a raft made of waterproof bags was pressed into service as a ferry. In due course a picquet was landed, a telephone installed, and a blockhouse set up; for, though no Abors were seen, precaution was necessary, as the spot was a favourite crossing for the villagers, both up and down stream.

As these movements were taking place the enemy were amusing themselves by ambuscading any isolated parties of troops that they came across, in attacking convoys, and in destroying the cables of the telegraph and telephone lines. On one occasion three thousand yards of cable were removed; on another the line was cut through in seventeen places, these signs of the times showing that the aggressiveness of the tribesmen had not yet been entirely quelled. For the moment, none the less, no actual movement was made against Panggi, whose inhabitants daily demonstrated their wish for peace by dispatching the headmen of the village to the outskirts of Yambung camp with presents of live pigs, *mithuns*, chickens and eggs, and in any other way that occurred to them. The fate of Panggi, however, lay on the knees of the gods, as its precise share in the responsibility for the massacre still had to be determined.

A feeling was growing that the time had come when the attempt might profitably be made to exchange the arts of war for the crafts of peace. Sooner or later, friendly relations had to be established with the quondam foe; and, with the capture of Kebang, it occurred to many that the right moment had now arrived. The first step in the direction of a cessation of hostilities was taken when three men from Pongging, the village which had harboured Narain Sing Thapa after the massacre, who had been made prisoners near Rotung, were presented with gifts of blankets, salt and food, and after being assured that only guilty villages would be punished, and that any friendliness would be rewarded, were released with instructions to return to their village and bring back their head-men. While these overtures proceeded, the Gams of Komsing and Riu, as the results of the exertions of friendly Pasis already serving with the force, summoned up courage to come and present themselves to Major-General Bower. Their arrival had a touch of tragic humour about it. They were accompanied by a slave behind whom they screened themselves, while he waved a flag, made out of a copy of the Calcutta *Statesman*, as evidence of good-will.

Less humorous was the fate of the Gam of Jaru. Killed by the people of Sissin while he was *en*

A PEACE ENVOY.

An incident at Yambung Camp.

A CAMP IN THE RIVER BED OF THE DIHANG.

route to Rotung camp, his death was avenged by the dispatch of two columns to the scene of the outrage. One column, composed of three hundred rifles of the 8th Gurkhas under Major Wilson, crossed from Yambung on December 21st, while the second column, composed of four companies of the 2nd Gurkhas under Major Sweet, went out from Rotung. Unfortunately neither party saw anything of the enemy, who had fled northwards up the Dihang River, though Major Sweet succeeded in recovering at Sissin some more of the late Mr. Williamson's property. As Sissin had been already burnt, its fields and fruit-trees were laid waste on this occasion : and when, a few days later, another Gam of Jaru started off with a similar object he was permitted to make his way in peace to British headquarters. Upon arrival at Rotung, this Jaru envoy was received impressively, the villagers of Pongging and of Jaru seemingly having combined to shield Mr. Williamson's unfortunate servant from the men of Kebang.

While the fate of Panggi was hanging in the balance, and the field columns were scouring the country in pursuit of the fugitive tribesmen from Kebang, achieving in spite of great efforts somewhat depressing results, an unexpected message from His Majesty King George made every one suddenly realise that Christmas Day had come round again.

All ranks were intensely gratified by the kindly condescension of the gracious message, which was received on Christmas Eve. The royal greetings read as follows :—

"To the General Officer Commanding the Abor expeditionary forces—

"I wish to express to you and all ranks under your command my hearty good wishes for Christmas and the New Year. I watch with interest the steady progress of your columns and look for a successful and speedy termination of the expedition.—George R."

In reply General Bower sent the following telegram :—

"To the Private Secretary of His Imperial Majesty—

"Please convey to His Imperial Majesty the profound gratitude of myself and all ranks for his most gracious message."

After the receipt of His Majesty's dispatch, it was perhaps natural that a happier note should have impressed itself upon the celebration of Christmas Day by the men of the Field Force. The day was observed, of course, as a holiday, and if the fare were not quite seasonable, at least there was no lack of joviality and good-will. Moreover, two days after the receipt of His Majesty's message, headquarters had further cause for rejoicing in a visit from no less a personage in Aborland than the supreme chief of Kebang, Takat Gam. Already old and decrepit, since the events which had brought about the dispatch of the expedition had taken place, Takat Gam had been deposed and had been living under the protection of the Gam of Komsing, who had turned him from his village a few days before the advent of the column at Yambung. As a representative of the Kebang men, Takat was a valuable medium for getting into touch with the tribesmen ; and, though it was obvious that he had lost his power and that he might not be able to exert any influence whatever upon the other villagers, much good was expected from the services which he offered.

Takat Gam was well known to Mr. Williamson, who had treated him with kindness and courtesy. In return, he now promised to use his good-will in securing the speedy and complete submission of Kebang. For what it was worth the offer of the old chieftain was accepted, and it was soon evident that the manner in which the gam had been received had gone a long way towards removing the suspicions which other gams had entertained about the column. At all events the visit of the Gam of Kebang was followed on the next day by the surrender of the Gams of Sissin, who readily agreed to be fined for having caused the death of the Gam of Jaru, and for other misbehaviour. Other gams quickly imitated the lead of those of Kebang and Sissin, until it became daily more apparent that the general submission of the Abors was not very distant.

In view of recent circumstances, however, it was impossible to say what proportion of the statements, made to headquarters about the Kebang tribesmen by the various gams who visited Yambung camp, was true. If the truth were spoken at all by any one of the gams at this time, it seemed to be contained in the repeated remark that the leaders of the onslaught upon Mr. Noel Williamson and Doctor Gregorson had lost their lives while fighting against the Ledum Column. What appeared to be most true was the fact that the leaders, at all events, were not available at this juncture, and that one and all of the gams who attended Major-General Bower expressed with singular unanimity their sense of relief at the break-up of the power of Kebang. Not only did they voice their satisfaction over the downfall of the village that had ruled this part of Aborland for nearly two generations, but each and every one of them welcomed the presence of the column, and begged that parties of troops might be sent on a visit to the various tribal areas. Under these conditions there seemed no reason to delay any longer the task of proceeding with the second phase of the work of the expedition, and active preparations for the dispatch of Missions, which should survey the country and establish friendly relations with the various sections of the tribes at the same time, were at once put in hand.

There were many directions in which it was desired to send small parties, either for survey purposes or for the purpose of paying a visit of inspection to some tribal centre. In regard to the former class there was, in the first place, the valley of the Dihang River, where the problem of the falls and the identity of the Dihang with the Tsan-po awaited settlement. In the second place, there was the valley of the Yamne to be explored ; thirdly, the course of the Siyom River and, finally, that of the Shimang River. There was, too, the general scale of the whole region to be corrected and adjusted to the survey of India ; while, in regard to the tribal centres which it was desirable to visit, such places as Geku, Riga, Damro, Komkar and Parong obviously claimed attention.

At the moment it was only possible to put two survey columns in the field. As no time was to be lost in taking advantage of the situation, they left simultaneously : the Dihang River party from Yambung camp and the Yamne River party from Rotung, on December 27th for their respective objectives. The Dihang River Survey was composed of Mr. A. Bentinck, in political charge ; Mr. Coggin

Browne, Government Geologist; Mr. Milroy, Forest Officer; Captain Hore, Intelligence Officer; Captain Trenchard, R.E., Survey Officer; six surveyors; one hundred rifles of the 8th Gurkhas under the command of Captain Giffard, and one hundred and fifty Naga coolies. The force was rationed for twenty-six days and in addition carried some ten loads of salt for the purpose of purchasing rice. The Yamne River Survey, which was under the charge of Lieutenant-Colonel MacIntyre, was accompanied by sixty rifles of the 2nd Gurkhas under Major Lindsay, with Lieutenant Oakes as Survey Officer. An interesting member of this latter party was Narain Sing Thapa, the survivor of the massacre.

While these Missions—whose work will be described in the next chapter—were proceeding towards their two goals, other parties were preparing to embark on somewhat similar excursions. Of all the columns getting ready for the field, general interest fastened for the nonce on a party of one hundred rifles of the 1st Battalion of the 8th Gurkhas, six British officers, six signallers, and one hundred and fifty Naga coolies that Lieutenant-Colonel Murray was leading to Komsing, where he was to unveil a cairn to the late Mr. Noel Williamson on January 10th. Although Komsing was the actual scene of the murder of Mr. Noel Williamson, the villagers had been let off with a fine, as inquiry showed that they were not accomplices in the crime. Rotung as instigators, and Kebang as participators, were primarily and directly responsible, Komsing only being associated with the affair because the men of Rotung and Kebang had followed Mr. Williamson until they came up with him and killed him in Komsing.

In his melancholy march Colonel Murray followed the path taken by the murdered officer on his last journey from Panggi to Komsing, the column being accompanied by Lal Bahadur, another of the survivors. Colonel Murray took with him a stone on which was carved the following inscription:—

"On this spot was murdered Noel Williamson,
Assistant Political Officer, Sadiya,
March 31st, 1911."

The villagers had been ordered to build a cairn and the stone was set up in it, the site chosen for the memorial being the exact spot where Mr. Williamson had fallen, while by ironic coincidence it faced the moshup, or guard-room, where the young warriors have their quarters and the greybeards instruct the village youth in the arts of fighting and hunting.

The unveiling ceremony was most impressive. On the left of the cairn stood a guard of sixty Gurkha sepoys with their British and Gurkha officers, and near it were the head-men and the villagers. The buglers sounded the "First Post," a general salute followed, and the troops presented arms. The cairn was then unveiled, after which Colonel Murray addressed the head-men, pointing out that for all time the upkeep of the memorial was their duty, and that they would be held responsible for its safety by the Indian Government. At the end of the address the buglers sounded the "Last Post"; when, as the British officers bared their heads, Mr. Williamson's memory received in a soldier's requiem a fitting tribute to the fearlessness with which he had sacrificed his life.

A few days later, with almost identical ceremony, a similar cairn, holding an engraved stone, was unveiled near the spot where Doctor Gregorson had met his fate. The river flood had carried away all traces of the second tragedy, with the exception of a frayed tent-rope; but the cairn was placed high above flood level and will offer its silent testimony for all time to the valour of a good man.

CHAPTER XVII

The Travels of Kinthup—The Problem of the Falls—The Dihang River Survey Party—The Yamne River Survey Party—Captain Molesworth's Party—The Submission of Kebang.

To understand the fascination of the problems presented by the mysteries of the river system of Aborland, it is only necessary to recall the excitement which gathered round the discussion as to the real nature of the Tsan-po some thirty years ago. If, in the long interval that has since elapsed, the Tsan-po has been identified with the Brahmaputra, there is still much to be elucidated about the riverine character of the region before we may regard our knowledge of the subject as at all complete. Briefly stated the question of the eighties was concerned with the precise relationship existing between the Tsan-po of Tibet, the Dihang of Aborland, the Irrawady of Burma, and the Brahmaputra of the Assam basin. At the time it was considered probable that the Tsan-po united with the Irrawady, though, as our knowledge of the region became more sure, it was recognised that it flowed in one continuous channel to the sea through the courses of the Dihang and the Brahmaputra.

No white man, nor any native surveyor, has ever traced the river from Tibet to the Assam frontier; though a few have mapped in the region both north and south of the belt that is still so entirely a terra incognita. Nevertheless the unknown area from north to south is but little more than one hundred and thirty miles in extent, though it is rendered difficult of access from the fact that the river flows at right angles to the mountains, which of themselves are some of the most inaccessible in the world. Such attempts as have been made, too, have proceeded from the north-western side of the water-shed, the recent expedition being one of the few recorded efforts to solve the problem from the south.

Prior to 1880, "G. M. N.," who is not regarded as a particularly trustworthy explorer, accompanied by Kinthup, or K. P., as he is known in the confidential archives of the India Office, reached Gya-La-Sing-Dong by way of Bhutan and Lhasa, while in July 1880, the late Captain Harman dispatched a Chinese lama of Giardong, again in company with Kinthup, to explore the country between the most extreme point reached by "G. M. N." and the Assam border. It is upon this journey that our knowledge of the region in the main depends, though it is to another explorer, Kishen or "A. K.," that the honour of proving that the Tsan-po had nothing whatever to do with the Irrawady by right belongs. "A. K.," after a long journey, in which his footsteps were beset with misfortune at every turn of the path, traversed the area across which the Tsan-po must have flowed if it had had any connection whatever with the Irrawady. "A. K.'s" journey reached eastwards as far as Rima. From this point he retraced his steps, as he was deterred from attempting to enter Assam by the valley of the Lohit, on account of the stories of the ferocity of the intervening Mishmi tribes, with which he was beguiled.

More valuable, because it is almost completely trustworthy, is the story of Kinthup's four years of wanderings in the savage fastnesses of this region. Before starting with his Chinese companion, he had been instructed by Captain Harman to throw a number of marked logs into the Tsan-po at the lowest place reached by the two travellers on the course of that river, Captain Harman, on his side, arranging to have the stream patrolled at the point where the Dihang flows into Assam, by men who would be on the look-out for the logs as they came down with the current.

Kinthup was faithful to his mission ; and, though turned from it by circumstances over which he had no control, he made repeated efforts to give Captain Harman the information he required. Hour after hour, too, for many weary days, the watchers of the gallant Captain Harman took up their stations by the troubled waters of the mighty river; but no message came, the arrangements that had been planned so carefully falling through in the end through the death of Captain Harman from malaria. Kinthup, of course, knew nothing of the death of his master; and, battling with the difficulties of his perilous journey, he clung with splendid courage for four years to the object of his mission.

His experiences were wonderful and afford unique testimony to his faith, loyalty and indomitable spirit. It appears that, shortly after starting, he was betrayed by his Chinese companion, and sold by him as a slave in the Pemakoi country. Kinthup served his time in slavery to a Tibetan household, from where in the end he contrived to escape to take refuge in a monastery. Once again he was sold to slavery and again he escaped; when, with no thought of turning back, he set himself the task of carving and releasing the logs which were to convey to the people on the banks below the proof that the Tsan-po and the Brahmaputra were one and the same stream. By now, of course, Captain Harman was dead; and no one knew aught of the significance of the logs, or remembered anything of the strange figure that had been lost to sight for so many years. In time, too, Kinthup realised for himself the futility of his efforts. Resuming his travels, the devoted explorer gained much further information for the Department of the

Survey of India before he thought of retracing his steps to Lhasa, from where he proceeded by a roundabout course to his home in India, modestly responsible for almost all present knowledge of the region in which he had passed such an adventurous time.

While Krishna proved that the Tsan-po and the Irrawady belonged to separate river systems, the journeys of Mr. Needham in 1886 and 1892, and that of Prince Henry of Orleans, brought further confirmation of the point. From this date then it came to be admitted that, though there was no connecting link between the Tsan-po and the Irrawady, the Tsan-po and the Brahmaputra were one and the same stream, and that the course of the Dihang was the connecting channel between the two rivers.

With this question settled, the next point to be determined was that concerned with the manner in which so vast a volume of water made its way to the plains; whether it swept with impressive grandeur over some enormous waterfall at Pema-koi-chang, or whether it flowed down from the eleven thousand foot elevation of the plateaux of Tibet to the five hundred foot level of the plains of Assam by a long series of rapids. In 1904, during the mission to Lhasa, it was proposed to send an expedition to follow the course of the river to the Assam plains, much as a party was sent westwards under Captain

Ryder and Captain Rawlings to locate its precise source in that direction. Unfortunately the proposal did not find favour with the authorities at the India Office though it was supported strongly enough by the Government of India; and, as Mr. Bentinck's Mission, which explored the course of the Dihang as far as Singging, failed to reach the supposed site of the falls, the question of their existence must continue to rank among the undetermined problems of the geography of this section of Asia.

While it is very much to be regretted that Mr. Bentinck's party failed to solve the problem, no blame can attach to a lack of success in this direction. The task set the Mission was humanly impossible in the time at its disposal and in the conditions which existed, for, when the party arrived at Singging, they found a seventeen thousand foot range of mountains, covered at the time with rapidly accumulating snow, lying between the Mission camp and the supposed position of the falls. To have continued the advance in the face of such a very serious obstacle would have endangered the lives of every member of the party, besides being a feat to which Hannibal's passage of the Alps could fairly be considered as child's play. In connection with the question of the existence of the falls, it is of interest to note that Major-General Bower himself believes that there are no falls. On the other hand Kinthup, in his official memorandum of the journey, writes as follows:—

> "We stopped at Pema-koi-chang three days in search of a road, and as we did not find one retraced our steps. There was a monastery with seven or eight priests at Pema-koi, but no other house. The Tsan-po is two chains distant from the monastery; about two miles further off the river falls over a cliff called Sinji-Chogyal, from a height of about one hundred and fifty feet. There is a big lake at the foot of the falls above which rainbows are always visible."

There is no reason to doubt Kinthup, and the conflict of opinion established by his description and the obiter dicta of other people does not suggest sufficient ground for mistrusting its accuracy. Somewhat similar differences, too, mark such native information as was obtained on the subject by the expedition. The Abors declare that there are no falls. Tibetans, who were serving with the Field Force, state that there are small falls, and beside the falls a large lake. It is improbable that the Abors who were consulted had been far enough afield to make their opinions conclusive; and, as Mr. Bentinck failed in his attempt, the mystery remains, the balance of probability tending in the direction of a series of large rapids with a low fall, in preference to a record-breaking repetition of the Zambesi's masterpiece.

Though the distance which the Dihang River Survey party had to cover in proceeding from Yambung camp to the supposed site of the falls was not very great, the nature of the route was as a closed book to every member of the little column. There was no road, of course, and both villages and patches of cultivation were few and far between, though the clearings were larger and the jungle freer on the upper reaches of the river than on those through which the main force had just come. Heavy mists overhung the river when the party moved out from Army Headquarters on December 27th, and masses of black cloud, rain-charged and evil-looking, lay heavily on the crests of the mountains. Here and there, through the curtain of fog that screened the face of Nature, glimpses were caught of the perpetual snows of the mountain ranges in the east and on the west, while from the open spaces came the moan of the wind and from out of the jungle the pit-a-patter of the rain on the leaves. The prospect was a little dreary and it was useless to deny or to make light of the difficulties which barred the attempt. At the same time, though they were known to be great, it was not thought that they would be sufficient to bring the progress of the column to a halt. Unfortunately, they were greater than all the wiles that the wit of Master Abor could have devised or the mind of man have conceived.

Photo] THE VALLEY OF THE DIHANG RIVER. [*Colonel Lumsden*.

Photo] CATARACT ON THE DIHANG RIVER. [*Colonel Lumsden.*

Photo] A REACH OF THE DIHANG RIVER. [*Colonel Lumsden.*

Day after day Mr. Bentinck's party continued, beating a way against the very face of Nature and frowned down upon by the mountains as, with slow progress, it skirted precipice and river, or, on occasions, was absorbed by the jungle. It was just a march into the sheer and utterly unresponsive unknown, and, before it had proceeded very far, the fogs, torrential rains, and deep snows which made themselves felt as the column daily struggled forward, united in the production of a concatenation of circumstances that showed that it would be impossible for Captain Trenchard and his colleagues to accomplish their object. As it was the column had to rely entirely on its own resources, everything being carried by the coolies who, in addition to portering the stores for the force, had to carry food for themselves as the country supplied nothing at all.

Although the party turned back, it is of interest perhaps to give a brief outline of the march up the valley of the mighty Dihang. From Yambung, the column followed for some five miles a track that ran parallel with the right bank of the river to the village of Pangin, which appeared to be a prosperous centre of about forty houses. The village lay about 1500 feet high in the centre of a considerable area of cultivation and was defended by a strong stockade. Not one of its three hundred inhabitants had ever seen white men before, and the troops were greeted by an enthusiastic crowd of both sexes, who, one and all, appeared only too anxious to assist in laying out the camp. Presents of *mithun*, pigs, chickens and eggs, as well as bowls of native liquor, were forthcoming, the greetings being the more cordial since Pangin was on bad terms with Kebang, because that centre barred the way to the plains. Pangin, therefore, regarded the column as its own deliverer insomuch that the fall of its rival implied that the way was open to the south.

Despite the reception given to the column, the day had not yet dawned when the Abor could be taken entirely on trust. Accordingly, camp was pitched beyond the village, and carefully enclosed within a high zariba. On the morrow the march was resumed, the Mission pushing up across the precipitous slopes of the mountains to Yekshi, where they were well received and whence they crossed the river by native rafts to Komsing. From Komsing a shift was made to Riu, the Komsing people assisting to transport the loads and speeding the column generally on its way. Riu was reached on January 5th. Two days later the little column arrived at Geku, where it halted until January 14th, while it surveyed the surrounding region from an adjacent hill.

From Geku, after a flying visit across the

river to Riga, there was a dash north, through Simong, much good work being done on Simong Hill, Getti, Puging, Rikor, Paling, which carried the head of exploration up to Singging. The distance between Simong and Singging was divided approximately into equal stages between the just-mentioned villages; Singging representing the farthest point reached to the north, while it was also half-way between the Tibetan border and Simong. The falls, if they existed at all, lay a further hundred miles north of Singging. Though the supposed site of the falls could not be visited, the march to Singging none the less produced important results, for the discovery of a big river, flowing into the Dihang from the west and found to be the Sigon, was made; while, away in the distance, was seen for the first time the summit of a 25,000-foot peak, round the base of which the Dihang swept to the south.

In addition to these two "finds" the journey to Singging proved that the prevailing knowledge of the country north of Yambung was quite inaccurate, and that the whole course of the Dihang as indicated on existing maps was in error. So far as being as it was shown, after breaking through the main range it was seen to flow south-south-west to Singging; south-south-east to Geku and south to Kebang, the windings being so incessant that the course nowhere ran from north to south. Many of the bends of the river's course were at right angles with the lie of the hills, the general character of the country showing beyond all doubt, if any at all has existed in recent years, that the Tsan-po and the Dihang were identical streams.

When the Survey party had finished all that it was possible to do at Singging it returned to Geku by its original route ; and, again crossing from Geku to Riga, proceeded to give attention to the villages on the right bank of the Dihang. Near Riga was a peak some 10,000 feet high, from where it was expected that a very useful view could be obtained. Much depended, however, upon the reception which the party was to receive in Riga village, as the place was large, populous, and addicted to slave-dealing.

Up to this point nothing had occurred to interfere with the peaceful progress of the column, and, as it happened, nothing was to occur for, if not enthusiastic, the Riga people were at least friendly, the gams offering much genuine assistance. From Riga, therefore, after a brief halt Mr. Bentinck turned west on a political tour of the Minyong region, accompanied by a single native surveyor, Subadar Shar Jang, no others being available. After halting at Arte Hill for survey work, Mr. Bentinck proceeded to Yibuk, which was the most distant of the villages on the Shimang River. The country was very steep ; broken by sheer descents and sharp rises, and the route of the party lay across the spurs of mountains which gave no foothold, and where a path had either to be cut or else to be blasted. In spite of the difficulties of the road, of sickness among the coolie transport, and the most appalling weather, the column continued on its way, penetrating as far west as Rangku, on the Siyom River, where there was a village of some thirty houses. From Rangku the column turned east to Pareng, which was the largest village on the Shimang River. From Pareng it moved to Riga, whence, after picking up the Survey party, Mr. Bentinck marched down the right bank of the Dihang to Yambung, his Mission at an end.

While Mr. Bentinck's party was proceeding with the survey of the Dihang, somewhat similar work was being carried out by the smaller mission under Colonel MacIntyre which had gone up the Yamne River. Moving out from Rotung on December 27th, this party, after crossing the Dihang, had encamped in the Yamne Valley between Pongging and Jaru with the object of getting into touch with the Panggi villages. From their camp of the first day they moved on to Jaru, where they arrived two days later, cordially greeted by the gams of the village. From Jaru the column proceeded to Peram, which they reached on January 1st, and from where they returned to Rotung.

From Peram, at an elevation of four thousand feet, on the next day, Lieutenant Oakes, who was responsible for the survey work of the party, secured his first glipse of a most instructive panorama. Away to the north-east, at the head of the Yamne Valley, the snow-clad peaks of a chain of mountains some sixteen thousand feet high could be seen standing out against the horizon and forming one wall of the valley of the Tsan-po, where it swept in a north-westerly course to an abrupt and almost right-angled bend. Further beyond the river, on the west, there towered a number of isolated peaks, the positions of which were noted by the surveyors of Mr. Bentinck's Mission, who also had got round and proceeded beyond the sixteen thousand foot range seen by the Yamne Survey. From the bird's-eye view which Lieutenant Oakes obtained, it was again apparent that the range of mountains that he had seen buttressed the course of but a single river, and that, while the waters of the Tsan-po and the Dihang mingled, the river was the same, irrespective of its name in the various stages of its course.

Although peace had not yet been definitely arranged with our erstwhile enemy, the villagers showed no ill-will to the Yamne River column, and no untoward incident marked its course. Signs of the times were still to be noticed in many places ; in stockades of recent construction by which the villages were defended, in the panjeed paths, and in many cunningly contrived rock chutes. Much good work was done by the party for, in general, the survey of the valley of the Yamne River was carried by Lieutenant Oakes to a point twelve miles north of its junction with the Dihang, while the valley of the Dihang itself was surveyed for fifteen miles beyond the same junction, and its course sketched in for yet another twenty-five miles. The region had not been visited before by any mission, and it was found with surprise that it differed considerably in character from the country through which the main column had been passing. Among other noticeable features was a village of two thousand inhabitants, while the lower slopes of the hills were clear of forest and periodically cultivated. Careful inquiry was made among the people as to their knowledge of the Dihang, which, by the way, Abors call the Siang, the "si" being a regular prefix to names of rivers and implying water, especially running water. All Abors apparently, as well as most of the tribes to the west, know the Dihang River as the Siang, and as nothing else. It was ignorance of this fact that gave rise to the conclusion that Siang and Tsan-po—"po" likewise meaning river—were identical terms.

With the return of Colonel MacIntyre from the Yamne Valley, a second mission was formed under the same leadership to proceed to Damro, the chief seat of the Padams. Colonel MacIntyre had with him Major Lindsay as Intelligence Officer ; Captain Macdonald as Medical Officer ; seventy rifles of the 2nd Gurkhas under Major Sweet, half a company of the 32nd Pioneers, a party of Military Police and a Survey party of which Lieutenant Oakes was in charge. As friendly relations had been established with the Aieng and Padam before the expedition set out, the art of the map-maker was on this occasion of more importance than the skill of the diplomatist.

It will be remembered that Damro was one of the objectives of a column, which took the field against the Abors in 1894, and was compelled to withdraw through the massacre of a hospital camp in the rear of the line of communications. In connection with the present disturbances, too, it will be recalled that the Padams expressly disassociated themselves from any participation in, or knowledge of, the murders of Mr. Williamson and Doctor Gregorson. Moreover, the tribesmen had agreed to cut a road to Damro, and to assist any visiting columns that proceeded thither as far as lay in their power. Considerable interest, therefore, attached to the visit to Damro, as not only was the village the metropolis of northern Aborland, but its inhabitants were of finer physique and of taller build than most of the southern tribes.

Leaving Rotung on January 20th, the column proceeded *via* Pongging to Damro, where a friendly welcome was offered to the troops. The place was found to resemble in great degree those centres which had already been visited by various columns, though it was larger and better built than the majority of Abor villages. Equally with them, however, its position proved to be incorrectly placed on the map, being much farther to the south, as also much more to the east than at first was thought. From Damro the party moved north on a reconnaissance of the snowy ranges which lie north-north-east across the Padam marches. Owing to a tribal feud between the Padams and the Simong Abors, it was impossible to get into touch with Mr. Bentinck's party on the Dihang, so, after completing the survey of the region, Colonel MacIntyre retraced his steps.

While Colonel MacIntyre was engaged on his visit to Damro, a small column of fifty rifles of the 8th Gurkhas under Captain Molesworth, with Captain Becher as Signalling Officer and accompanied by Mr. Kemp, the Zoologist, made two short journeys along the Siyom and Shimang Rivers. They proceeded on the first trip to Parong, from where the Shimang River, which has its origin in the snows and springs of Peak 10,090, was explored; and, on the second journey, to Peak 10,090, including an examination of the source of the Siyom, which is a big river. As Captain Molesworth was occupied with this work, Captain Sir George Duff-Sutherland-Dunbar, Bart., and a detachment of military police visited a number of centres in the Galong country, including the large and important place, Kombong. At the same time, another column of police moved out of Mishing for the purpose of visiting the Minyong villages to the south-west of Yemsing. Here again no trouble was experienced, such difficulties as had been encountered by any of the field columns being concerned almost solely with questions of transport, and with the task of maintaining touch between Major-General Bower's headquarters at Yambung and the almost daily shifting camps of the advanced parties.

Up to this point, the signalling arrangements had been in two parts: one a telephone phase as far as Yambung, and the other when flags and helios were called into service. It has already been shown what an important part the telephone played in the operations, but other arrangements were necessary for maintaining touch with the various movements to the north, east, and west of Yambung. Lieutenant Knight, however, was equal to the occasion, for he soon organised a very capable flag and helio service from various peaks in the rear of the exploring columns. With Yambung as the base point he established a chain of stations that not only picked up the movements of the Dihang and Yamne Survey parties, but kept in touch with all the smaller operations. Near Yambung itself a fine position was found on a two thousand foot hill to which was given the name of Signal Hill. From its summit the signallers picked up a peak above Komsing ; from there a peak near Geku, while an intermediate station was dropped at Riu. In due course the field telegraph was carried to Riu, when Signal Hill and Komsing Peak stations were shifted further forward and Riu became the signalling base. When the lamp and flag work became hindered by an ever-prevailing mist, one of Lieutenant Knight's feats was to run a flying line of seventeen miles of telephone cable from Geku to Simong, the combination of field telegraph and field telephone, flag and helio, together with the enterprise of the signallers and their officer, keeping headquarters in direct touch with every movement.

While the greeting accorded the Survey columns showed that the temper of the tribesmen was no longer hostile to the expedition, the most noteworthy indication of the trend of events at this juncture was the submission of the Gams of Kebang, who one day waited on Major-General Bower for the express purpose of arranging the cessation of hostilities. From this visit to the surrender of the Gam of Rotung, with which began the final act of the drama on which the curtain had risen so many months before, was but a brief space. Encouraged by the reception given to the Gams of Kebang the

Gam of Rotung presented himself at headquarters, and declared that the village accepted full responsibility for the troubles which had come upon the country. Extenuating nothing and denying nothing, he stated that his men had been entirely to blame, and that their impetuosity had carried away the braves of Kebang and Babuk. He admitted, too, as the narrative of events already given has shown, that the Rotung men in the main were responsible for the resistance which the column encountered, both at the Egar River stockade itself and in the little action at Kekar Monying. With these matters adjusted, there remained only the question of the surrender of the actual murderers of Mr. Williamson and Dr. Gregorson, and the precise character of the penalties, to be inflicted upon the offending villages, to be determined. In due course the murderers were secured, tried and sentenced, the gams of the guilty villages meanwhile bringing in their fines.

CHAPTER XVIII

The Value of the Operations—Work of the Survey—The Return of the Troops—The Mishmi Mission—The Miri Mission—Captain Graham's Gallantry—A Final Word.

WITH the events recorded in the last chapter it was obvious to every member of the Field Force that his days of activity in Aborland were numbered. Much had been done in the past few months to bring home to the tribes the consequence of their misdeeds, but with the submission of the principal gams, the capture of the murderers and the destruction of the chief tribal centres, the punitive part of the expedition had been accomplished. There remained only the requirements of the Survey to be considered; when these were satisfied, and the field columns one by one repaired to Yambung from their objectives in the valleys of the Dihang, the Yamne and Shimang Rivers, the signs of the times indicated a speedy return to India.

There were few expressions of regret at the termination of the labours of the force; for, if the work of the columns had been thankless, it had also been rather unsatisfactory, insomuch that our friend the enemy had not stood in any one position sufficiently long to receive effective punishment. Furthermore, the difficulties of transport had necessarily inflicted much hardship on the troops, who also experienced the strain of great extremes in matters of temperature. While the earlier marches were made in a tropical heat, many of the survey columns had toiled through snow, the movements of Mr. Bentinck's party being hampered very much in this respect. The effect of these conditions was felt the more, too, because the operations were conducted on bivouac scale. Consequently, to the hard work of the day the misery of a wet camp at night had usually to be added. In the face of these things it is really remarkable that so much was done in so short a space of time; and it is impossible to give too great praise to officers and men who, alike, bore themselves very cheerfully in most trying circumstances.

If the course of the operations in the field was without many of those elements which attract the attention of the "man in the street," very gratifying results were obtained nevertheless by the work of the Survey officers. An accurate series of triangulation emanating from the Assam longitudinal series of the great trigonometrical survey of India was carried over the outlying ranges to the latitude of Kebang, terminating in the base Sadup H.S. Namkam H.S. From this series, and an extension of reconnaissance triangulation to the latitude of Simong, several large snow-peaks were fixed on what appeared to be the main Himalayan divide. One of these was the 25,000-foot peak to which reference has been already made. Other peaks were fixed on the watershed between the Dihang and the Subansiri Rivers which seems to be a prominent spur of the main water-parting. It was, of course, only possible to obtain a mere approximation of the topography of these snow ranges ; but, none-the-less, the results which were forthcoming will be of great future value. Three thousand five hundred square miles of country in all were correctly mapped on a scale of four miles to the inch. This area included the whole of the valley of the Dihang as far north as Singging, the whole of the Yamne Valley, the whole of the Shimang Valley and a portion of the Siyom River.

While the might of Kebang has been destroyed and a serviceable road opened as far as Yambung, it is perhaps early yet to expect that the latter will become a caravan route of any pretensions. India is far removed and the trade of the Abor country small, so of necessity the development remains in the womb of the future. Whether or no it will ever occur, depends in great measure on how long the peace of the borderside will be kept. In general the whole of Aborland was visited ; and, while the guilty villages were punished, friendly relations were established with the tribes that took no part in the massacres. Moreover the punishment administered was not vindictive and, though the domination exercised by Kebang was crushed, it is safe to say that no smouldering animosity has been left behind on this account. At the same time it is difficult to think that the effect of the operations will remain if steps are not taken to provide visible evidence of the power of the Sirkar. It is all very well to move into and out of the country, but the mere passing of a force is not sufficient if lasting results are anticipated. The tribesmen, naturally protesting eternal vows of good behaviour while the columns were encamped about their villages, are but human. It is folly to think that they will maintain the attitude when all coercive means have disappeared.

Oppression of the weak is to the Abor an elemental principle of life. If we wish to see the influence of the expedition preserved, strong posts should be established in all large centres. In fact such a series of posts is the logical corollary of the policy which sanctioned the dispatch of the expedition in the first place, and it is impossible to have a second opinion on the signal blunder which has brought about the evacuation of the posts at Kobo, Rotung, and Yambung. Much labour, considerable money and no little ingenuity were spent on these places, which for all practical purposes wore the appearance of permanent camps. The abandonment

AFRAID OF NOBODY.

Two Mishmi children who became the pets of the Mishmi Mission.

THE EVER-NECESSARY STOCKADE.

Sepoys of the Lakhimpur Military Police are standing along the face of the post.

TAKING THE ROLL-CALL OF THE COOLIES.

of Rotung, in particular, is serious, for it occupied a central position, and had become so strong under the delicate attentions of the engineers who were responsible for its construction, that, in every sense of the word, it was a border keep. From its walls sentries could have looked out upon the tribal marches, while its maintenance as a frontier outpost would have supplied all that is required to keep alive the lessons of the operations.

While the columns of the expeditionary force were reassembling at Yambung for their homeward march, the two political Missions which were operating east and west of Major-General Bower's forces were likewise retracing their steps. In spite of the many rumours about the presence of marauding Chinese in the valley of the Lohit, the Dundas Mission failed to find either Chinese officials or any parties of Chinese soldiery within the limits of the frontier zone. Though the difficulties of the route were very great, the progress of the party down the valley was entirely peaceful and the Mission succeeded in establishing very cordial relations with the various Mishmi tribes. No untoward incident occurred to mar its course and much good work was accomplished, though neither the road, which the Mission was constructing, nor the surveys, which were considerably advanced, were completed. Similarly, no cairn was set up to mark the frontier which, it would appear, cannot materially differ from that already recognised by the Chinese.

While the work of the Mishmi Mission proceeded in an atmosphere of perfect peace, the troubles which attended the Miri Mission very strongly support the contention that the effect of the Abor operations in general will be inconclusive if Aborland is left without some permanent indication of the mailed fist. It was assumed, before the Miri Mission took the field, that the Miris would be friendly; and it should not be forgotten that one of the grounds for the Abor operations was to put an end to the persecution with which the Abors for so long a time have treated the Miris. It would seem, however, that the Miris were not particularly impressed by the punishment inflicted on the Abors, for it was only with great difficulty that they could be induced to give any assistance to the Mission. Time and again the attitude of the villages was hostile; while, from first to last, there was behind the reception accorded the parties engaged on the survey signs of mistrust and suspicion which the tribesmen hardly took the trouble to veil. If matters succeeded as satisfactorily as they did, and for so long, it was by sheer luck, for the Miri Mission was given an impossible task to carry out with the means placed at its disposal.

The policy adopted by the Government towards

the Miri Mission was one of half-measures, for though they dispatched the little force for the purpose of surveying the Kamla-Subansiri region, they fettered the action of the commander with restrictions that, together with the inadequate organisation of the expedition, made failure probable. The mistake arose through the Foreign Department of the Government of India having left the arrangements for the Mission in the hands of the Assam Civil Government, who, instead of giving the matter to the military authorities, attempted to run it for itself, without expert advice.

In the first place the Assam Civil Government established a dual control between Mr. Kerwood, who was the Political Officer, and Captain Graham, who commanded the escort, and was wholly subordinate to Mr. Kerwood until, and unless, actual fighting occurred. Mr. Kerwood was an officer of only three years' standing ; and, if it had not been for the loyal manner in which Captain Graham worked with him in matters about which there should have been no divided authority, the results of the work accomplished would have been even less than it is, as Mr. Kerwood's very limited experience did not allow him to realise the inefficiency of the arrangements that he was accepting.

In the second place the Assam Civil Government having appointed Mr. Kerwood to the control of the

Mission, failed either to support him or to trust his judgment, with the result that a further expedition will be necessary if work on the region is to be completed, when, unless organised on very different lines, it, too, will meet with failure. Further, the Mission was hampered at every turn owing to the smallness of the escort, the lack of coolies and the insufficiency of stores. In regard to the hospital arrangements, moreover, it is difficult to think that mismanagement could have gone further.

The column carried no base hospital; no arrangements were made for the sick to be conveyed to the rear, the duty of attending to the sick and wounded in the various advance camps, and up and down a line of communication two hundred miles in length, being entrusted to a single native hospital assistant! Those responsible for this disgraceful state of affairs may, perhaps, realise the gravity of their blunder by reflecting upon what would have happened had the fighting around Tali resulted in any loss to the Mission forces. As it was one man, who was wounded by a poisoned arrow from a bamboo spring-trap, died; while the sick, who had to be carried along with the column as it moved on its daily march, suffered terribly. Had Mr. Kerwood more experience, or his representations been given proper attention by his departmental chiefs, many of the defects from which the Mission suffered might

HEADQUARTERS OF THE MIRI MISSION AT CHIMIR.

THE CAMP OF THE DETACHMENT OF THE ASSAM VALLEY AND SURMA VALLEY LIGHT HORSE, ON THE BANKS OF THE BRAHMAPUTRA, DIBRUGARH.

MISHMIS FROM THE LOHIT VALLEY.

have been remedied before the start took place. As it was the Miri Mission supplies a most illuminating example of official carelessness and, if Mr. Kerwood had not had the advantage of the well-tried experience of Captain Graham and of Captain Beauchamp Duff, there is little doubt that the Miri Hills would have witnessed a signal disaster. When the trouble did come, it developed with extraordinary swiftness, the situation breaking down just as the various field parties had concentrated at Seitom, a village which lay across the Kamla.

Up to the arrival of the Mission at Seitom, the party had not encountered any direct opposition, though the attitude of the villagers fell just short of open enmity. The first column to arrive at Seitom was that led by Mr. Kerwood, the little party reaching the place on January 31st. Three days later they were joined by Captain Duff and Lieutenant Wahab. Up to Seitom all had been well, though there had been frequent reports that the villages ahead intended to combine against the Mission. A few miles north-west of Seitom the signs of opposition were no longer to be ignored for the men of Rugi and of Mei were reported to be laying *panjees* on the jungle tracks. As the situation seemed threatening the Mission halted to await supplies, upon arrival of which, as the little force numbered some fifty rifles, it was felt that a further step forward could be taken. Accordingly, Seitom was left on February 9th, when Mr. Kerwood, Captain Graham and Lieutenant Lewis, with thirty rifles, moved out with the intention of establishing a post a few miles farther on.

While the main column proposed to follow the direct route, Captain Beauchamp Duff and twelve men went out as a flanking party to clear the jungle of a large body of tribesmen who were reported to be lying in ambush where the road had been blocked. Captain Duff started some few hours before the main column, and, making a wide detour by a path which they had to cut for themselves through dense jungle, he turned the position of the enemy, who immediately withdrew. From the ambush Captain Duff continued acting on the flank of the main column, which maintained its advance to Rugi and Mei. These places were reached without incident; Mr. Kerwood and Captain Graham halting near Rugi while Captain Duff returned to Seitom, as the temper of that centre was very doubtful.

Moving forward from Rugi, the main column after camping between Talung and Tali, was near Tali on February 11th, when, as the column breasted a ridge, Captain Graham found that a party of two hundred natives was closing in on the head of his little force. For a moment the position was serious. The convoy was straggling and the strength of the troops available was by no means sufficient to hold the position if a sudden attack were made. There was, therefore, no alternative to immediate action and Captain Graham, putting a bold front upon a bad situation, cleared the field after firing half-a-dozen shots. Once again the tribesmen bolted, and the column reached Tali village in safety. Tali lay in three sections. Each was situated half-a-mile apart, the head-men vying with one another in finding explanations for the conduct of their " bad men," and in making overtures of friendship.

The situation now died down, though it revived rapidly on the intelligence that Rugi was contemplating an attack. Acting on this information, Captain Graham sent word to Captain Duff to take a party from Seitom and to endeavour to bring Rugi to terms, as there was no doubt that the Rugi villages were the principal instigators of the opposition. The orders had barely reached Captain Duff when Seitom itself again began to show an ugly attitude. From the first appearance of the column in the neighbourhood, the villagers of Seitom had deserted the place and taken refuge in the jungle, from which, under cover of night, some of them, including the head-men, returned to their houses. Recognising that the evil at hand was as great as that farther afield, Captain Duff decided before proceeding to Rugi to deal with Seitom by arresting the head-men as they slept.

Accompanied by fifteen men, Captain Duff and Lieutenant Wahab surrounded the houses of the head-men during the night, and, as dawn broke, surprised the two gams together with seven other men who were asleep at the time. Opposition, naturally, was offered to this venturesome act, for the uproar had aroused the jungle, whence volleys of arrows were directed on the sepoys from the concealed tribesmen. A few rounds of rifle fire, however, provided for the safety of the party, who managed to get their prisoners into camp without further resistance.

Captain Duff's action had an immediate and very salutary effect, the more so when he proceeded to release half the prisoners on their promise that they would secure the submission of the village. Matters once again moved more smoothly ; and, for the moment, such a calm settled upon Seitom that Captain Duff proceeded the next day to Rugi. At Rugi he was given assurances that all obstructions would be removed from the roads and that the village would return to its good behaviour. From Rugi, therefore, Captain Duff proceeded to join Captain Graham at Tali, where Mr. Kerwood was confident that the trouble was over. For the moment, too, it seemed that this might be the case ; and arrangements were made to continue survey work towards some high snow ranges which lay seven marches up the Kamla in a north-westerly direction. At the same time, it was decided to make an attempt to reach Mora, a village in an east-north-easterly direction on the Subansiri, north of which there was reported to be a pass into Tibet.

In order to prepare for the forthcoming journeys, for Captain Graham, Mr. Kerwood, and Lieutenant Lewis were to move up the Kamla while Captain Duff and Lieutenant Wahab made their way towards Mora, it was necessary for Captain Duff to return to Seitom to collect stores. Captain Duff and his little party proceeded to Seitom via Rugi, which village was found to have failed in its promises to remove obstructions from the route. At Seitom all was quiet, and a convoy was immediately dispatched to Tali. Soon after they had started, however, sharp firing was heard from the direction of Rugi, which made it apparent that the convoy was being attacked. Captain Duff, Lieutenant Wahab, and thirteen men at once proceeded to the assistance of the convoy, and succeeded in bringing it safely back to Seitom, though not without inflicting some little loss on the enemy.

Events were now moving very rapidly. While Captain Duff was rescuing the convoy from the attack of the Rugi villages, a similar movement was being carried out by Tali men against Mr. Kerwood and Captain Graham. At the moment, dawn had scarcely broken and the camp was hardly awake.

Captain Graham was lying in his blankets at work; Mr. Kerwood was asleep; the sepoys, except for a guard, were either cooking breakfast or cutting wood some little distance away. All was peaceful when suddenly the sentry fired his rifle and shouted, "Sahib, the enemy are upon us." Captain Graham, seizing his revolver, jumped out of his blankets to find but very few yards away a party of three hundred tribesmen, armed with swords and spears, charging down upon the camp. Firing as rapidly as possible, Captain Graham held the enemy at bay, as, with extraordinary gallantry and coolness, he dropped men shot by shot, the last few falling as near as eight yards from him in the actual perimeter of the camp. It was a fine and plucky action, and saved the situation until the sepoys were able to reach their rifles. So soon as the rifles began to speak, the raiders fled. Twenty dead were left behind in the field, no less than ten being killed by Captain Graham in his single-handed defence.

News of the attack on Captain Graham reached Captain Duff by special courier on the evening of the day on which it took place, and but an hour or two after he had returned from rescuing the convoy. Collecting all the available men once again, Duff was in readiness to dash to Captain Graham's support, when his own camp in turn was attacked. A large body of tribesmen, after firing several rounds of arrows, rushed to close quarters, but were driven off with a loss of some six killed. As the enemy retired Captain Duff, Lieutenant Wahab and fifteen men proceeded through to Tali, which they reached without opposition as the villages *en route* had been deserted. The reunited column now proceeded to punish Tali and Rugi. During the next three days both places were burnt, together with the supplies of grain which the villagers—so certain of success were they—had failed to remove. As the column had been ordered not to take the initiative in any fighting, no further punishment could be inflicted on the tribesmen for their gross treachery, though it was now obvious that any further survey work was out of the question. While efforts were made to complete as far as possible what had been done, the return of the column was inevitable, the abandonment of the proposed journeys northwards being very much regretted. At the same time there was no alternative, for the column was not strong enough to proceed in the face of resistance, while most positive orders were against it.

The journey *via* the Apa Tanang and the Ranga River to civilisation from the Miri Hills was uneventful, though opportunity was taken to continue the survey work. The change, after the many weary months that had been spent on the steep slopes and in the dense jungles of the hills region, to the cultivated oases of the Apa Tanang plateau was very delightful, the vista of pine woods, broad open cultivated valleys, stretches of rice-fields, nestling villages and grassy knolls, forming a picture that rejoiced the hearts of the sepoys as well as those of the weary transport coolies. Every one was pleased to be returning, the safe arrival of the column being the closing incident in the Aborland operations.

The moment, too, had now arrived for the writer to say farewell. As Government in its wisdom had decreed that only one correspondent, and he an officer, should be permitted to follow the troops in the field, the writer had to turn his face homewards, without sharing the vicissitudes of the troops which he has endeavoured to describe. If mistakes have occurred, as is not impossible, the responsibility must be visited upon him, though it should be said that the proofs of this book have been submitted to the various authorities concerned in the operations, with a view to presenting a correct account of what has taken place.

APPENDIX I

In his dispatch to the Government of India, dated Kobo, April 11th, Major-General Hamilton Bower, C.B., brought to favourable notice the names of the following officers and men from among those serving with the Abor Expedition.

Staff.

Major C. A. R. Hutchinson, 41st Dogras, General Staff Officer, 2nd grade :—I am greatly indebted to this officer for much valuable assistance. He has shown himself a hardworking and capable Staff Officer.

Captain L. S. H. Smithers, 17th Infantry (the Loyal Regiment), was acting Brigade-Major, Assam Brigade, at the time preparations were being made and a great deal of general staff work devolved on him during the expedition. He has often been of considerable assistance in other capacities than that of orderly officer. He is well fitted for staff employment.

Captain W. Hore, 120th Rajputana Infantry, Intelligence Officer, has an exceptionally good knowledge of the Abor and Miri languages and was of the greatest assistance.

Captain H. S. Becher carried out the duties of Provost Marshal efficiently.

I am much indebted to Mr. A. Bentinck, I.C.S., Assistant Political Officer, for useful advice and assistance. He has an extensive knowledge of the tribes on this frontier and conducted under difficult circumstances several exploration parties, showing tact in his dealings with the villages. His services are well worthy of commendation.

Lines of Communication.

Colonel D. C. MacIntyre, Indian Army, base command, and Inspector, Line of Communications, has performed his duties to my complete satisfaction. He conducted missions to the Panggi and Padam countries, being in both political and military charge. Largely owing to his tact in dealing with savage people, these missions were most successful and resulted in the establishment of excellent relations and a large addition to our geographical knowledge.

Corps and Departments.

Assam Valley Light Horse, Dismounted Detachment.—The members of this detachment showed a most soldier-like spirit in volunteering, in many cases at great personal inconvenience and pecuniary loss, to accompany the expedition. They underwent considerable hardship in a most cheerful spirit and played an important part in the taking of the Kekar-Monying position. Captain C. L. Lovell commanded the detachment in an efficient manner.

No. 1 Company K. G. O. Sappers and Miners.—The work done by this company is above all praise, and it is to the skill and energy displayed by all ranks that the success of the expedition is largely due.

During six months of arduous work their energy has never flagged. Major E. C. Tylden-Pattenson is an officer of exceptional ability and his advancement would be to the good of the Service.

Lieutenant W. C. Cave-Brown did much good work, particularly in the hazardous enterprise of getting a steel cable for rafting across the Dihang.

1st Battalion 2nd K. O. Gurkha Rifles.—This corps well maintained its reputation for efficiency, both on the Ledum column and guarding the line of communications. An excellent spirit pervades the regiment. Colonel J. Fisher, commanding the Ledum column, acted for some time as officer, G. Defences, lines of communication. He performed his duties to my satisfaction.

Major A. B. Lindsay is a very capable officer with great enterprise. He acted as staff officer with the Ledum column and accompanied the Panggi and Padam missions as intelligence officer and brought back very useful reports. He has all the qualities that go to make a good staff officer and his advancement would be to the good of the Service. Lieutenant H. F. Marsh is also mentioned.

32nd Sikh Pioneers.—This corps has done much useful work on the line of communication. Lieutenant-Colonel H. Peterson, D.S.O., is an officer of sound judgment and has commanded his regiment and carried out the duties of officer commanding defences, line of communication, to my satisfaction. The good work done by the following was noticeable :—Major E. H. S. Cullen, M.V.O., Captain the Hon. M. De Courcy.

1st Battalion 8th Gurkha Rifles.—On this corps devolved most of the fighting and the very hard work involved in escorting expedition parties. I cannot speak too highly of the manner in which it carried out its different duties. A better corps for jungle warfare it would be hard to find. Lieutenant-Colonel F. Murray, D.S.O., commanded to my complete satisfaction and carried out various important detached duties in a most capable manner. His services are well worthy of recognition. He was invalided as a result of the hardships involved in campaigning in such a difficult country. Major J. A. Wilson commanded when Lieutenant-Colonel Murray was invalided and carried out his duties to my satisfaction. He has shown energy and enterprise throughout, and has commanded detached bodies on several occasions. Captain J. F. S. D. Coleridge is a most reliable officer of sound judgment and has done excellently in military charge of exploration parties. Captain A. L. Molesworth has done well in command of exploration parties. Lieutenant M. A. C. Kennedy is a good officer and distinguished himself at the taking of the Egar stockade.

Signal unit from No. 31 (Divisional) Signal Company had great difficulties to contend with in the nature of the country and the long periods during which visual signalling was impossible. In spite of these difficulties its work was of the greatest assistance to me. Lieutenant J. H. Knight is a most enthusiastic signaller, and I could always feel that if it was at all possible he would maintain communication with any detached parties.

Supply and Transport Corps.—Questions of supply and transport to a great extent govern operations, and in a trackless country there is a great deal to contend with. I attribute the state of efficiency maintained by the force largely to the excellent *personnel* of the Supply and Transport Corps. Major E. G. Vaughan, Assistant Director, Supply and Transport, is an officer who always keeps in view the comfort and efficiency of the troops, while being careful of the financial interests of the State. Major H. M. Broke did good service at the base. Captain W. B. Dunlop has done good work with the advanced supply columns. The five Naga Carrier Corps well justified their enlistment. Better men for the duties they were called upon to perform it would be difficult to find. They were taxed to the utmost of their physical powers, but were always cheery. There never was any trouble with them, and on several occasions they showed themselves quite willing to engage the Abors. These satisfactory results I largely attribute to the tact and firmness with which they were treated by the Corps Commandant. Where all did well it may appear invidious to select any for special mention, but perhaps I may be permitted to mention Captain G. W. Bond and Captain C. W. Hext, whose work came more immediately under my notice.

Lieutenant A. B. H. Webb, 5th Gurkha Rifles, under great difficulties did excellent work in charge of the boat transport between Kobo and Pasighat. The good work done by the following was noticeable :—Captain C. E. Edward Collins, Commandant, 26th Mule Corps, Hony. Lieutenant J. Foy, Indian Medical Service.

To the efficient carrying out of sanitary and other medical duties, the comparatively good health and absence of epidemic is largely due. Major J. Davidson, Assistant Director, Medical Service, has done well in that capacity. Captain C. W. F. Melville is a very good officer and well worthy of advancement. He acted as Staff Surgeon and also accompanied exploration parties. Captain J. S. O'Neill is also mentioned.

Lakhimpur Military Police.—On this corps, ever since the massacre of Mr. Williamson's party, has devolved the duty of keeping the North Lakhimpur district free from Abor raids. The difficulties and hardships involved in carrying out this duty during the rainy season can only be realised by those having knowledge of the country and climate. The battalion also did good work in the operations near Mishing. Captain Sir George Duff-Sutherland-Dunbar, Bart., 31st Punjabis, has commanded to my satisfaction, and his services have also been brought to notice by Colonel Fisher, commanding the Ledum column.

The untimely death of Captain A. M. Hutchins, as the direct result of continuous hardships during a long period, is much to be regretted. He was a capable and gallant officer.

Surgeon-Captain J. M. Falkner, Assam Valley Light Horse, served as a volunteer medical officer with the Ledum column and Lakhimpur Military Police. He has served throughout without remuneration, and I consider his services worthy of commendation. Captain J. Masters is also mentioned.

The Survey party under Captain H. B. Trenchard, R.E., did good work. The good work done by the following was noticeable:—Lieutenant G. F. T. Oakes.

The Telegraph Department under Mr. G. E. O. De Smidt did very useful work.

The following are also mentioned as having done good work :—

No. 1 *Company (K.G.O.) Sappers and Miners.*—Acting Sergeant-Major J. F. Eltham Jemadar Sultan; Havildar Diwan Ali.

1*st Battalion* 2*nd* (*K.E.O.*) *Gurkha Rifles.*—Subadar-Major Delman Ale, I.O.M.; Havildar Siri Lal Thapa ; Rifleman Budhiman Gurung ; Rifleman Deosur Thapa, have been the subject of a separate communication.

32*nd Sikh Pioneers.*—Subadar Sundar Singh ; Havildar Budhe Singh.

1*st Battalion* 8*th Gurkha Rifles.*—Subadar-Major Nawalsing Rana Bahadur, I.O.M.; Jemadar Makansing Gurung; Jemadar Narbahadur Gurung; Havildar Bhairab Sahi ; Lance-Naik Chitrabir Rana; Rifleman Kalia Pun.

Signal unit from No. 31 (*Divisional*) *Signal Company.*—Lance-Naik Dharm Singh ; Lance-Naik Dost Mahammad.

Supply and Transport Corps.—Conductor W. C. Hayman ; H. Wright ; J. Ballen, 26th Mule Corps.

Indian Medical Service.—First Class Sub-Assistant Surgeon Mahadeo Parshad ; Second Class Senior Sub-Assistant Surgeon Nirunjan Cas.

Lakhimpur Military Police.—Subadar-Major Dorward ; Jemadar Jangbir Lama ; Havildar Dal Bahadur Thapa.

Survey Party.—Surveyor Sher Jang ; Surveyor Hamid Gul.

The Ordnance Base Depot, under Conductor F. I. Williams, was most useful and met all requirements.

Telegraph Department.—Sub-Conductor W. Dacies; Private W. Rouse, 2nd Connaught Rangers.

The postal arrangements were satisfactory.

Corps of Military Staff Clerks.—Sergeant A. Park.

APPENDIX II

Return of Casualties

Casualties received in action, from 6th October, 1911, to 11th January, 1912, were :—

Officers.—*Nil* killed, *nil* died of wounds, 1 wounded, *nil* missing.

Indian Officers, British and Indian Rank and File.—Non-commissioned officers and men, 2 killed, *nil* died of wounds, 2 wounded, *nil* missing.

Followers.—2 killed, 1 died of wounds, 3 wounded, *nil* missing.

APPENDIX III

Honours List

In recognition of their distinguished services during the operations in Aborland, the King has given orders for the following promotions and appointments of officers of the Indian Army :—

To be K.C.B.: Major-General Hamilton Bower, C.B.

To be C.B.: Colonel (temporary Brigadier-General) Donald Charles Frederick MacIntyre; Colonel John Fisher.

To be Companions of the Distinguished Service Order: Major James Davidson, M.D.; Major James Alban Wilson, Major Edward Gyles Vaughan, Major Ernest Henry Scott Cullen, M.V.O.; Lieutenant Miles Arthur Claude Kennedy.

To be Colonels: Lieutenant-Colonel Frank Murray, D.S.O.; Lieutenant-Colonel Frederick Hopewell Peterson, D.S.O.

To be Lieutenant-Colonels: Major Alexander Bertram Lindsay, Major Charles Alexander Robert Hutchinson, Major Edwin Cooke Tylden-Pattenson, Royal Engineers.

To be Major: Captain Charles Edward Edward-Collins.

APPENDIX IV

Acknowledgments

THE author desires to render acknowledgments to Colonel Sir Thomas Holdich, R.E.; Mr. Needham, Mr. W. Crooke, Captain Poole, D.S.O.; Lieutenant-Colonel W. T. Boyer and Mr. L. A. Waddell, the authors of books and papers on some aspects of the tribal life of the north-west frontier of India; to Mr. Gennings, Managing Director of the Central News Agency, Limited, for permission to use photographs taken by the author in his capacity as correspondent for the Central News Agency ; to Colonel Lumsden, C.B. ; Colonel F. Bailey, Captain Poole, D.S.O., and those, whose names may not be mentioned, for the loan of photographs which materially enhance the value and character of these pages ; to those officers who assisted in the correction of the proofs ; to Mr. W. C. M. Dundas and Major Charles Bliss of the Mishmi Mission, to Captain Graham of the Miri Mission, to Captain Hutchison, Doctor Roberts, Mr. Lamb, and Mr. Evans of Dibrugarh, for much hospitality and many kindnesses.

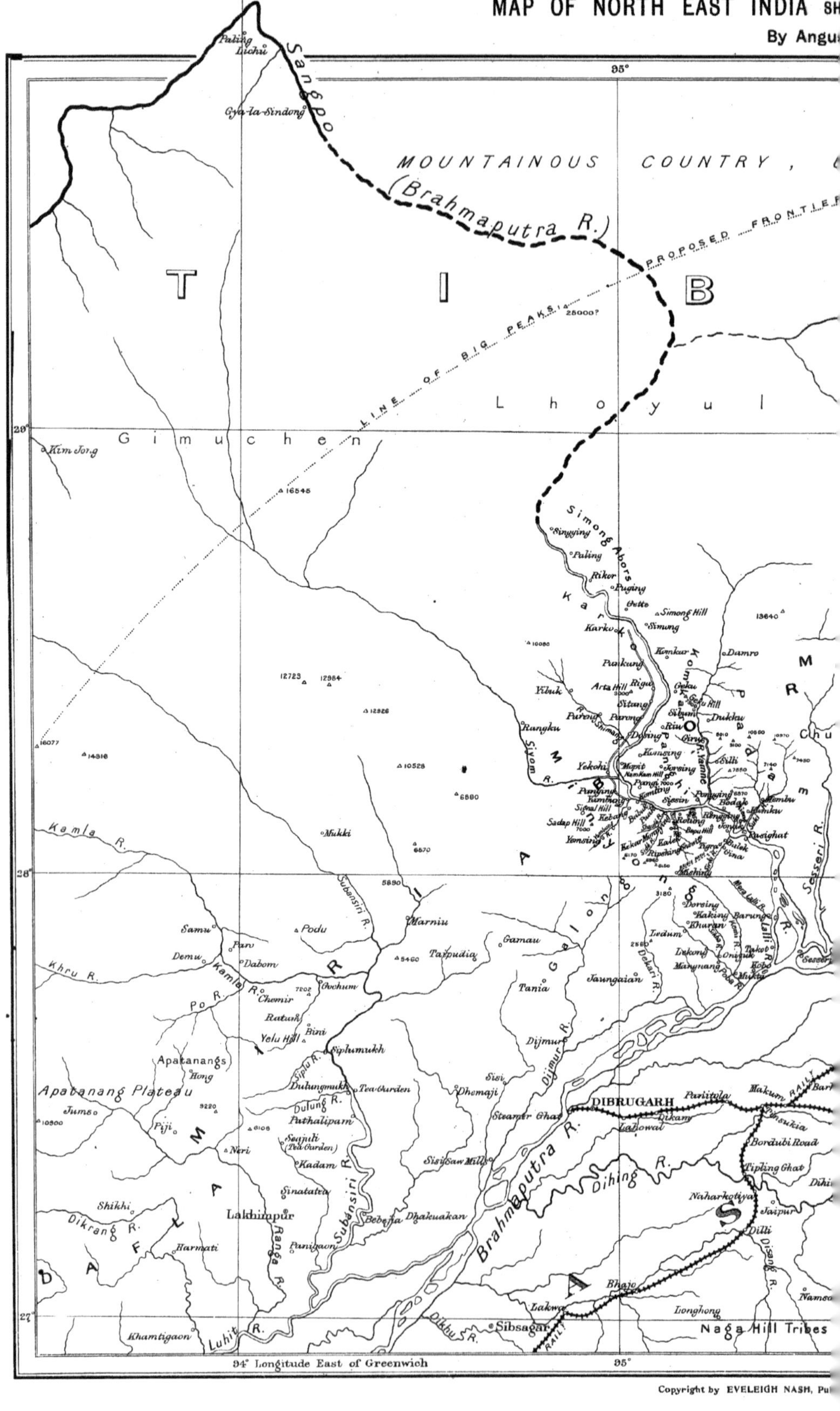

Copyright by EVELEIGH NASH,

R, MISHMI, & MIRI REGIONS

.R.G.S.

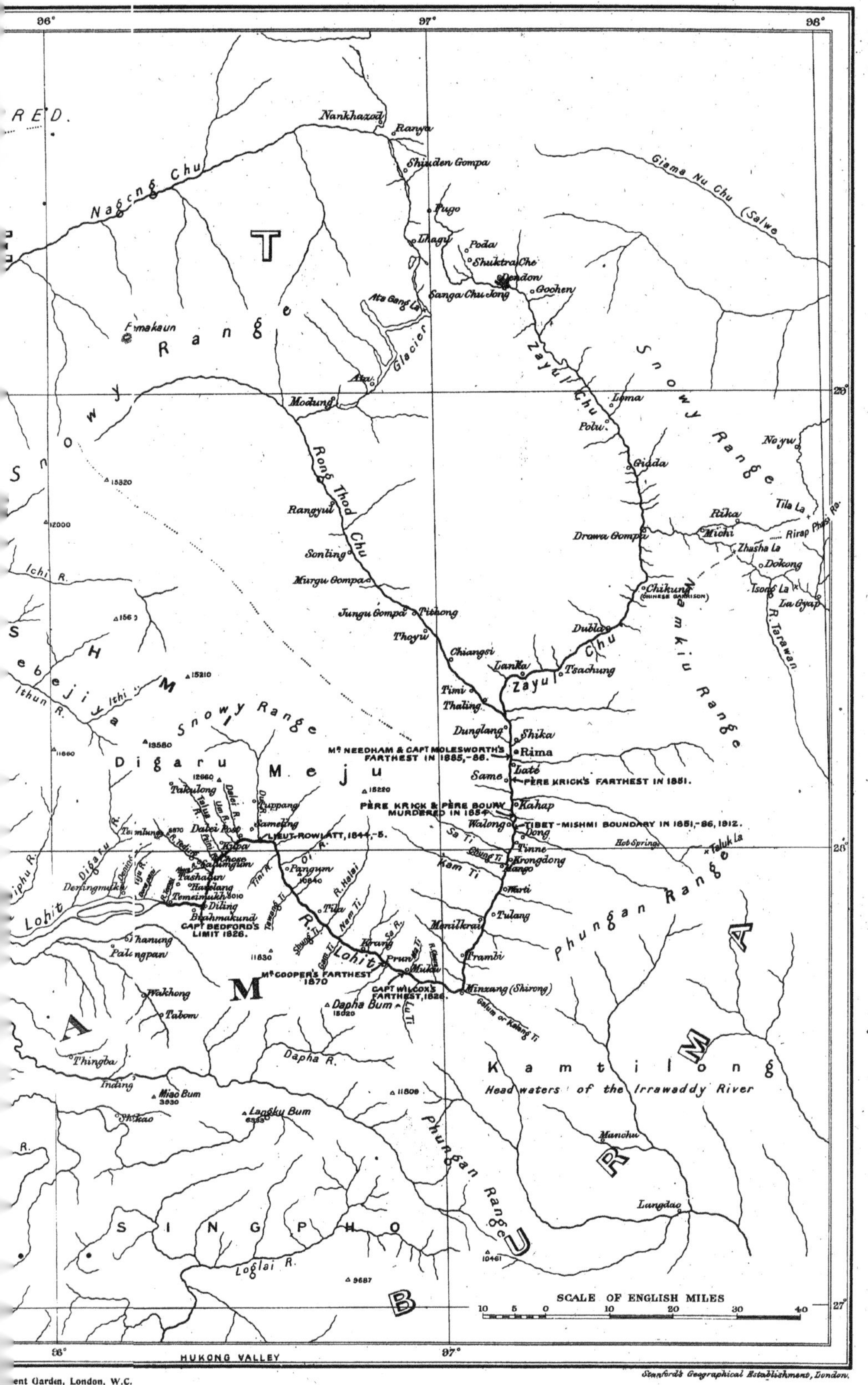

ent Garden, London, W.C.

Stanford's Geographical Establishment, London.

www.ingramcontent.com/pod-product-compliance
Ingram Content Group UK Ltd.
Pitfield, Milton Keynes, MK11 3LW, UK
UKHW022324190726
13856UKWH00001B/204

9 781843 424987